PARIS
SHOPFRONTS

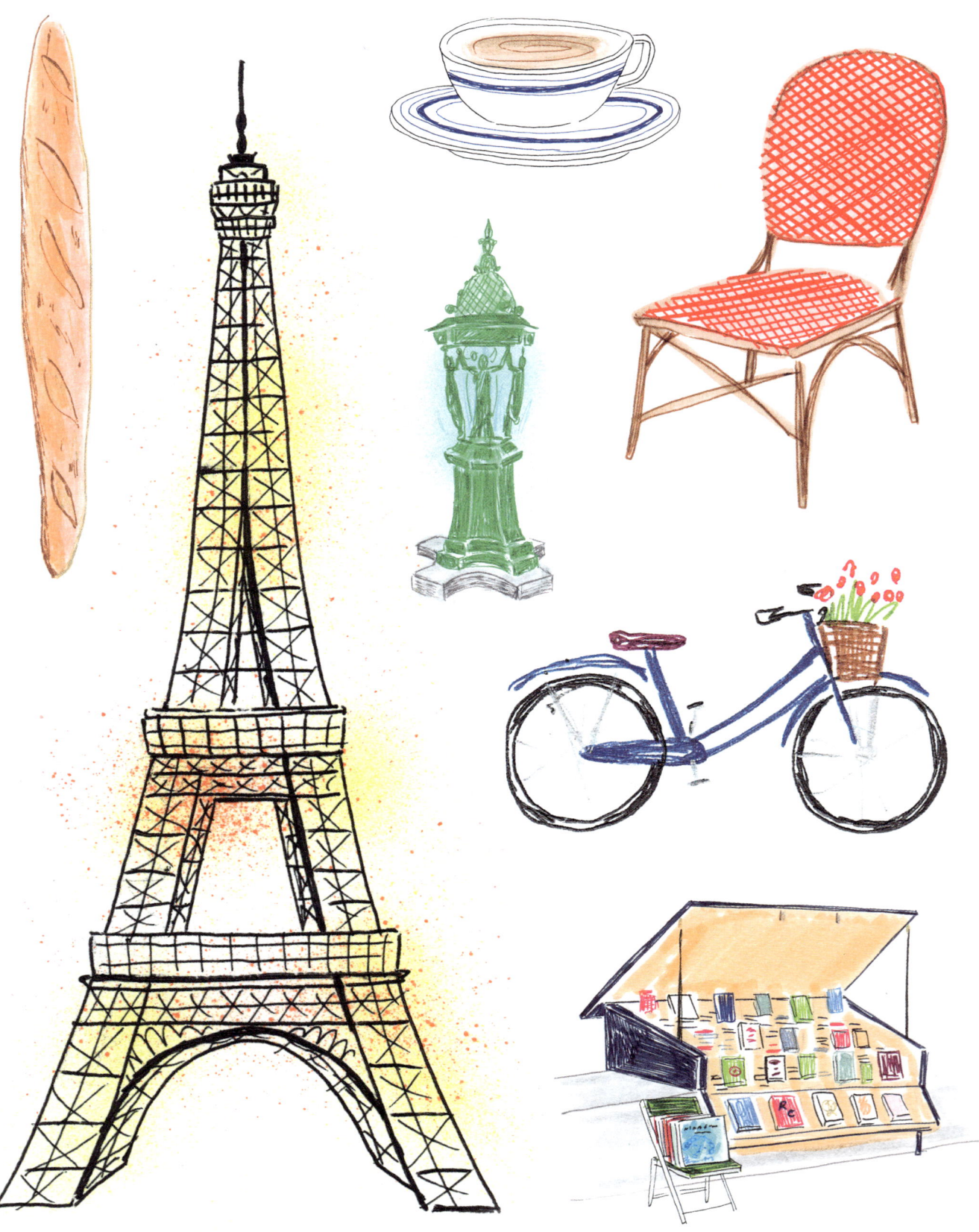

PARIS SHOPFRONTS

Illustrations of the City's Best-Loved
Boutiques, Brasseries, Bars, and More

JOEL HOLLAND

words by
VIVIAN SONG

foreword by
SARAH ANDELMAN

PRESTEL
Munich • London • New York

Contents

LE PENSEUR DE RODIN

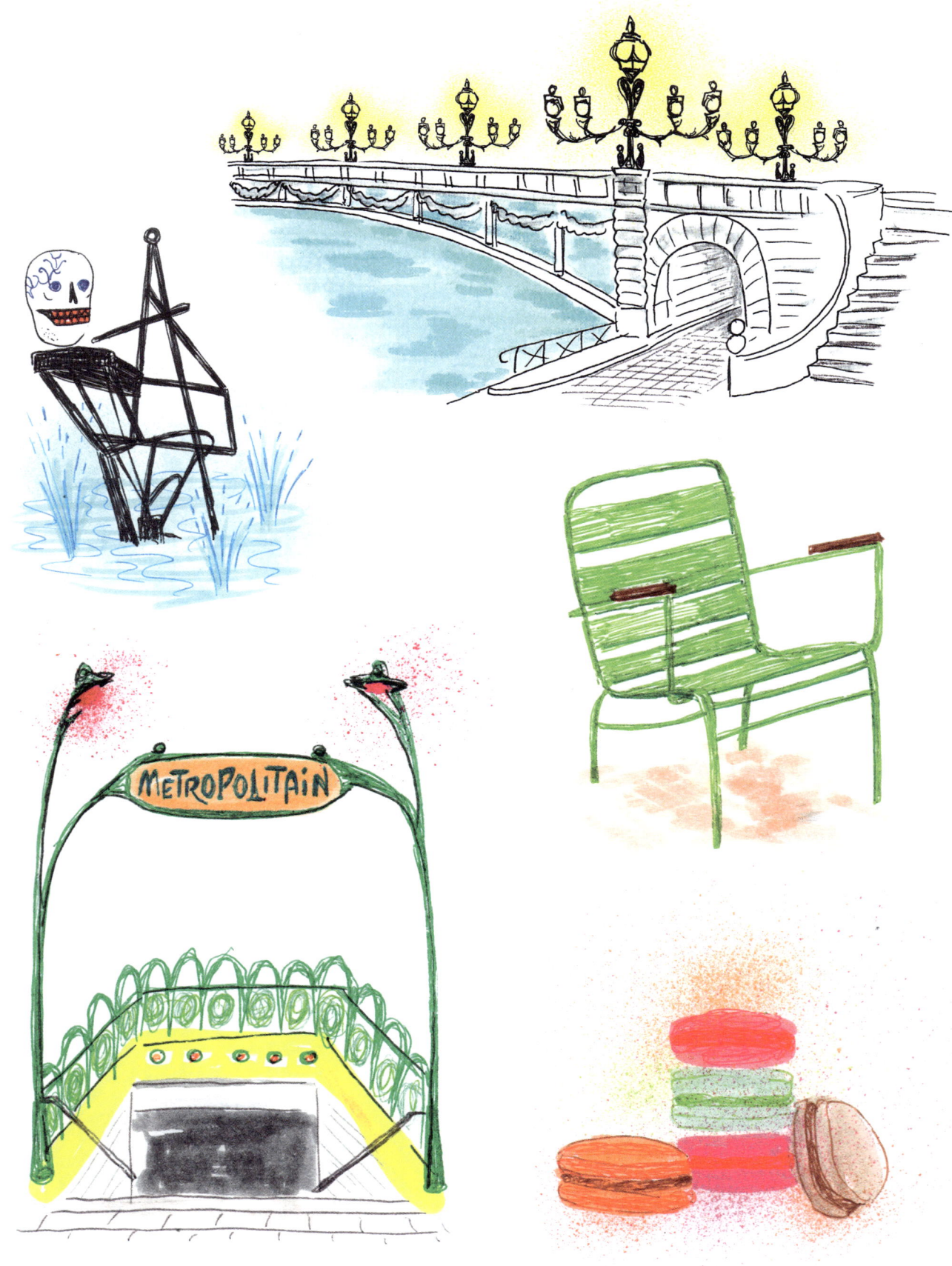

Foreword

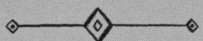

Flipping through Joel Holland's exquisitely drawn *Paris Shopfronts* is like taking my favorite bicycle ride through the city. Each of these destinations is meaningful, and I love the delightful journey through them. The book is not organized into lists of arrondissements, cafés, shops, or hotels—rather, we just naturally flow from surprise to surprise. *This is Paris!*

You'll likely recognize some of the more famous places, like Café de Flore, Shakespeare and Company, or Ladurée, but you'll also discover so many (*so many*) Parisian secrets. Joel—with the help of local journalist Vivian Song—illustrated not only the city's "best-loved" spots, but also the *real* spots, the ones that only a few people know (and if you know, you know). I'm thinking of Lastre Sans Apostrophe, for example. This gourmet shop is very near to my home and I'm just obsessed with their cuisine. So many friends in Paris don't know about this place and what they are missing out on. When I'm in line there, patiently waiting for the *plat du jour*, I marvel at the people quietly pouring in from all corners of the country because of just how special it is.

When I admire the windows of shops like À la Mère de Famille, Buly, Folderol, Café Nuances, and Marin Montagut, I reflect on my friends who founded and run them—Steve, Victoire, Jessica and Robert, Charles and his brother Raphaël, Marin—and I realize how these places flourish because of the people behind them. They exist as the result of family stories, love stories, and you can feel the emotions as you visit them.

Paris is my city, and there is a personal memory attached to every street corner. It's where I co-founded the concept store Colette, which was located at 213 rue Saint-Honoré and lasted from 1997 to 2017 (I secretly dream it would have been drawn by Joel). When it was still up and running, we worked with the cheese shop Barthélémy, with Berthillon for ice cream, with P. Legrand for the wine selection, with Maison Goyard for one-off collaborations, and they'll all remain part of my life forever. Just like the places that punctuated my earliest dates with my husband Philip: Charvet, Deyrolle, Café Verlet, Harry's New York Bar, Caractère de Cochon. And now, years and years later, he continues to rave about G. Detou and E. Dehillerin (despite complaining about almost everything else in France—he's American).

As I flip past the last page and close the book, there's only one thing I want to do: run to all the locations I don't know yet! Trains? How is it possible I've never been there with my son? La Boutique Sans Argent? *What's that*?!

Sarah Andelman co-founded Colette in Paris in 1997. For over 20 years, the concept store was globally renowned for its creativity at the intersection of style, design, art, and food. After closing it in 2017, she launched JUST AN IDEA, a consulting and curating company focused on brand collaborations and retail experiences. In 2021, she created the publishing company JUST AN IDEA BOOKS.

Introduction

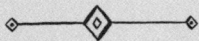

My first visit to Paris was for a quick 23 hours. I had extra time before flying back to Manhattan via London, so I Chunneled over and squeezed in as much as I could. I was really not prepared for just how beautiful the city was. It surpassed all literary and film-based expectations; I was gobsmacked.

I got a room at Delhy's Hotel (since renovated and now called Le Clos Notre-Dame) near the Notre-Dame Cathedral in the Latin Quarter. There were no amenities, other than an amazing view. I checked in, took a breath, and started walking.

I went past where the old Les Halles food market had been, by the bookstore Shakespeare and Company, stared at the Pompidou Centre, and kept going. I wanted to see as much as I could; it was so pretty. Eventually, I needed to break for a *café au lait* and a croissant. I could've stayed in that spot all day to soak everything in. But there was falafel to eat, art to see, and more to explore, so I carried on.

I walked over bridges decked out with golden statues and spotted unique newsstands, flower shops, tons of cafés, yellow mailboxes, and buildings with incredible histories. I passed so many stores, including brilliant oddities like a taxidermist's, a puppet shop, an exterminator, and art supply stores that knocked my socks off.

In the evening, while looking at my map to find another destination, I glanced up from the tree-lined residential street I was on and saw the Eiffel Tower. It had just started to twinkle. Starstruck, I just stood there. It was dinnertime, and I could hear the sounds of cutlery clinking on plates through open windows. Eventually, I walked up to the famous tower and marveled.

Exhausted—but not tired—I found my way back to my hotel room with a half-bottle of wine, a demi-baguette, and a few hours in which to sleep. I leaned out of the window to try to absorb all the sensations of being there, attempting to connect my prior expectations of this place to what I had actually seen.

My first book, *NYC Storefronts*—which featured illustrations of some of the city's best-loved stores—was published in 2022, and was followed by *London Shopfronts* in 2023 and *Brooklyn Storefronts* in 2024. Paris felt only natural as the next installment in the series, since visiting had been so inspirational.

Exploring a city while on vacation is much different than traveling for other purposes, and this is even more so when you live there. If you reside somewhere, your day-to-day experiences give you a unique wisdom. This is the gift that Paris-based journalist Vivian Song bestows on this book. Yes, we've included numerous heavy-hitter historic cafés and famous fashion outposts, but we've also covered an extensive array of diverse, unique businesses that show the city's wonders, both new and old. Thanks, Vivian!

Paris isn't a big city by traditional measurements, but it feels immense when you're tucked in it. The narrow passageways and skinny streets that snake along the Seine justify its romantic reputation supremely. Here, we've aimed to capture some of the pieces which make up the lovely, complex puzzle that is Paris. Take me back.

Joel Holland

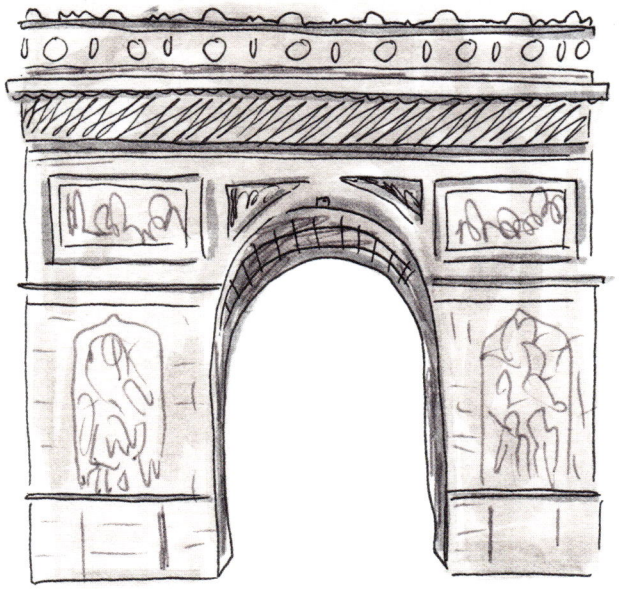

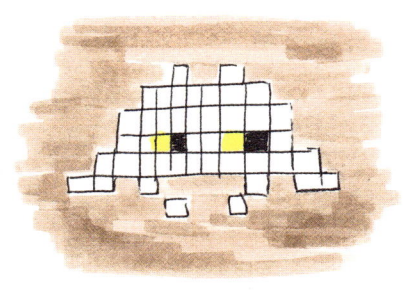

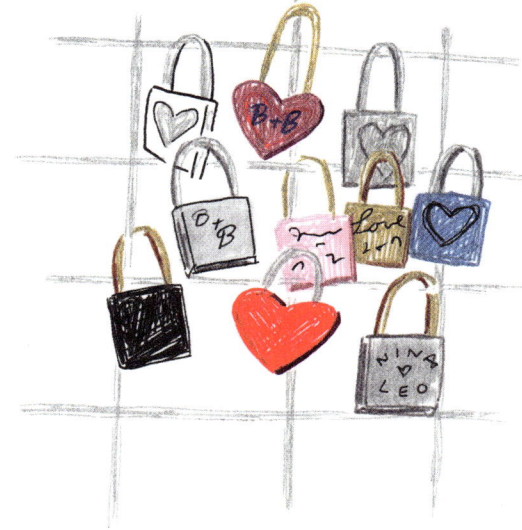

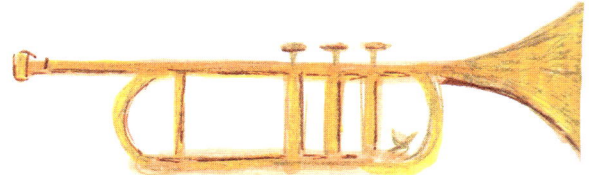

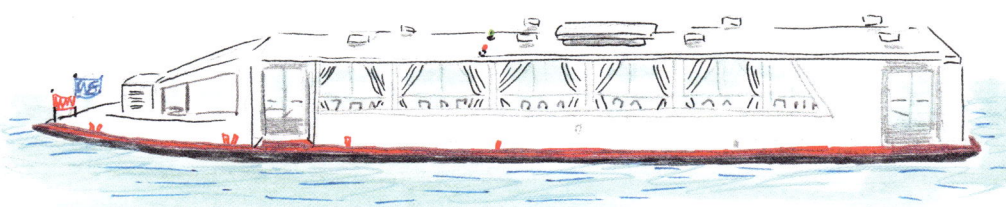

Note to the Reader

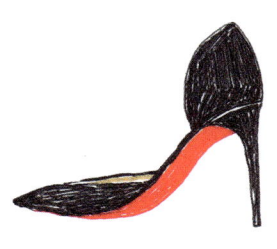

Paris is known for many things—among them, constant change. Care has been taken to provide current addresses for the shopfronts in this book, but some may have since moved or closed. Certain illustrations depict places that have permanently closed. In these cases, the old address is provided, and the text notes that the business has shuttered. Other shops changed locations after the illustration was made, during the process of creating this book. For these, the old shopfront is depicted, but the new address is provided to direct readers to the current location (to help keep it open there).

Café de Flore

——

Café de Flore's start as one of Paris's most important literary cafés can be traced back to one of its regular customers, French poet Guillaume Apollinaire, who turned the main floor into a newsroom for his journal *Les Soirées de Paris*. Apollinaire is also famous for having coined the term "Surrealism," and the café lays claim to being the cradle of this art movement.

About 50 years after its opening in 1887, a new owner installed a large stove in the middle of the café, offering artists a warm alternative to their cold, damp apartments. Some of the business's pseudo-tenants included Jean-Paul Sartre and Simone de Beauvoir, who revamped the second floor into their personal offices. The café has also been a favorite among movie stars and filmmakers (Jane Fonda, Jack Nicholson, Sofia and Francis Ford Coppola) and people in the world of high fashion (Yves Saint Laurent, Karl Lagerfeld, and Hubert de Givenchy).

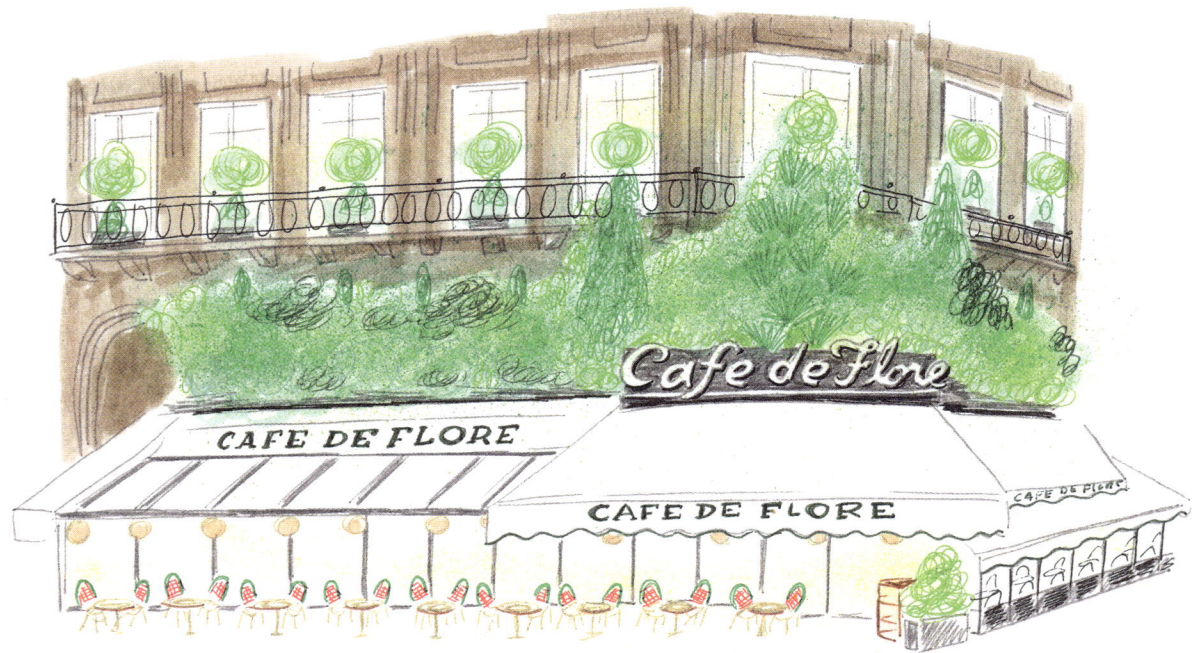

Les Deux Magots

———

While Les Deux Magots shares several characteristics with its next-door neighbor, Café de Flore, it boasts a slight edge in terms of age, having opened three years earlier. While the business was initially a novelty store, in 1884 it became a liqueur bar where French poets Arthur Rimbaud and Paul Verlaine met to exchange ideas on symbolism over glasses of the "green fairy," or absinthe. Many of the same giants of English and French literature who frequented Café de Flore were also customers of Les Deux Magots: Ernest Hemingway, Jean-Paul Sartre, Simone de Beauvoir, Guillaume Apollinaire, and Albert Camus. Since 1933, the café has organized a yearly literary prize that favors early and under-the-radar writers, as well as hosting readings and monthly writers' workshops, building on its heritage as one of the most influential literary cafés in Paris.

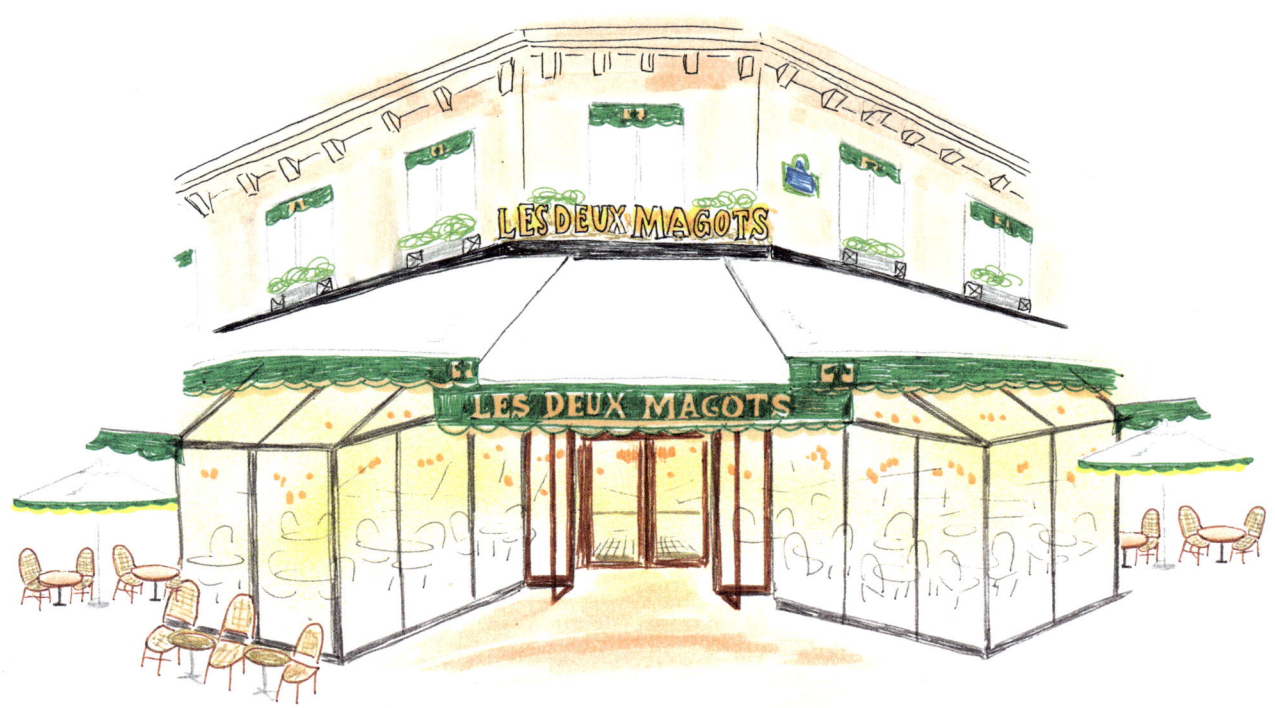

Antoine

———

The oldest cane and umbrella shop in Paris, Antoine is a testament to a bygone era, when walking sticks were *de rigueur* for men but umbrellas were considered a cumbersome and feminine accessory. In 1745, an enterprising couple, the Antoines, came up with the idea of opening an umbrella rental service at Pont Neuf, a bustling bridge lined with merchants and tradesmen. On rainy days, instead of having to carry around the unsightly item, Parisians could rent an umbrella "chez Antoine" at one end of the bridge, then leave it at the shop at the other side. The business moved to the Palais-Royal district before shifting to its current location in 1886, where mother-daughter duo Dominique and Sophie Lecarpentier continue the tradition, selling canes, umbrellas, hats, and folding fans made in France.

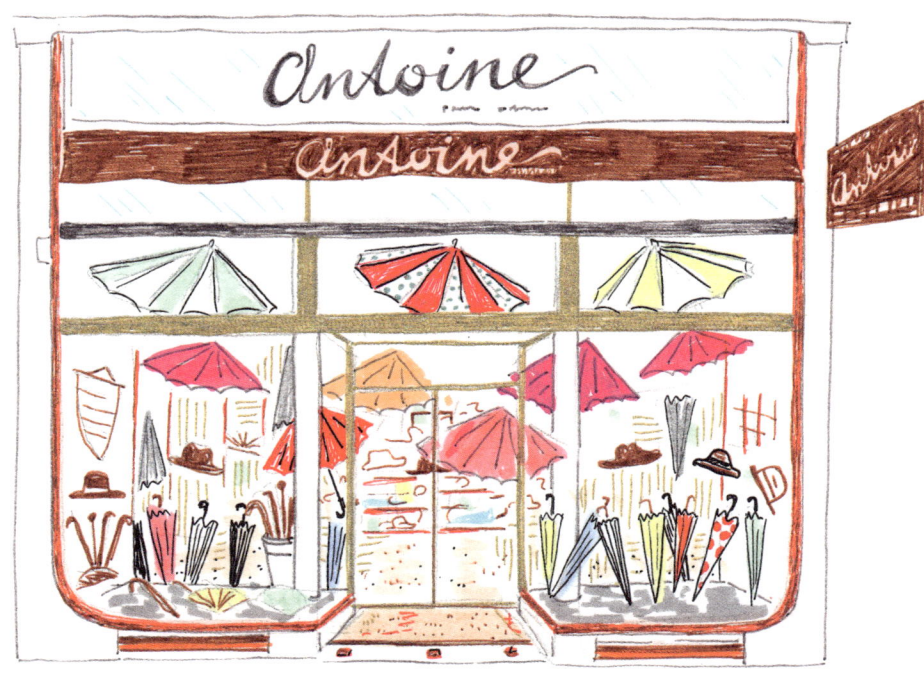

Ines de la Fressange Paris

A fashion icon of the 1980s, when she was the muse of Karl Lagerfeld and the face of Chanel, former supermodel Ines de la Fressange is often described as the archetypal *Parisienne*. It was only natural, then, that the French beauty would turn her name into a bankable brand, opening her own boutique in 2015 on the posh part of the Left Bank. Located in a former foundry, her clothing line is a high-end *prêt-à-porter* collection for the modern woman. It's not hard to find Chanel-inspired pieces, like tweed blazers and LBDs (or little black dresses). The brand also produces leather handbags, shoes, and accessories. In classic French—and Ines—style, pieces are chic, but don't shy away from color or prints. Products are made in Paris, and a workshop is located within the store.

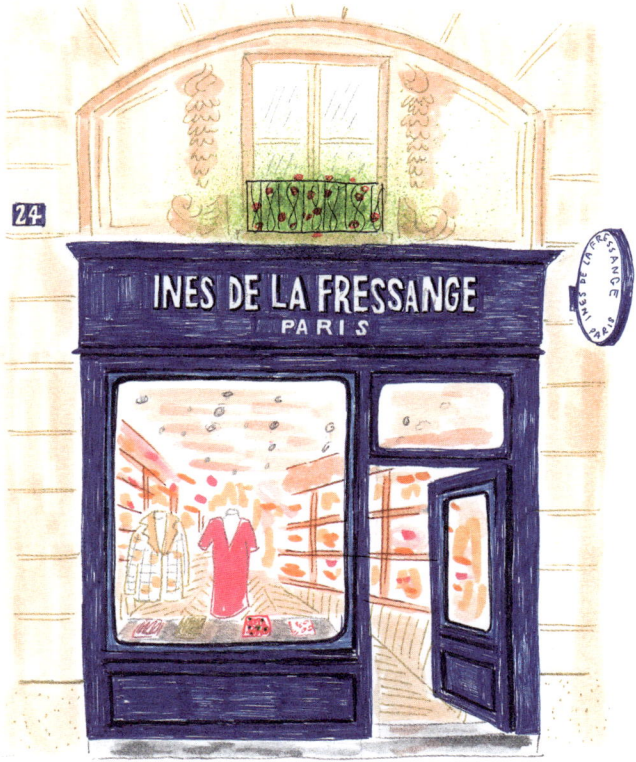

Laulhère

———

Aside from elderly French gentlemen, Parisians don't generally wear berets. In fact, one of the easiest ways to identify a tourist or influencer among the crowds is to look for the tops of brightly colored, souvenir-style flat-crowned caps. That said, there *is* a place for the right type of beret, styled in a way that honors French heritage and doesn't perpetuate stereotypes.

Enter Laulhère, a business comprised of master craftspeople that has been producing handmade berets for almost 200 years. Their hats have topped the heads of celebrities including Madonna, Emma Watson, and Rihanna. Founded in 1840 in the French Pyrenees from the marital union of a merchant who specialized in wool stockings and a woman from a family of beret makers, Laulhère is the last remaining beret factory crafting caps that are 100 percent produced in France.

Each headpiece takes around two days to create and passes through the hands of about a dozen local craftspeople in Laulhère's workshops in southwest France, who reshape every one by hand.

The brand produces about 200,000 berets a year for the public, but also for *haute couture* houses like Gucci, Saint Laurent, and Dior. Laulhère is also the official beret supplier to the French army, and their products have been worn by Belgian, Norwegian, and African soldiers. The company's flagship Paris store is hidden in a courtyard off the rue du Faubourg Saint-Honoré and another location is in the 18th arrondissement.

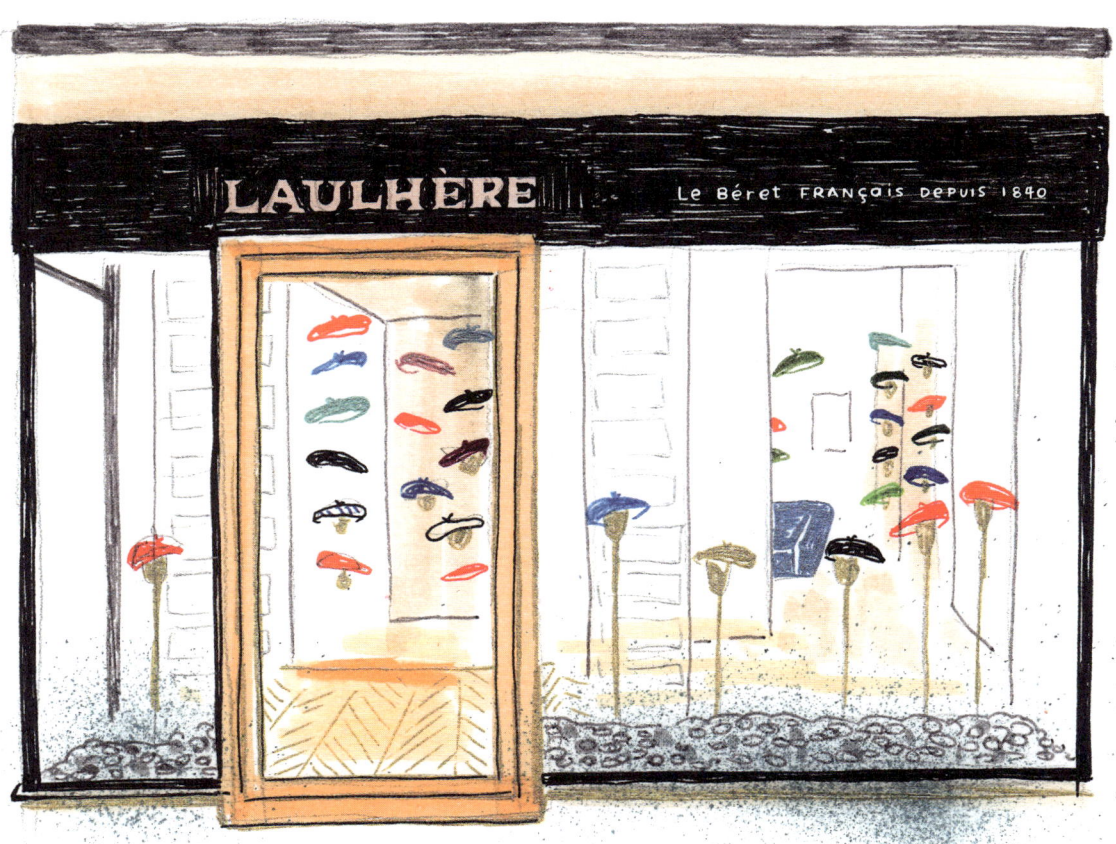

L'Officine

—

While its vintage signage reads "Homeopathie" and "Allopathie," this former pharmacy no longer dispenses anything medicinal— although it does cure hunger and thirst. Today, it's a bistro serving steak *béarnaise*, duck confit, and molten chocolate cake.

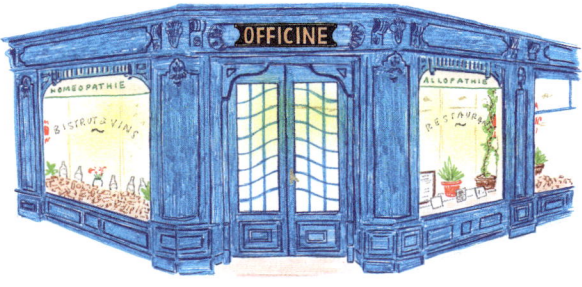

9 rue de la Monnaie
1st arr.

La Samaritaine

—

When it opened in 1870, La Samaritaine was the go-to department store for Paris's working class. After a painstaking 16-year renovation, the property reopened in 2021 under LVMH as a luxury department store in the city center.

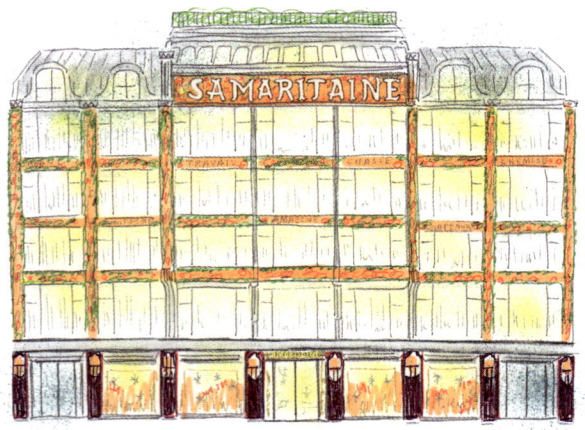

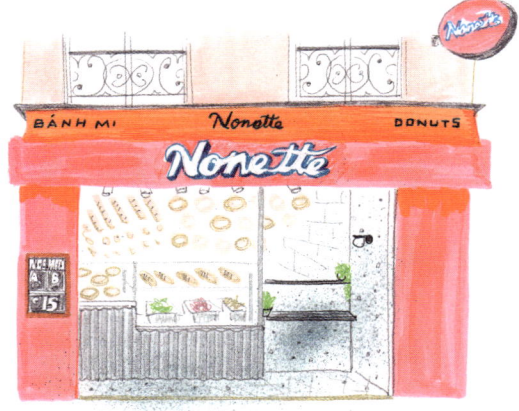

71 rue Jean-Pierre Timbaud
11th arr.

Nonette Bánh Mì
& Donuts

—

This takeout shop is a lunchtime favorite for its homemade *bánh mì* sandwiches and donuts in flavors like pork floss and durian. The concept is meant to reflect the Vietnamese, French, American, and Singaporean heritage of its female founders.

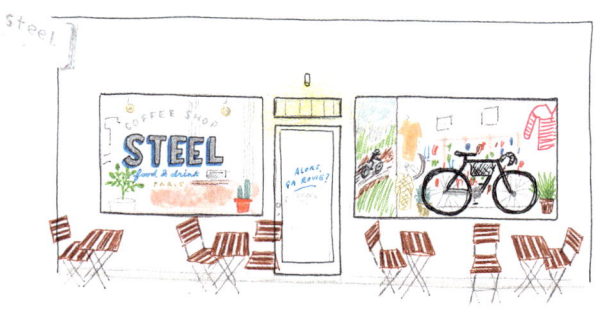

58 rue de la Fontaine au Roi
11th arr.

Steel Cyclewear
& Coffeeshop

—

Born out of a French lifestyle magazine for city cyclists called *Steel*, this concept store and coffee shop opened in 2015, selling high-end products to a community of passionate urban bikers.

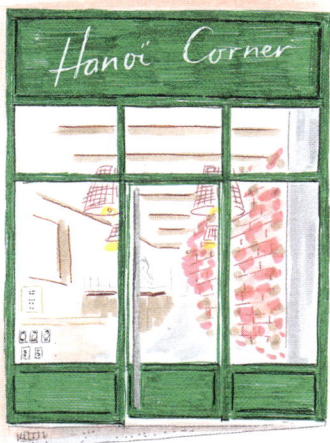

7 rue Blanche
9th arr.

Hanoi Corner

—

This café and lunch spot, which sadly closed in late 2024, claimed to be the first Vietnamese coffee shop in Paris, with pour-over coffees made with imported *cà phê* carefully selected by the shop's Vietnamese owners.

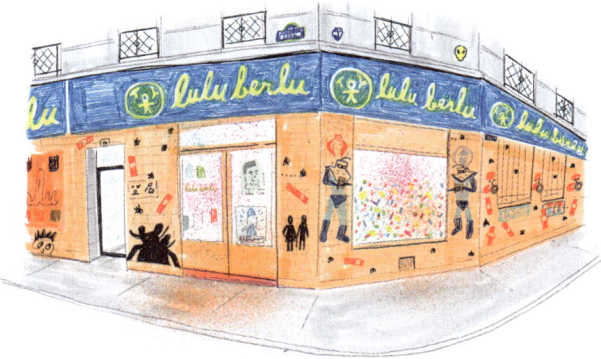

2 rue du Grand Prieuré
11th arr.

Lulu Berlu

—

The largest vintage and collectible toy store in Paris, Lulu Berlu is the place to go to relive moments of your childhood. Here, the shelves are lined with action figures and pop culture memorabilia (think *ThunderCats*, *Astro Boy*, and Care Bears).

29–31 rue Saint-Louis en l'Île
4th arr.

Berthillon

—

If you spot long lines outside a shop on Île Saint-Louis in the summer, odds are that you've stumbled on Berthillon, the city's most famous and enduring artisanal ice cream maker. They've been at it since 1954, and their signature flavor is wild strawberry sorbet.

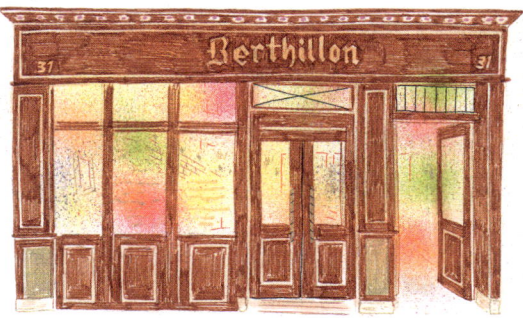

3 rue Charles Robin
10th arr.

Gumbo Yaya

—

Since 2015, Gumbo Yaya has been catering to homesick US expats and curious Parisians unfamiliar with American soul food. On the menu: chicken and waffles drizzled with maple syrup, mac and cheese, fried pickles, and biscuits.

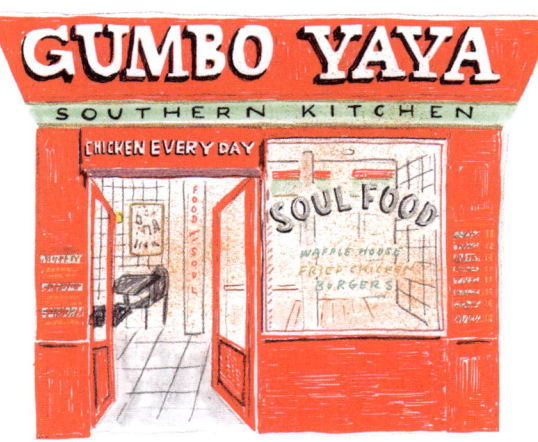

Little Red Door

———

On the international cocktail scene, Little Red Door has long been acknowledged as one of the top bars in Paris. Since opening in 2012, it has appeared on the influential World's 50 Best Bars list no fewer than 10 times and first cracked the top 10 in 2022.

Like any good speakeasy, it's easy to miss: its walls are painted a discreet slate gray, there's no signage, and its namesake entryway is cleverly recessed into the façade. Inside, the space is warm and inviting, with candlelight, brick walls, and New York vibes. The bar's locally sourced produce and "Farm to Glass" ethos made it an industry leader in sustainability. In July 2024 it changed hands, and is now run by the duo behind The Cambridge Public House in the same arrondissement, who promise equally inventive and masterful cocktails.

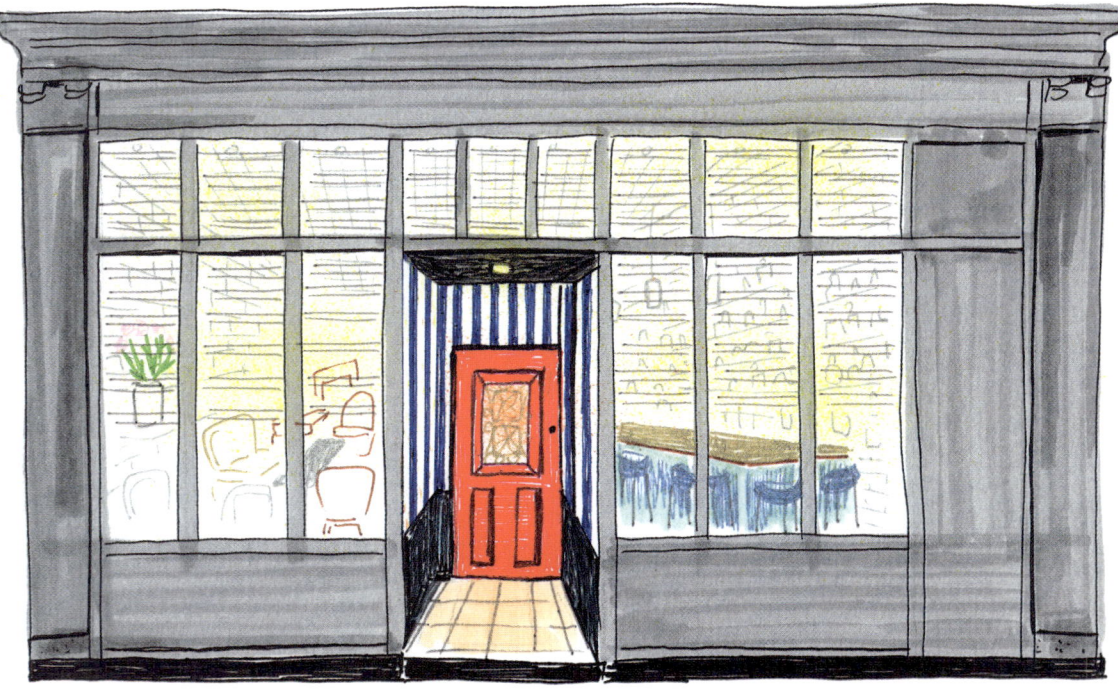

Delhi Bazaar

——

French friends Bastien Peccoux and Alexis Gracio opened Delhi Bazaar because they felt that Indian cuisine in Paris was mostly either represented by the cheap and spartan canteens near Gare du Nord and La Chapelle, or high-end restaurants, with few good options in between.

Almost as soon as it opened, the restaurant was hailed as one of the most successful new spots of 2023 thanks to its modern decor (no Taj Mahals here), stylized plating, and flavorful dishes like roasted broccoli *makhani* and chicken korma, made with up to 40 spices under Bangladeshi chef Eqbal Hossain. That said, a meal at Delhi Bazaar is less likely to whisk diners to India and more to London, where the founders scouted the dynamic Indian food scene for inspiration.

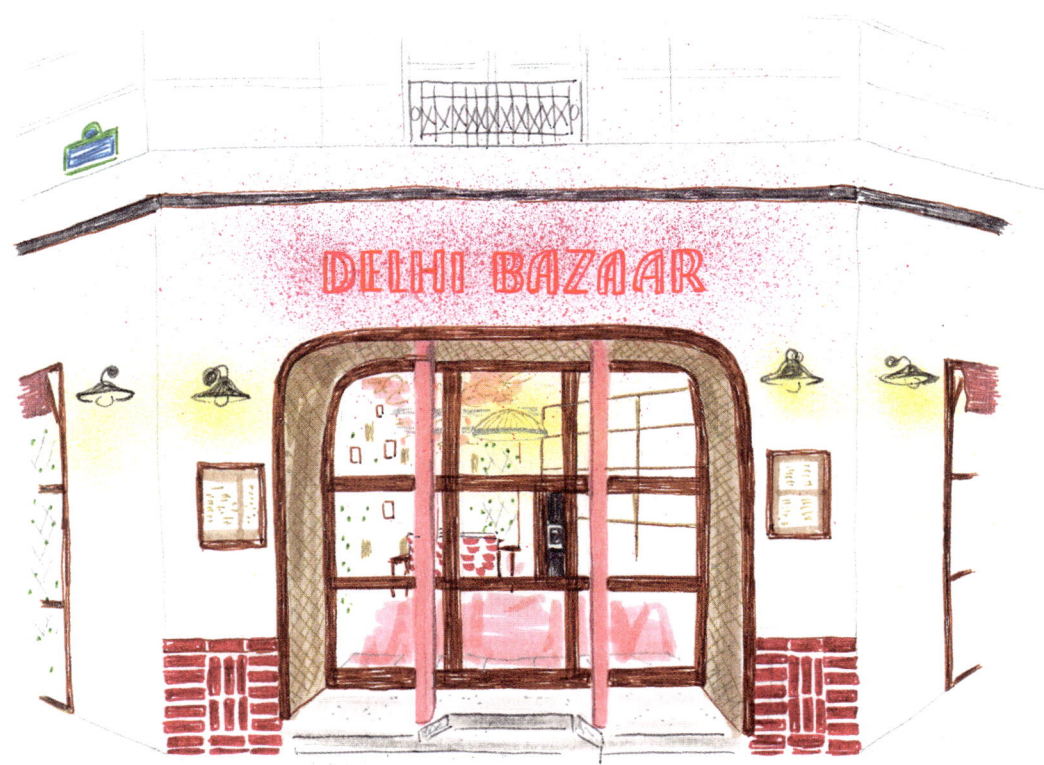

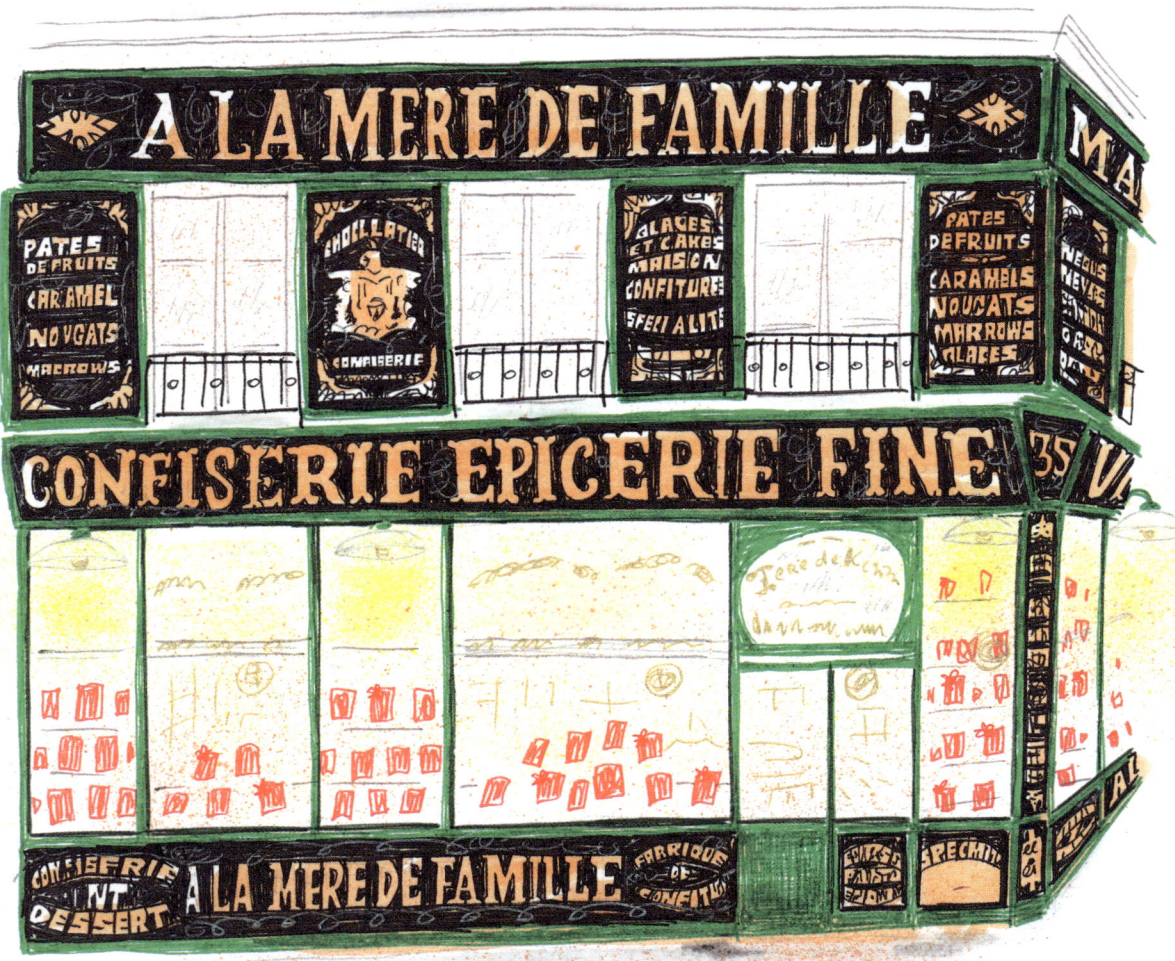

À la Mère de Famille

———

À la Mère de Famille could be described as the chocolate shop of fairy tales. Originally a neighborhood grocery store, it has been steered by eight different generations and families since being founded in 1761. But it was in the 1850s, under the ownership of the Bridault sisters, that it pivoted to chocolates and confectionery, with the proliferation and democratization of sugar in France. The storefront was eventually listed as a historic monument by the French government in 1984.

Today, four siblings of the Dolfi family serve as its guardians. Besides being the oldest *chocolaterie* in Paris, the shop at rue du Faubourg Montmartre is also one of the prettiest, with its bottle-green façade and gold-leaf lettering announcing its goods from candy and confectionery to chocolate and desserts. Window displays serve as portholes into a universe of bonbons, sugar-crystal-crusted *pâté de fruits*, sachets of caramels, candied chestnuts, and artisanal marshmallows.

À la Mère de Famille has been beckoning passers-by for centuries, turning them into modern-day Hansels and Gretels as they press their noses up against its windows.

Along with pushing the brand's expansion—there are now 16 locations across Paris and its suburbs—the Dolfis added another local institution to the family when they bought Stohrer, the oldest pastry shop in Paris, in 2017 (see p. 153).

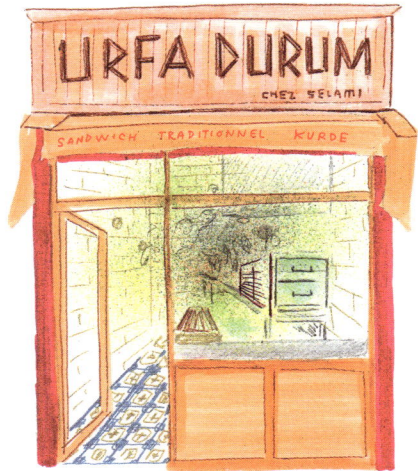

58 rue du Faubourg Saint-Denis
10th arr.

Urfa Dürüm

This popular Kurdish wrap shop has been serving up homemade flatbreads stuffed with doner kebab meats like lamb, chicken, and beef since 1987. Expect long lines of late-night drinkers looking to soak up the booze.

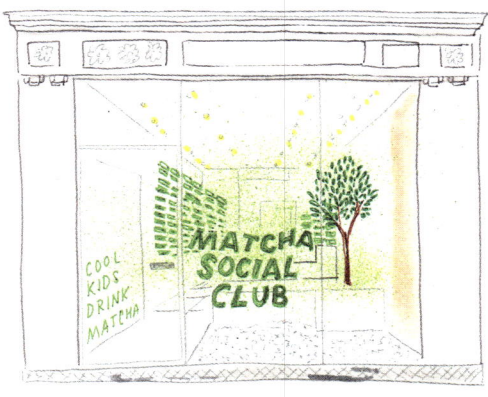

39 rue des Petits Champs
1st arr.

Matcha Social Club

Matcha connoisseurs know to come here for an authentic hit of Uji matcha, one of the most premium grades from Japan. Along with matcha lattes, the takeout café offers matcha cakes and soft serve.

62 rue de Sèvres
7th arr.

Fromagerie Quatrehomme

Marie Quatrehomme became the first female cheesemaker to take the title of Meilleur Ouvrier de France (MOF) in 2000, a prestigious designation that honors the best craftspeople of their trade. Her gourmet shop boasts a line-up of 250 cheeses, and she has four other locations in France.

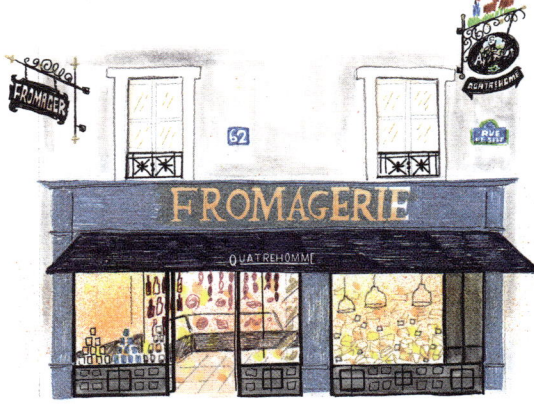

16 rue Guisarde
6th arr.

Au Plat d'Etain

Since 1775, this boutique has been selling hand-painted figurines and toy soldiers to avid collectors keen on recreating historic battle scenes. The story goes that former French president Charles de Gaulle was one of the shop's regular customers.

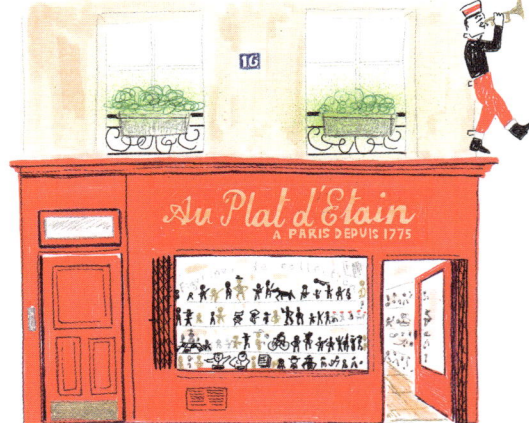

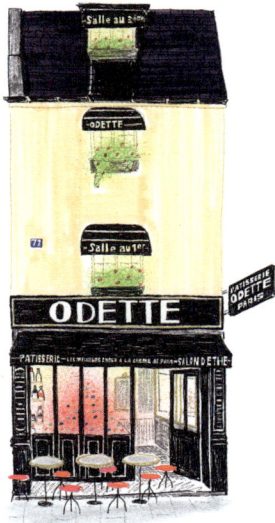

77 rue Galande
5th arr.

Odette

—

Located near Notre-Dame at the end of a lovely side street in a 17th-century building, this charming tea salon sells dreamy, bite-sized cream puffs in flavors like chocolate, passion fruit, and salted butter caramel. There are two other locations in Paris.

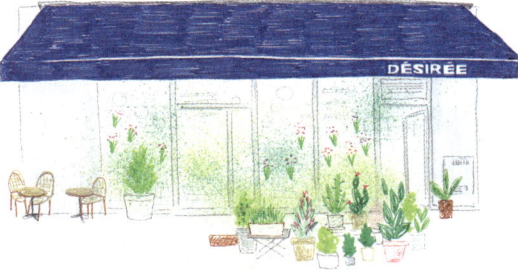

96 rue de Meaux
19th arr.

Désirée

—

It's estimated that 85 percent of flowers sold in France are imports. But this florist café works exclusively with French horticulturalists for its artistically assembled bouquets, which also respect the seasons. The menu is both sweet and savory. There are two other florist-only locations in the city.

21 Bd du Temple
3rd arr.

Trains

—

Specializing in model and miniature toy trains, this store has been described by many visitors as a journey back to childhood. Owner Citerne Maurice-Victor can customize and repair model trains, but also toy planes, helicopters, and boats.

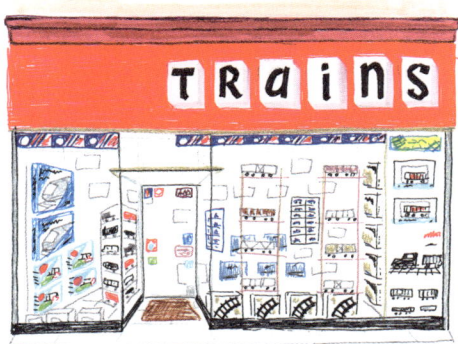

7 Bd de Port-Royal
13th arr.

La P'tite Cave

—

At "The Lil' Wine Shop," it's the fall grape harvest year-round—at least according to the yellowing leaves and grapes painted on the façade panels that lend the store its charm. It stocks biodynamic and natural wines.

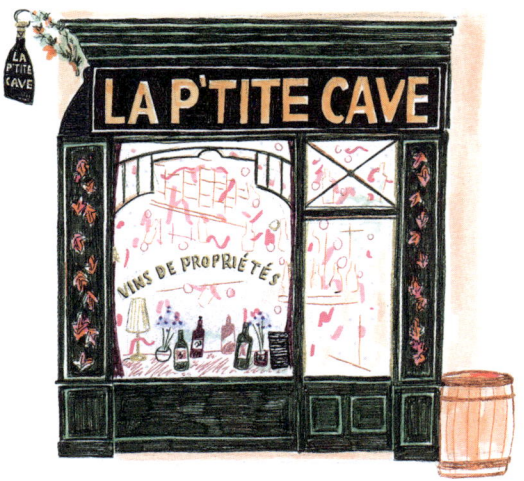

La Tour d'Argent

As one of the most historic restaurants in Paris, La Tour d'Argent has welcomed heads of state (John F. Kennedy), royalty (Queen Elizabeth II), and A-list celebrities (Angelina Jolie and Brad Pitt) over the years. It claims to have a heritage that goes back to 1582 and is famous for its signature "bloody duck" dish, prepared in a centuries-old press that crushes the animal's carcass to extract the juices and create a sauce.

In 2023, third-generation owner André Terrail reopened the restaurant following extensive refurbishments and additions. Along with a new cognac bar, luxury hotel suite, and rooftop bar, the sixth-floor dining room now features an open kitchen. La Tour d'Argent is also famous for its 300,000-bottle wine cellar, its panoramic views of Notre-Dame, and inspiring the 2007 Pixar movie *Ratatouille*.

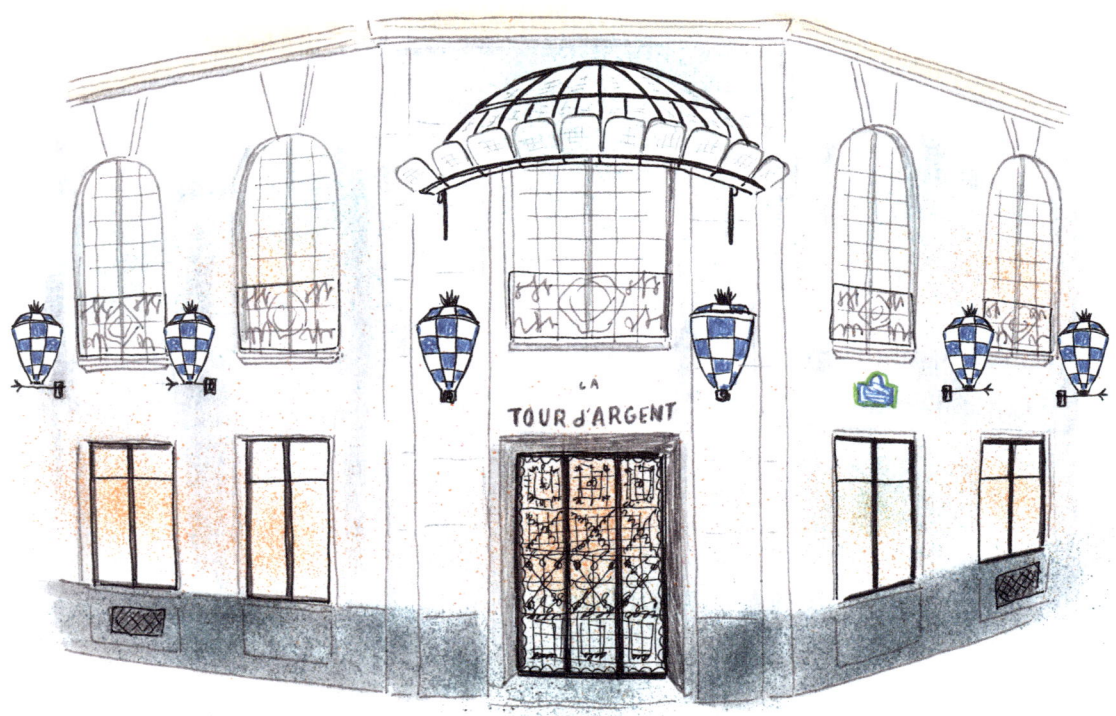

Lastre Sans Apostrophe

———

This takeout charcuterie shop specializes in one very particular, centuries-old French delicacy: *pâté en croûte*, a meat terrine that's wrapped in a pastry crust and baked until golden brown. For years, the dish had become obsolete and outdated, until the arrival of the "World Championship in *Pâté en Croûte*" event in 2009, aimed at reviving the traditional appetizer.

After winning the 2012 title, Yohan Lastre, who had worked in some of Paris's top high-end restaurants (including La Tour d'Argent—see opposite—and the Ritz Paris), opened Lastre Sans Apostrophe in 2016, helping to make *pâté en croûte* fashionable again. Along with classics like pork, chicken, and pistachio, he also creates elaborate recipes that include seven types of game meat, foie gras, sweetbreads, and truffles in one terrine. The average *pâté en croûte* takes four days to make.

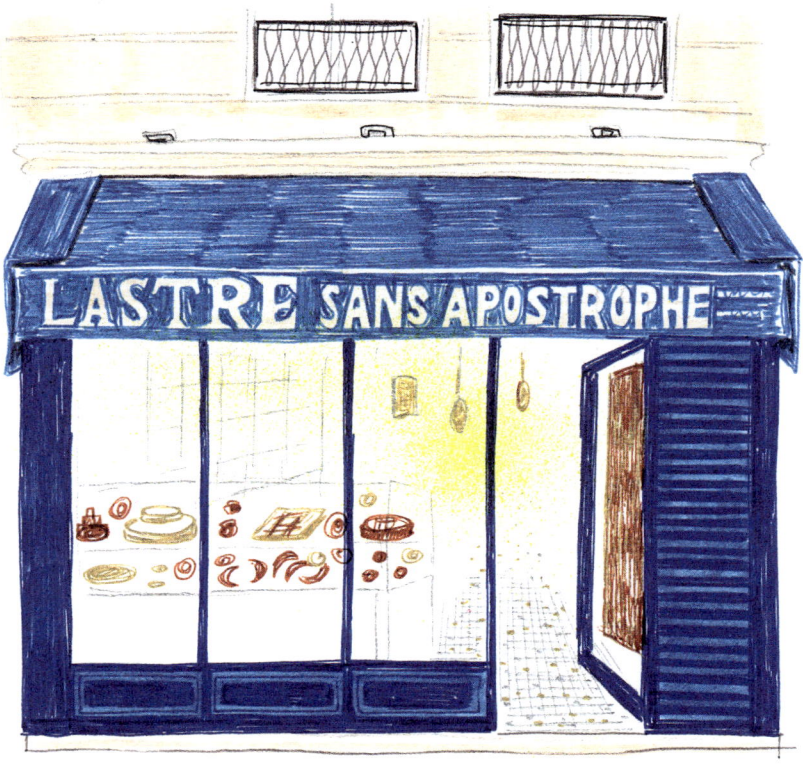

Nina's Vendôme

———

Every sip of Nina's Marie-Antoinette tea is a taste of royalty—quite literally. The shop is the exclusive partner of the Gardens of Versailles (created in the 17th century by Louis XIV) and uses the fruits of the gardens to flavor their teas. This extraordinary privilege can be traced in part to Nina's 1986 acquisition of the historic Distillerie Frères, founded by Pierre Diaz in 1672, who earned the favor of the king and queen for his mastery of blending fragrances. He also became famous for distilling lavender and rose essences to perfume ladies' gloves. Nina's signature Marie-Antoinette tea is made with rose petals and apples from the royal gardens (a scent created for her by Diaz), which boast 200 varieties of apples alone. The boutique also has a lovely sit-in tea salon.

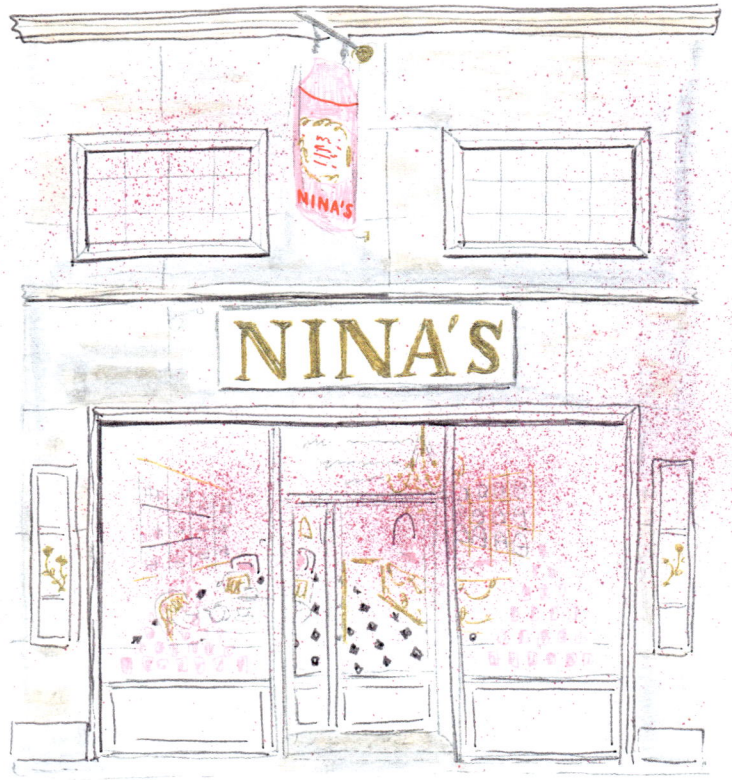

Shakespeare and Company

———

The most famous English-language bookshop in Paris, Shakespeare and Company was founded by American expat George Whitman in 1951. George sought to continue the legacy of the original Shakespeare and Company run by another American bookseller, Sylvia Beach, a few streets over. Before the Germans shut down Sylvia's shop during World War II, it had been an important gathering place for anglophone writers, including Ernest Hemingway and James Joyce. George wanted to create a similar space for expat writers of his generation, bringing together the likes of James Baldwin, Allen Ginsberg, and Anaïs Nin.

Today, the store is run by George's daughter Sylvia, named after Sylvia Beach, who also organizes literary festivals, writing competitions, and readings with authors such as Zadie Smith and Jennifer Egan. The shop has had star turns on the big screen in films like *Before Sunset* and *Julie & Julia*.

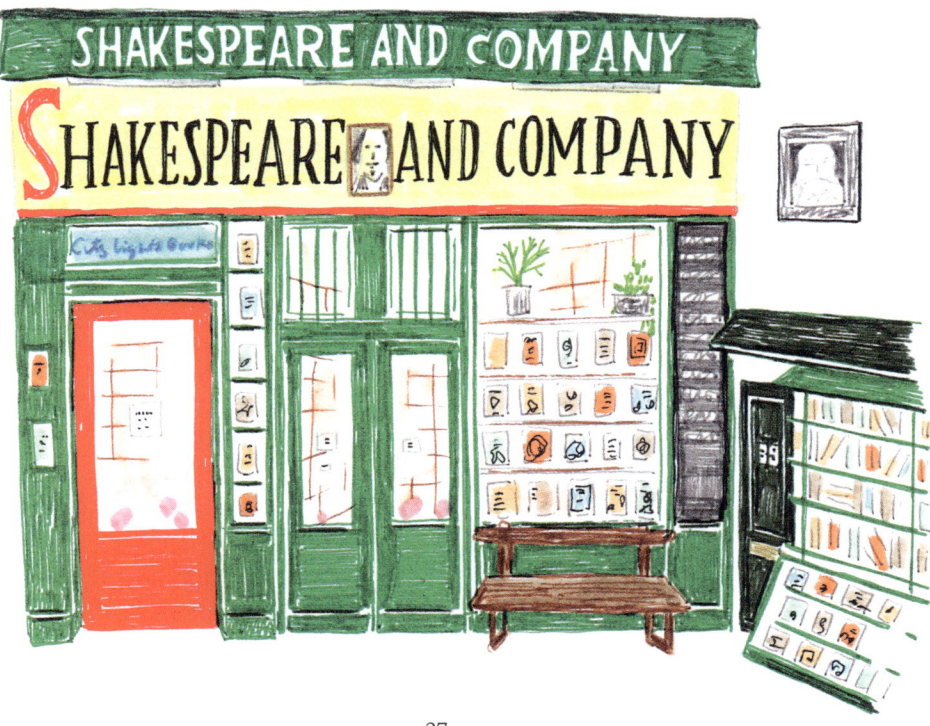

Le Dôme

Of the four big brasseries and cafés that line either side of Boulevard du Montparnasse and compete for the attention of passersby—La Coupole, La Rotonde, Le Select (see p. 123), and Le Dôme—the last was the first to open, and transformed the Montparnasse neighborhood into a literary and artistic hub on the Left Bank.

Founded in 1898, the café became so popular among influential writers and artists over the decades that regulars were known as the "Dômiers."

They included Paul Gauguin, Pablo Picasso, and Vladimir Lenin, along with members of the Lost Generation: American writer expats such as Ezra Pound, Henry Miller, Ernest Hemingway, and Gertrude Stein. So pivotal was the café in their lives that Hemingway made reference to it in his book *A Moveable Feast*, and Édith Piaf in her love song to the city "Paris," singing: "Creamy coffees in the morning / Montparnasse, the Dôme café."

In 2018, after 30 years of service, chef Frank Graux ceded his place to Japanese chef Yoshihiko Miura, who was recruited by Le Dôme's owners Edouard and Maxime Bras to modernize the restaurant. The menu includes classic French seafood dishes like bouillabaisse, sole *meunière*, and roasted blue lobster flambéed in cognac, but it's also known for its towering fresh seafood platters featuring different varieties of oysters, shrimp, crab, and lobster.

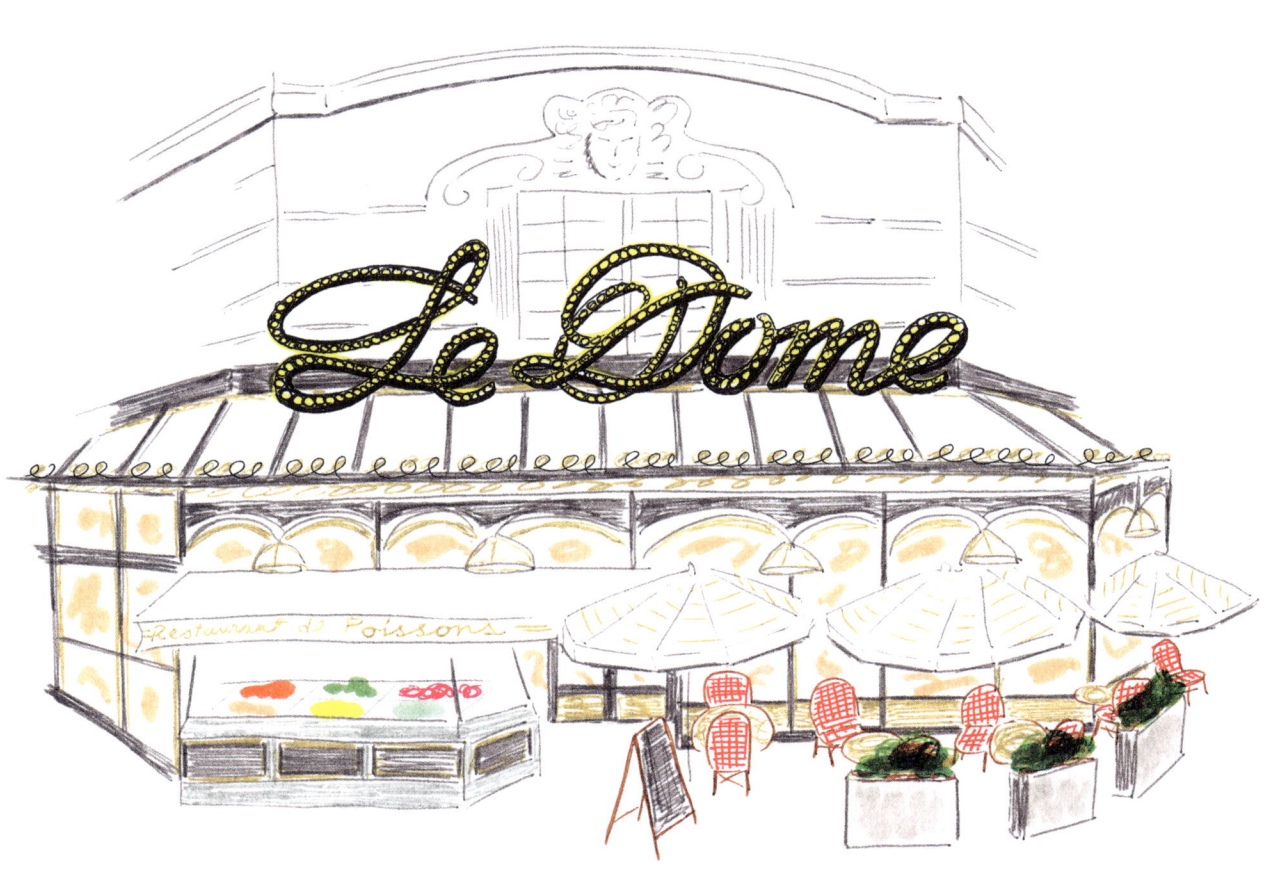

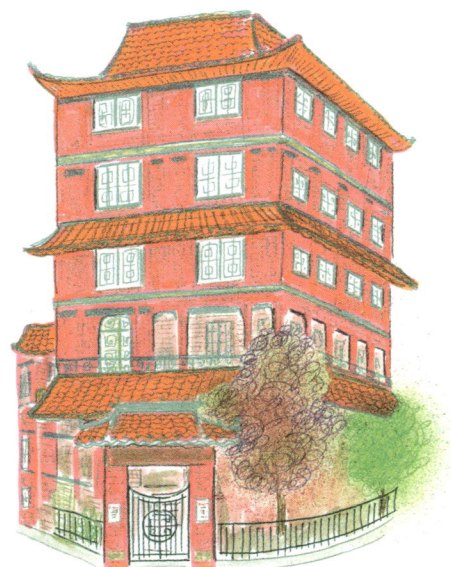

48 rue de Courcelles
8th arr.

Pagoda Paris

—

This stunning pagoda is the legacy of Chinese art dealer Ching Tsai Loo, who immigrated to France in 1902 and built the venue to house his art collection. Today, it's rented out for private events.

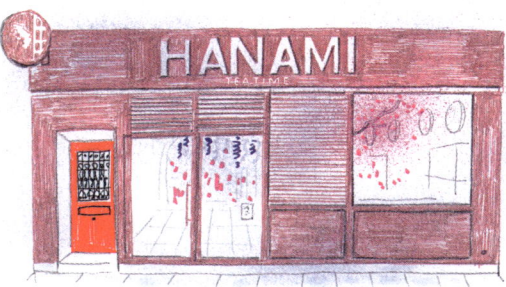

50 rue des Gravilliers
3rd arr.

Hanami Teatime

—

Inside this Japanese tea salon, cherry blossoms are in bloom year-round, and the menu specializes in one dish: fluffy pancakes. Cloud-like offerings come in flavors such as matcha and red berries, tiramisu, and crème brulée.

30 rue des 5 Diamants
13th arr.

Chez Gladines

Regulars of this neighborhood restaurant come here for the authentic Basque cuisine of southwest France. Signature dishes include roast chicken, omelets, and squid in a *Basquaise* sauce of tomatoes, red peppers, onions, and chilis.

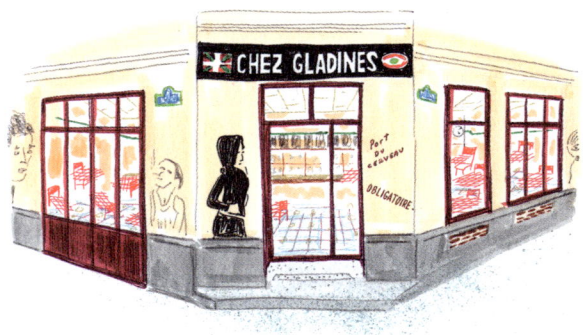

19 rue du Pont aux Choux
3rd arr.

Boot Café

—

Formerly a shoe repair shop ("*cordonnerie*" means cobbler), this has been one of the most popular coffee destinations in Paris since 2014 due to its espressos and Chemex pour-over brews, as well as its weather-worn vintage aesthetic.

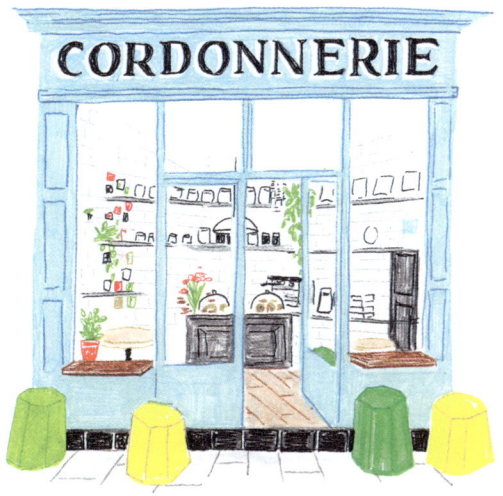

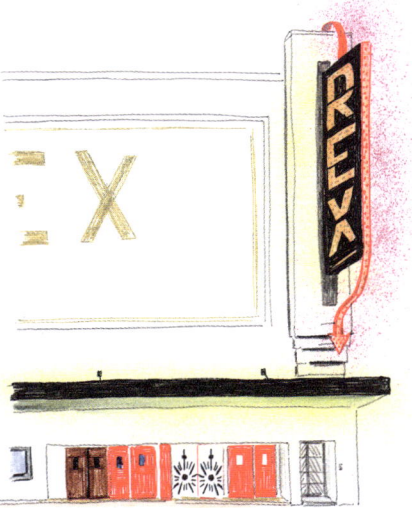

5 Bd Poissonnière
2nd arr.

Rex Club

—

Originally a disco venue when it opened in the basement of the Grand Rex (see p. 145) in 1973, today the Rex Club is known as the launchpad for lauded DJs like Laurent Garnier, David Guetta, and Daft Punk, and is considered Paris's temple of electronic music.

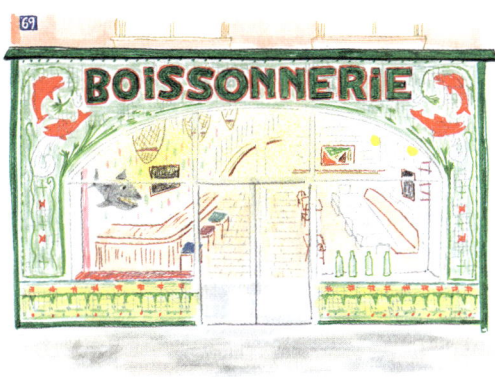

69 rue de Seine
6th arr.

Fish La Boissonnerie

—

Amazingly, this mosaic-tiled façade that's striking enough to be appreciated as a work of art was once home to a humble fishmonger. Today, it houses a popular restaurant known for honest, generous bistro fare.

2 rue Edouard Robert
12th arr.

La Boutique Sans Argent

—

Who said nothing in life is free? At the eco-minded "Moneyless Boutique," which opened in 2013, *everything* is free—with the aim of giving old clothes, toys, and dishware a second life, no strings attached.

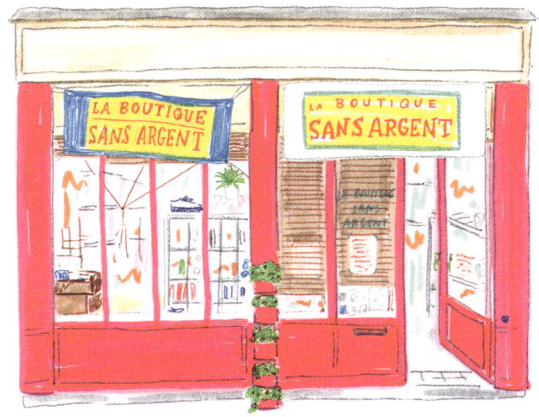

85bis rue de Charenton
12th arr.

Boulangerie Bo

—

Ideally located steps from the famous Aligre farmer's market, this corner bakery is classified as a historic monument due to its painted panels depicting a wheat harvest outside, and original ceramic tiles inside.

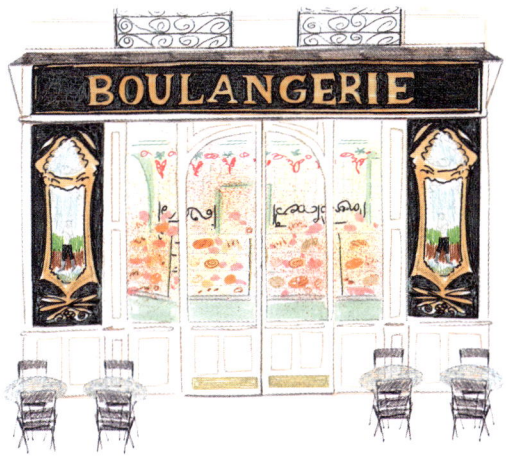

61 rue de Meaux

19th arr.

Le Paon Qui Boit

———

After staying away from alcohol during the pandemic, Augustin Laborde decided to make it a way of life, but was frustrated by the lack of options for non-drinkers and the social pressure to imbibe. After some research, he opened Le Paon Qui Boit in the spring of 2022—the first booze-free wine shop in Paris. It caused quite a stir: after all, a huge part of France's cultural identity lies in its winemaking heritage and romanticized drinking culture. But the opening of a boutique selling 450 non-alcoholic wines, beers, and liquors resonated strongly with the growing part of the population that was moving away from booze, and the teetotalers who had always been excluded from the local drinking culture. The shop is popular among pregnant women, Muslims, and people with health problems.

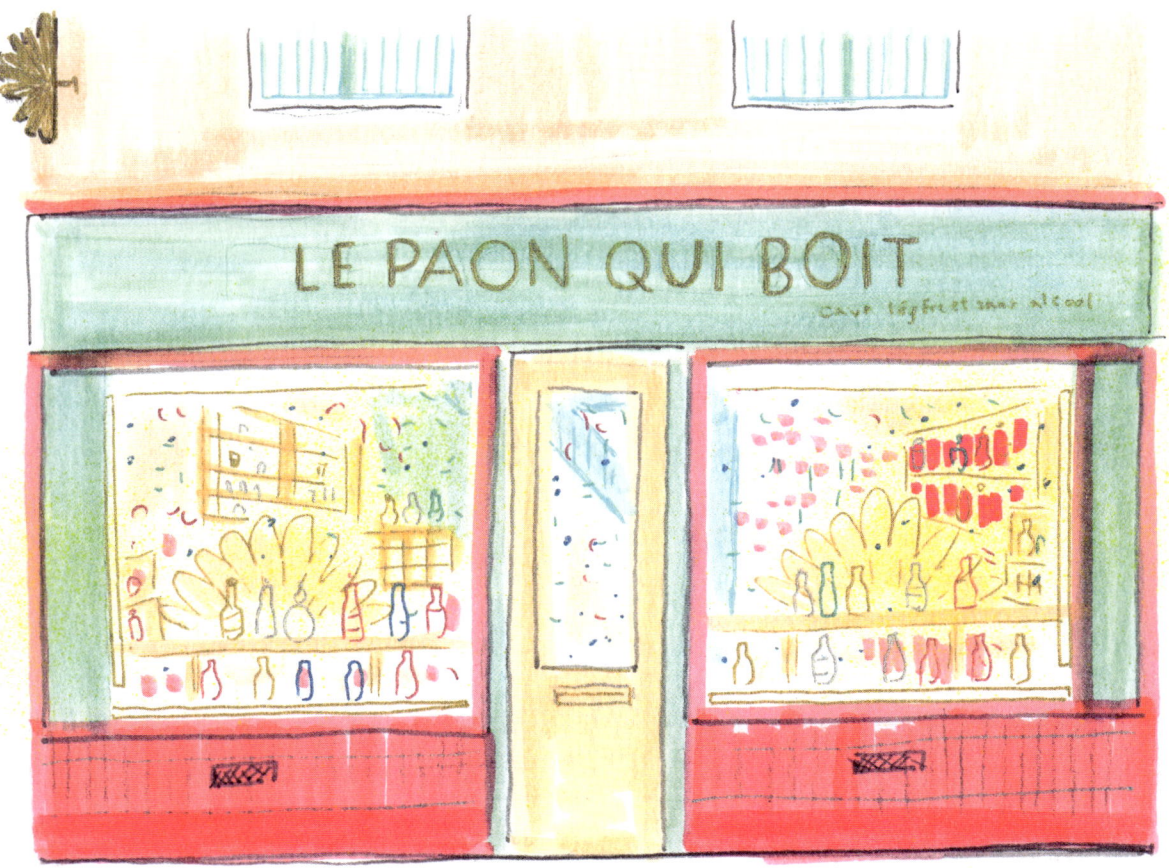

Boneshaker Donuts

———

American pastry chef Amanda Bankert ignored the French naysayers (mainly banks) who pooh-poohed her idea of bringing donuts to Paris, and opened a small takeout counter in 2016 after a successful pop-up experiment. Since then, not only has she proven her critics wrong, but she's helped make donuts a bona fide favorite pastry in the city: nowadays, it's not uncommon to find them sharing shelf space with *éclairs* and lemon tarts in neighborhood bakeries.

Boneshaker's takeout counter has since evolved into a sit-down store that sells artisanal handmade donuts in flavors like cinnamon sugar, peanut butter glaze and chocolate drizzle, and speculoos. New flavors are introduced every season. In keeping with her own lifestyle, in 2019, Amanda tweaked her recipes: now, all the offerings are vegan.

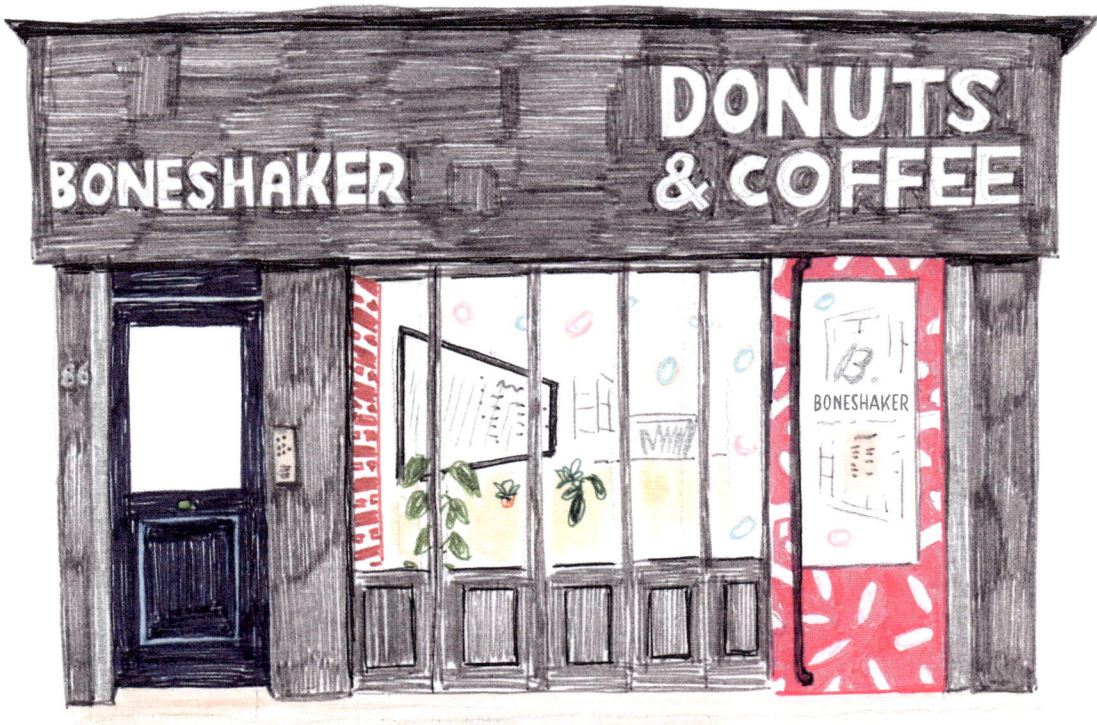

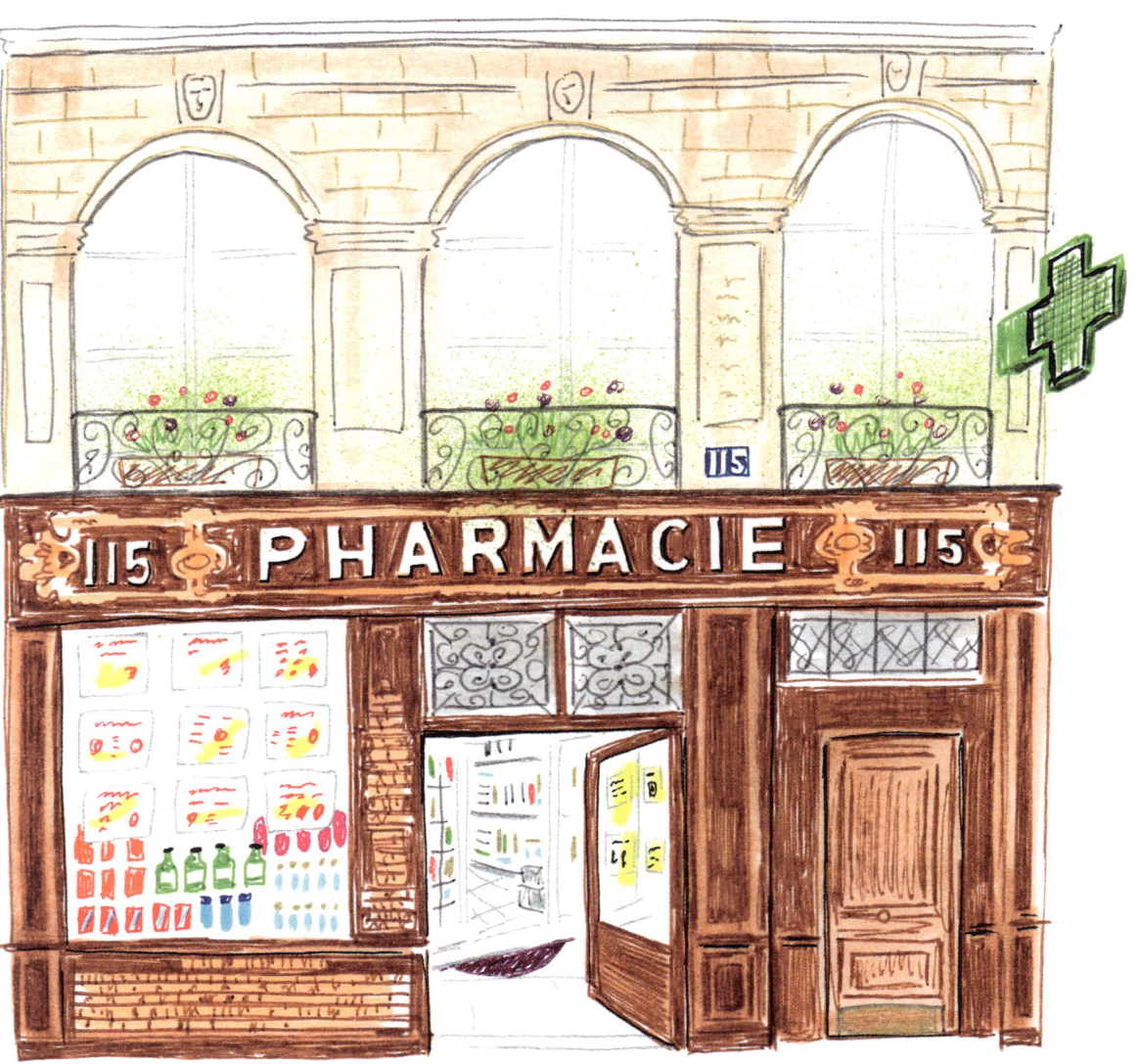

La Pharmacie Saint-Honoré

———

This pharmacy lays claim to being the oldest in Paris, with a history that can be traced back to the 1700s under the ownership of one of France's most renowned pharmacists and chemists of the time, Louis Claude Cadet de Gassicourt. Along with stints as the chief pharmacist for the armies of Germany and Portugal, Gassicourt was an apothecary at Hôtel des Invalides in Paris, where injured soldiers were treated, and served as the king's commissioner for chemistry at the famous Sèvres porcelain factory.

In 1762, he opened his own pharmacy at 115 rue Saint-Honoré, which went on to become one of the most sought-out apothecaries among the French.

Its reputation even drew Count Axel von Fersen, who, as the story goes, purchased invisible ink there so that he could write to his beloved Marie Antoinette in secret (the Swede was known to hold the special attentions of the queen, and rumors were rife of the pair's relationship).

The pharmacy was also popular for stocking mineral water from Passy, reputed for its laxative properties. Archival images show that, aside from new coats of paint and the addition of automatic doors, the façade has changed little over the years.

Florence Kahn

———

With its bejeweled blue-and-white mosaic façade, this Jewish delicatessen and bakery is a literal and figurative cornerstone of the Marais neighborhood, having anchored the corner of rue des Écouffes and rue des Rosiers since 1932. But it wasn't until Florence Kahn took it over in 1988 and started offering Ashkenazi delicacies that it started to draw crowds. Locals and tourists alike now seek out its famous pastrami sandwiches, eggplant caviar, *tarama* (fish-roe-based dip), bagels, challah, cheese *bourekas*, chopped liver sandwiches, and chocolate babka. In fact, the menu begs comparison with another iconic Jewish delicatessen just a few shops over, Sacha Finkelsztajn, also known as the "yellow shop." That's because Florence learned all the trade secrets there when she was married to the owner's son. (Though the marriage ended, the business rivalry is friendly.)

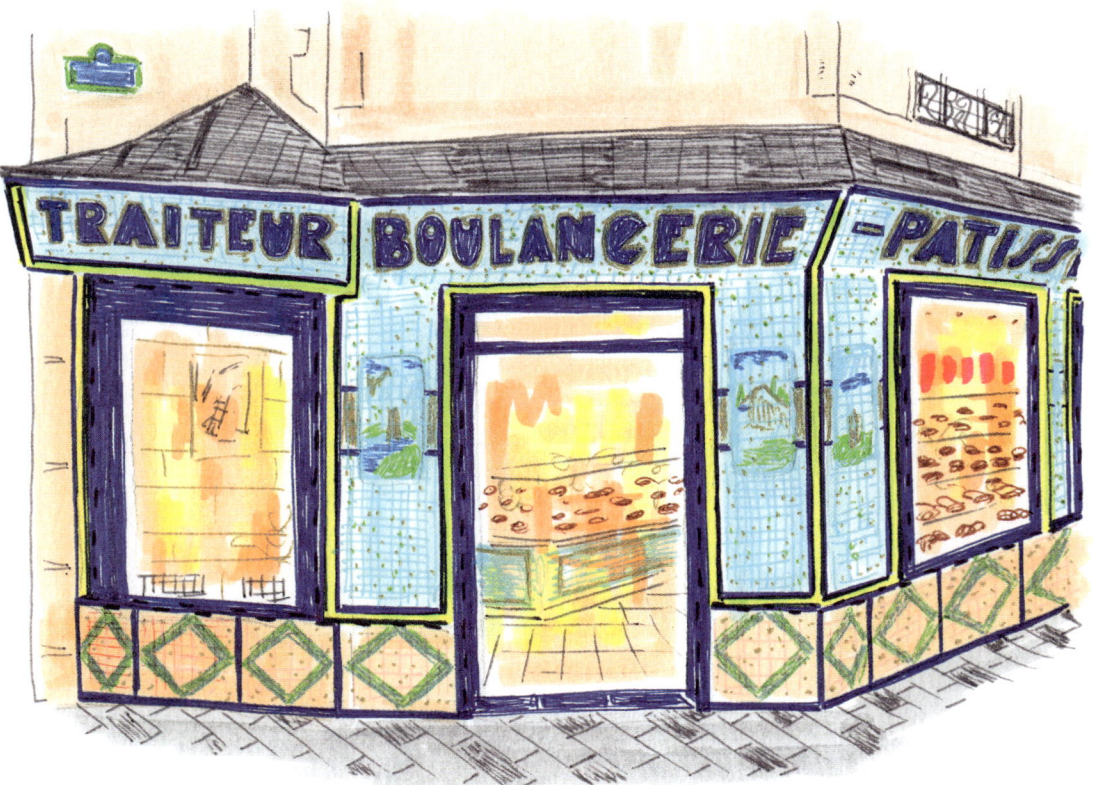

HARK

———

When the Franco-Taiwanese DJ, NTS Radio host, and international queen of nightlife Louise Chen announced that she had a hand in opening a new record store in Paris in 2023, people listened, and people came. Chen, who *Vogue France* calls the "emblem of new feminine cool," announced the store's opening on Instagram, saying it's meant to give "nerds of all horizons" a space to "mingle, debate, question, trade points of view, and leave inspired." Along with an eclectic selection of new, old, and collectible vinyl, a second repair shop one street over specializes in the restoration of vintage hi-fi equipment. HARK has also developed its own in-house brand of loudspeakers that are made in Paris.

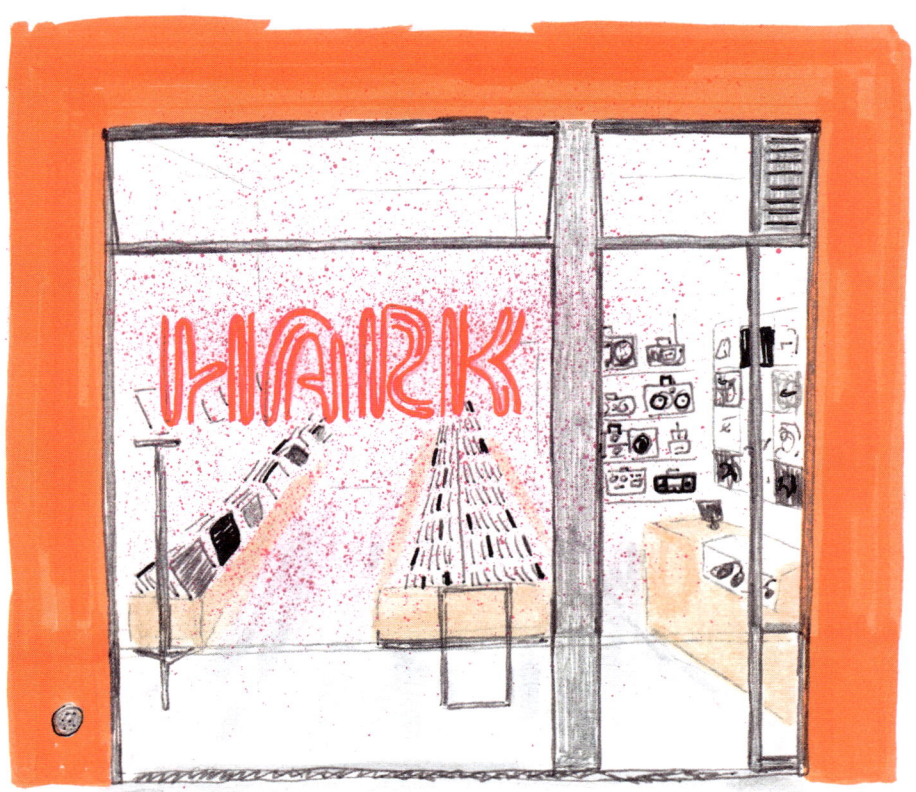

Librairie Delamain

———

As the oldest bookshop in Paris, Librairie Delamain has served as a repository of the written word for more than three centuries. Founded in 1708 by André Cailleau, the store first opened near Palais-Royal, the former royal palace in the 1st arrondissement, before moving to its current location in 1906, where its handsome green façade and classic striped awning beckon curious pedestrians passing through Place Colette.

More than 25,000 books from literature to the humanities, fine arts, and graphic novels line the floor-to-ceiling oak shelves, and wooden stepladders from the store's early days are still used to reach titles on the top level.

Along with a sizable section for kids and young adults, the shop also boasts a collection of 5,000 rare books that date as far back as the 18th century. The quality and diversity of Librairie Delamain's offerings helped it obtain the title of "reference independent bookstore" from the Ministry of Culture's National Book Center.

The bookstore's reputation over the centuries has earned the loyalty of customers like French writers Alexandre Dumas, Guy de Maupassant, and Colette; actors and playwrights from the nearby Comédie-Français theater; and French politicians, including former president François Mitterrand. It was also here that director François Truffaut bought a copy of the obscure book *Jules and Jim* and turned it into one of the most iconic films of the French New Wave movement, with Jeanne Moreau as its star.

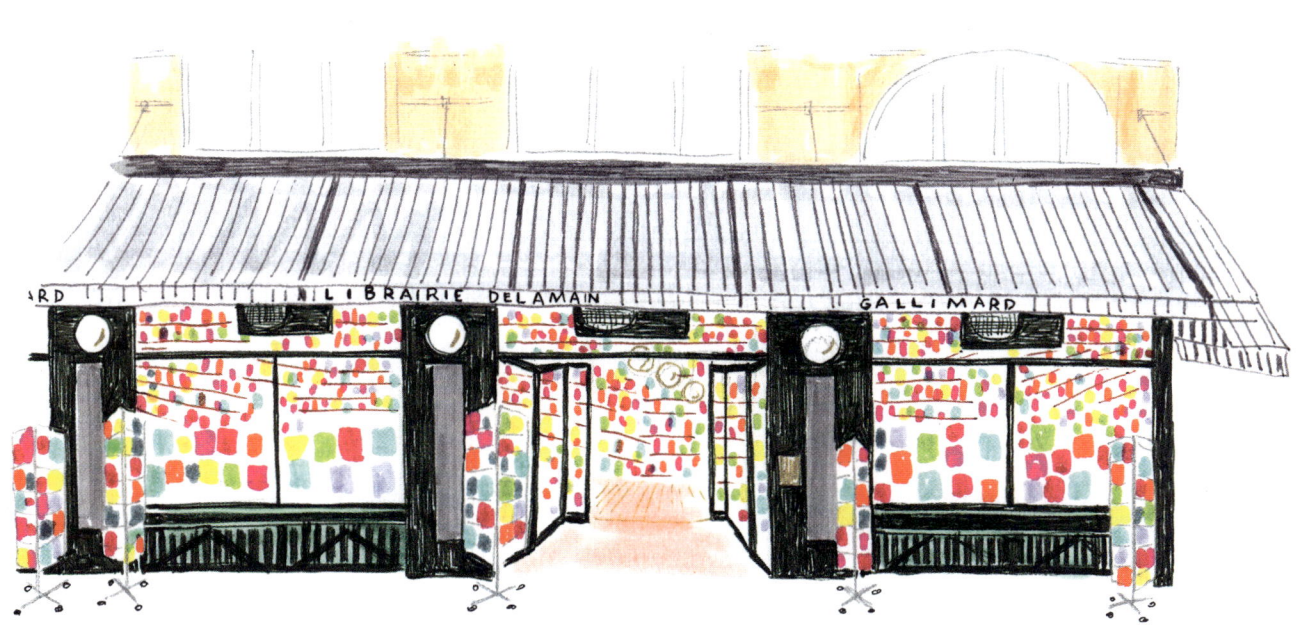

Folderol

———

After Folderol became a viral TikTok sensation for its novel ice cream and wine pairing concept, owners Jessica Yang and Robert Compagnon, a Parisian power couple who also run Le Rigmarole restaurant, were forced to do something unusual in the summer of 2023: hire a bouncer. This person was tasked with clearing the sidewalks of customers—often young content creators from out of town who had taken over the neighborhood, much to the annoyance of locals. Victims of their own success, the couple have even implemented a strict social media policy: a sign on the shopfront warns, "No TikTok. Come here to have fun, not to take pictures." But if Folderol became a hit, it's also because its artisanal ice creams in flavors like raspberry pomelo and rose saffron, as well as its highly edited organic wine list, are just that good.

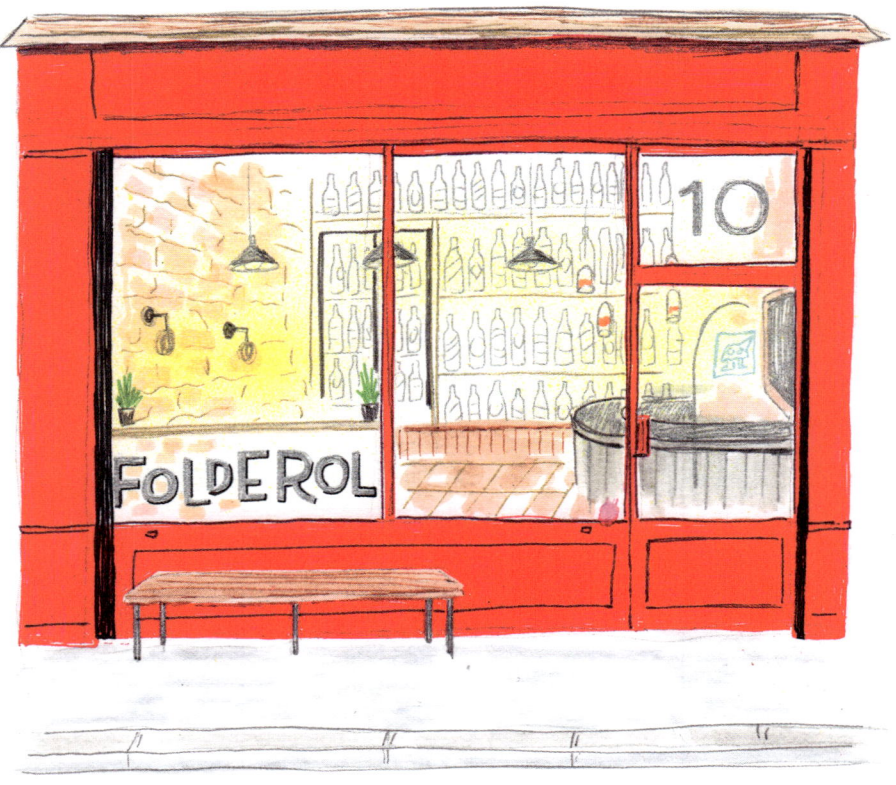

Aurouze

———

In the 2007 film *Ratatouille*, this historic pest control shop is used as a macabre cautionary tale for young Remy, who is warned about what happens to rats who get too "comfortable around humans." The animated depiction of the storefront is surprisingly and impressively accurate. Its deceptively charming façade displays stuffed rats that have been hanging in the window since 1925.

Located in central Paris near Les Halles, former site of the city's largest wholesale market, Étienne Aurouze opened the shop in 1872 and was the go-to expert among local restaurateurs and residents for exterminating all manner of pests. Aurouze is also described as one of the earliest inventors of the spring-loaded mousetrap (though others beat him to patenting it). Today, the shop is managed by his great-grandchildren, Cécile and Julien.

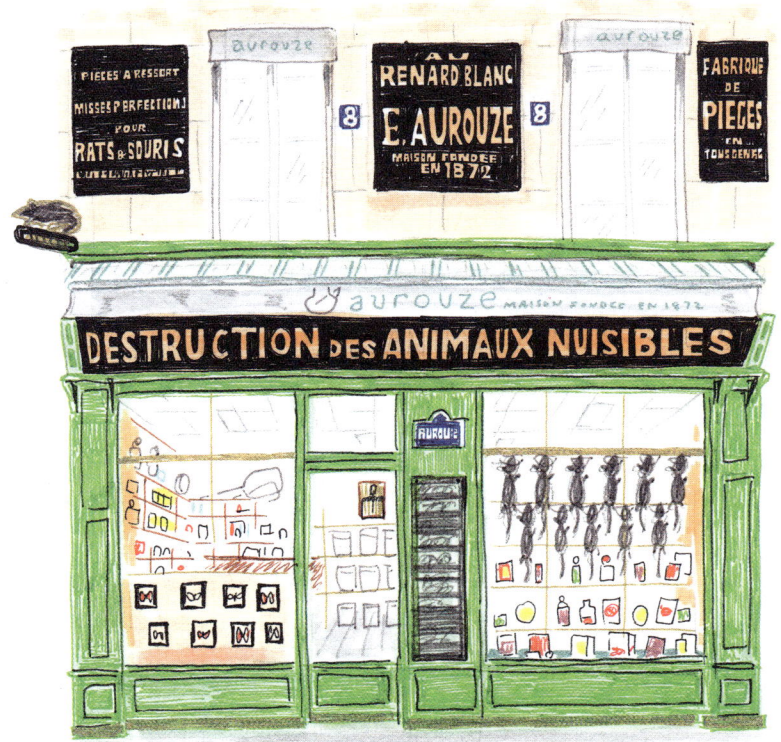

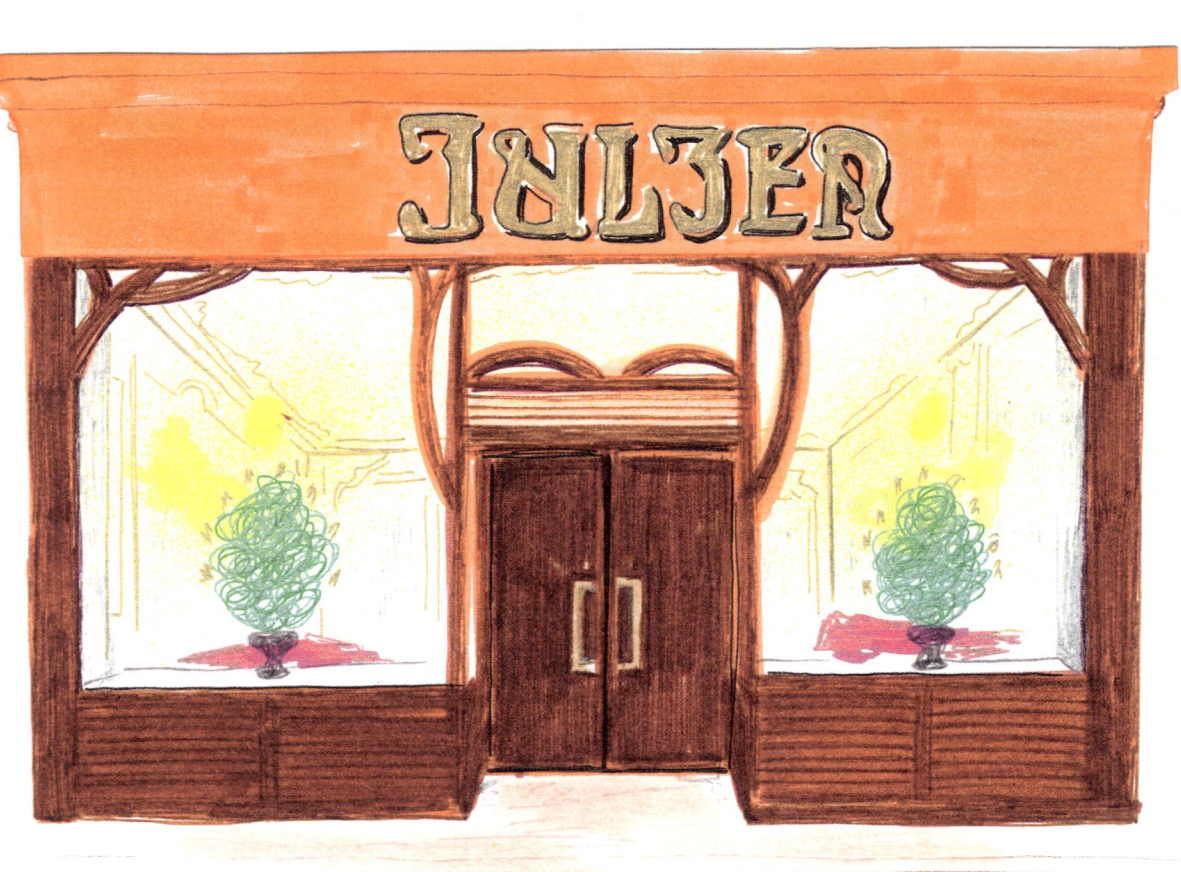

Bouillon Julien

———

Appreciating the heritage of this establishment requires first understanding the concept of the *bouillon*, a restaurant style that was unique to 19th- and 20th-century Paris. It originated when a butcher working in Les Halles (the city's central wholesale food market) came up with the idea to boil leftover meat scraps and sell the broth—or *bouillon* in French—as a cheap and restorative meal for working-class Parisians. The concept was a hit, and the formula was replicated throughout the city. Around the same time, the Art Nouveau movement gained momentum in France, giving rise to establishments like this one.

Opening in the early 1900s under a different name, it became a regular haunt of Édith Piaf and her lover Marcel Cerdan, who dined at table number 24.

Like most trends, the *bouillon* concept eventually petered out and the restaurant operated as a brasserie for decades. But somewhere around 2017, a city-wide revival of *bouillon* restaurants led to new openings, including Bouillon Julien, which abandoned its last identity as a brasserie and reopened as a *bouillon* in 2018.

The restaurant's façade, with its stylized gold lettering and curved wood embellishments, is modest compared to the interior, a painstakingly restored example of Art Nouveau architecture with ornamental moldings, glass panels depicting fairy nymphs, a stained glass skylight, and unique celadon-green walls. In true *bouillon* style, the menu features French comfort foods like leeks vinaigrette, roast chicken, smoked pork loin and sauerkraut, and crème brulée on the cheap.

Au Vieux Paris d'Arcole

—

A historic French restaurant set in a 16th-century building steps from Notre-Dame, Au Vieux Paris d'Arcole's bewitching façade becomes even more enchanting in spring, when the wall explodes with hanging lilac wisteria.

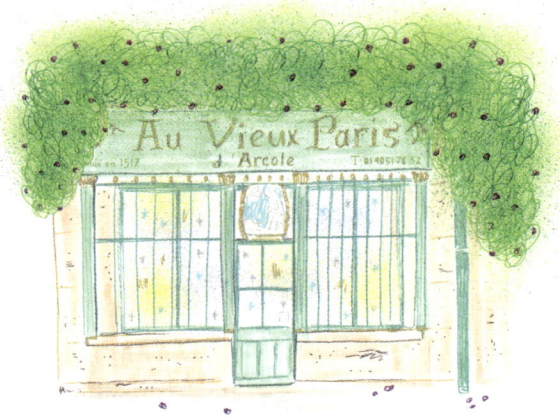

Land&Monkeys

—

The creaminess, butteriness, and flakiness of the pastries here are all the more remarkable because everything is vegan. Breads and cakes are made with organic flour and seasonal products, and packaging is plastic-free. There are four other locations across Paris.

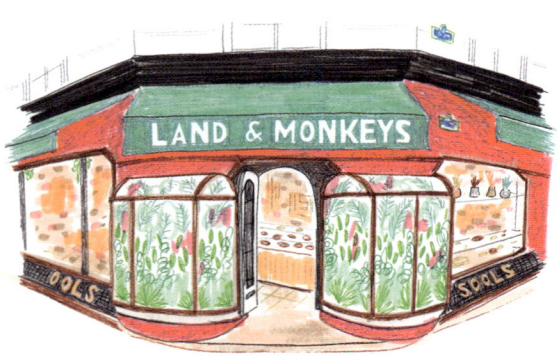

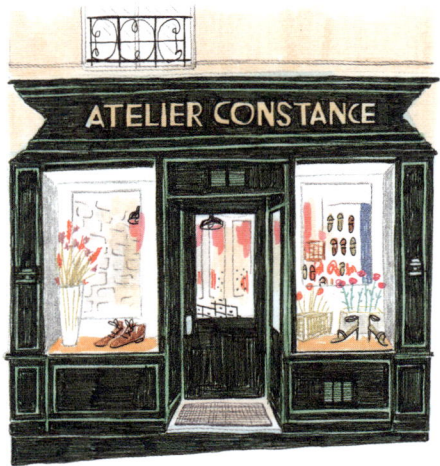

Cordonnerie Atelier Constance

—

For decades, in-the-know Parisians have entrusted their designer shoes to Atelier Constance near Montmartre for repairs. Once run by a shoemaker from luxury French brand Berluti, today, the shop is operated by alumni from Christian Louboutin.

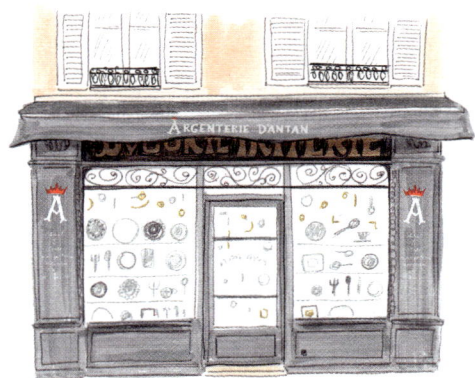

Argenterie d'Antan

—

Parisian brides- and grooms-to-be, as well as expectant mothers, head here to register for their wedding and baby shower silverware. Specialists in vintage silverware and table-ware, the shop also does engravings and cleanings.

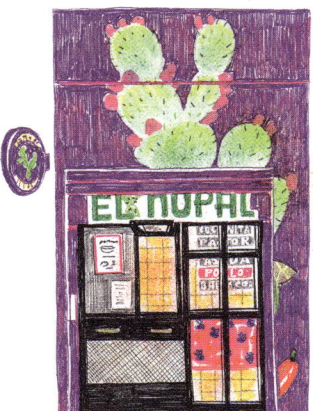

3 rue Eugène Varlin
10th arr.

El Nopal

This tiny Mexican takeout counter opened in 2010 as the city's first taqueria, and can be credited with introducing Parisians to authentic Mexican cuisine. In warm weather, its burritos and tacos are best enjoyed along the Canal Saint-Martin. There's a second location in the 9th arrondissement.

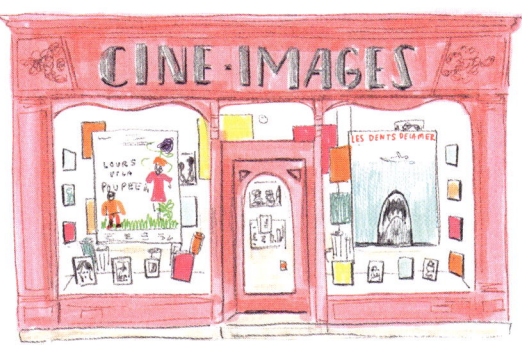

68 rue de Babylone
7th arr.

Ciné-Images

Movie buffs may want to bookmark this niche shop that has been specializing in film posters since 1975. Vintage, original, and contemporary posters are on offer in categories including New Wave, *Star Wars*, James Bond, and superheroes.

27 rue du Bourg Tibourg
4th arr.

L'Appartement Français

After creating six test pop-up shops starting in 2017, a pair of entrepreneurs finally opened a brick-and-mortar version of their business concept, aimed at promoting indie French brands, in 2019. Its artisan home decor and clothing is 100 percent made in France.

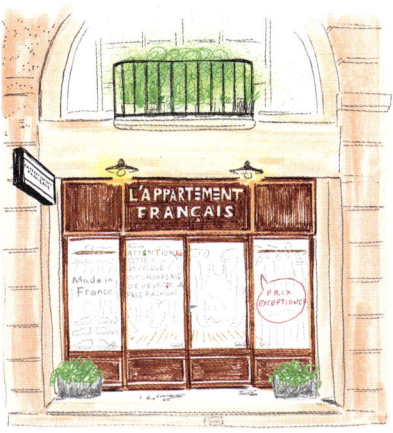

4 rue Grégoire de Tours
6th arr.

Buci News

Tucked away on a side street off the bustling rue de Buci in the Saint-Germain-des-Prés neighborhood is this bright yellow-green shop, which sells a good variety of English-language newspapers, magazines, stationery, and souvenir trinkets.

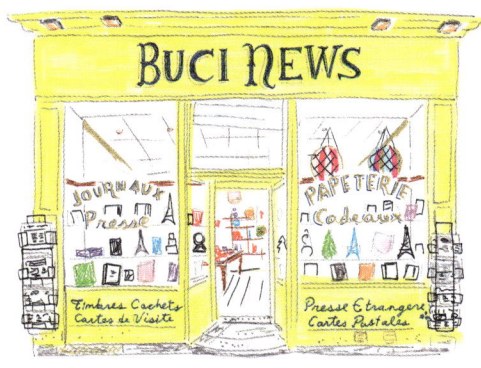

Kodawari Ramen-Yokochō

——

Look up any "best ramen in Paris" list, and odds are high that Kodawari Ramen-Yokochō will figure at the top of the rankings. Despite the dozens of Japanese ramen shops to choose from, this address in the sixth arrondissement has distinguished itself for its lively decor, which recreates an izakaya and bar-lined alleyway (*yokochō*) in Tokyo's Shibuya neighborhood. Jean-Baptiste Meusnier, a former fighter pilot who became obsessed with ramen, learned the trade secrets from masters in Japan before opening his first restaurant in 2016. His rich, fragrant broths are brewed using free-range chicken, and noodles are made with wheat flour grown and milled at a French farm near Ardennes. The black sesame and Iberian pork *chashu* ramen is a standout dish. A second, seafood-themed ramen restaurant can be found in the first arrondissement.

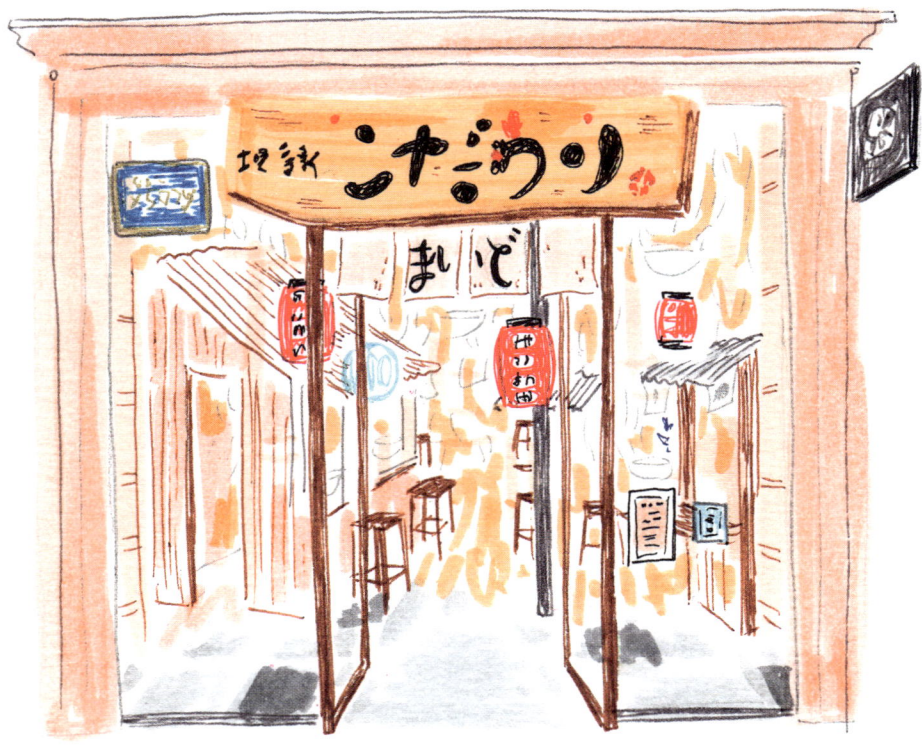

Player One

At this retro gaming and pop culture bar, the worlds of Harry Potter, *Dungeons & Dragons*, *Star Wars*, *Pac-Man*, and *Super Mario* collide. Spanning two floors and around 1,200 square feet, Player One has been popular within Paris's geekdom since it was opened in 2018 by Michal Pichel, founder of the tech and geek culture blog Hitek.fr. On the ground floor, visitors can get nostalgic playing games and arcade machines from the 1990s, or read manga. Downstairs, Harry Potter fans will appreciate the replica of the Weasley family car seen in the film franchise, and the moving portraits from Hogwarts. The bar also boasts the world's first 3D version of the game *Pong* and a huge selection of board games, good for large groups. The drinks menu features fun cocktails with names like "Stormtrooper" and "Iron Man," as well as 50 bottled and draft beers.

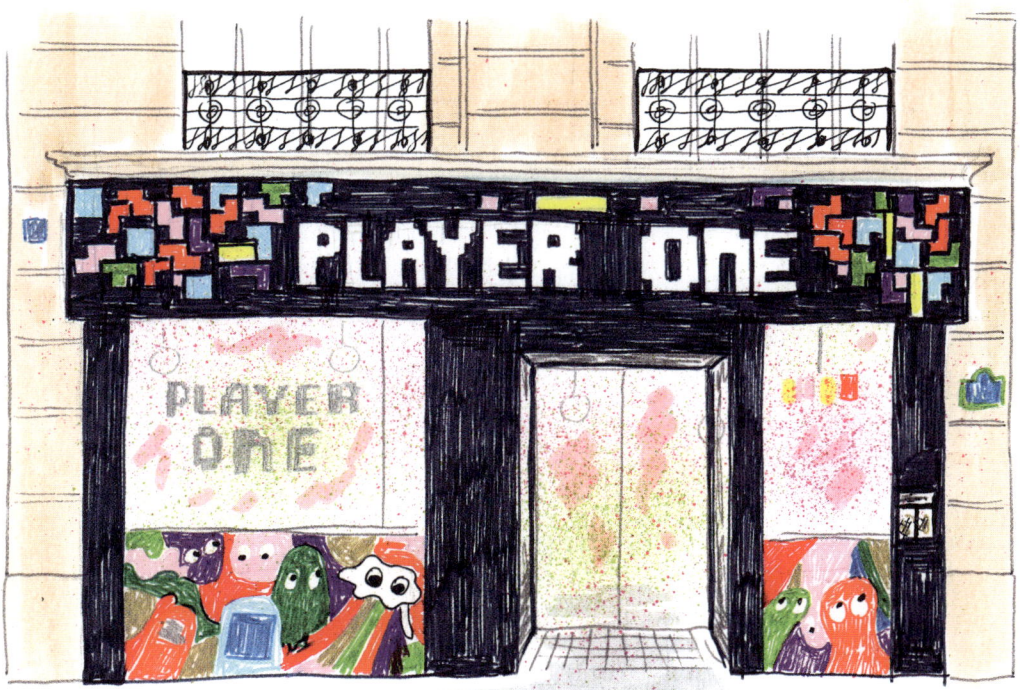

Cadolle

———

The modern-day bra owes some of its existence to the founder of this luxury lingerie boutique. Herminie Cadolle was a fierce 19th-century feminist who fought for women's rights during a violent people's insurrection in 1871, a bloody episode in Parisian history. After serving six months in jail for her role in the uprising against the French government, Cadolle fled to Argentina where she used her previous experience working in a corset factory to launch a successful lingerie business. Inspired by her feminist sensibilities, the designer came up with the idea to split the corset in two and "liberate" women from the tyranny of the stomach-strangling straightjacket. In 1889, she returned to France and introduced women there to the *corselet-gorge*, the predecessor of the *soutien-gorge* (the French word for bra).

Six generations of Cadolle women—the latest being mother-daughter duo Poupie and Patricia—have since led the boutique and brand into its modern-day iteration as an *haute couture* clothier to the stars.

Clients include celebrities like Rihanna, Vanessa Paradis, Scarlett Johansson, and Beyoncé, who wore one of its corsets in the music video for "Apeshit," which was shot in the Louvre.

Cadolle's clientele is typically comprised of wealthy women who don't bat an eye at four-digit price tags for corsets and three-digit ones for a single pair of silk panties. A team of seamstresses can also create bespoke pieces with on-site fittings and custom finishes.

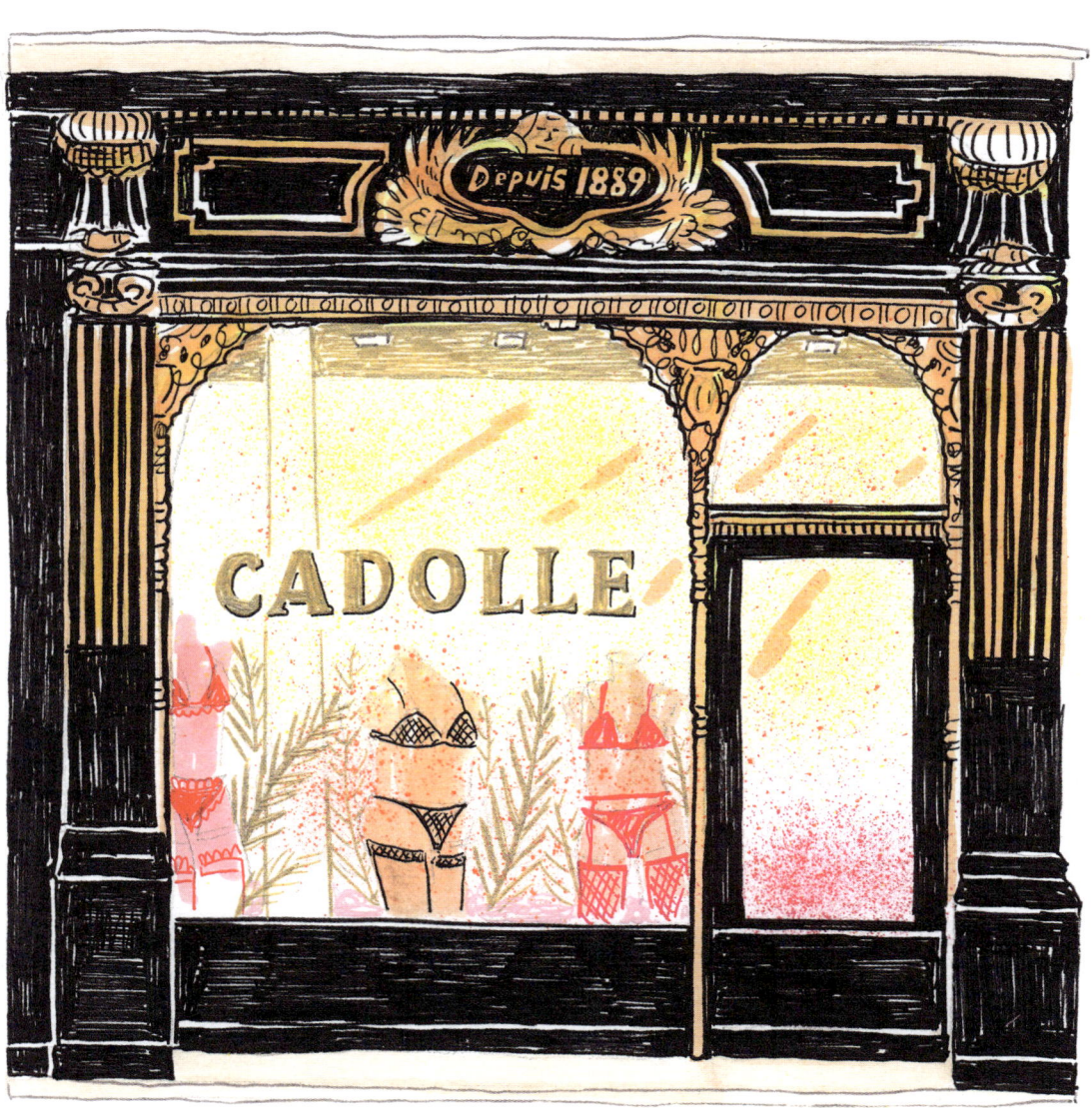

Charvin

———

Charvin was founded in 1830 in the French Riviera, where it continues to produce extra-fine oil paints using some of the same techniques it employed when it first began. (By adding ingredients like lapis lazuli and linseed and poppyseed oils, colors are prevented from yellowing.)

French painters including Paul Cézanne, Pierre Bonnard, and Pierre Ambrogiani all used Charvin oil paints for their masterpieces. But the brand is best known for the intensity and range of its color selection, which, at 208, is one of the largest offerings of any manufacturer. Charvin's extra-fine oils are ground for twice as long as fine oils, and are particularly popular among *plein-air* painters, who work outdoors in the style of Cézanne. There is a second shop in Nice.

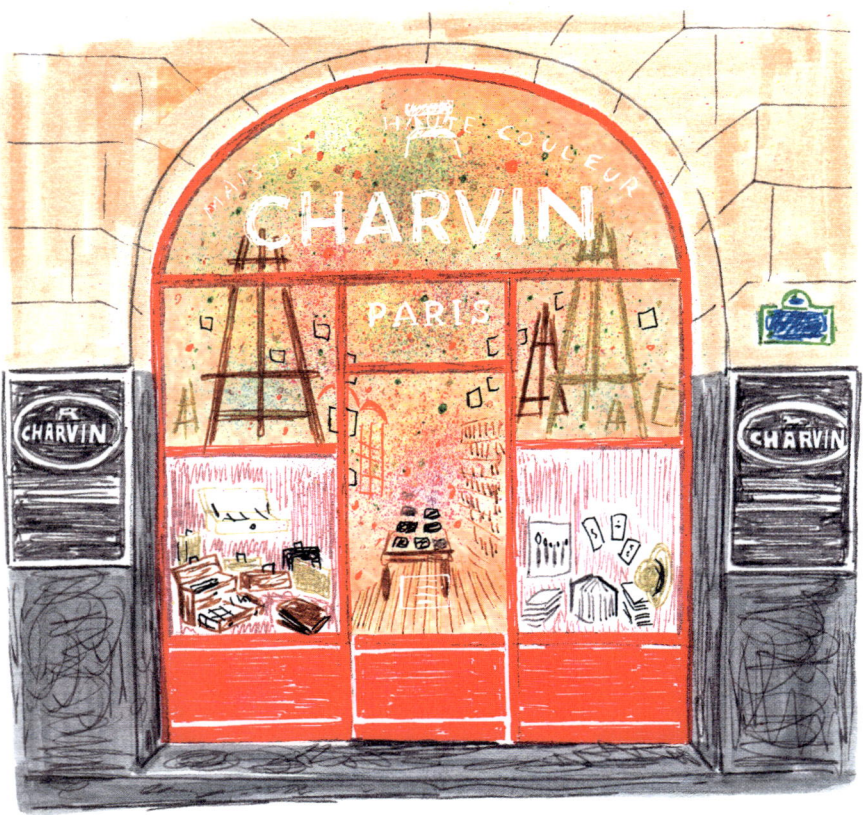

Ladurée

─────

While Ladurée can be found in more than a dozen countries and emirates around the world, it's on rue Royale that the famed macaron brand got its start. In 1862, Louis-Ernest Ladurée opened the bakery in the Madeleine neighborhood, then home to many of the city's luxury craftsmen. The company stakes a claim to having created the French macaron as we know it, via the founder's grandcousin Pierre Desfontaines, who came up with the idea of putting two macaron shells together and stuffing them with a jam or ganache filling. The base recipe remains the same today.

Louis-Ernest's daughter-in-law, Jeanne Souchard, can also be credited in part for pioneering the concept of a female-friendly Parisian tea room, at a time when public spaces for women were few and far between. In the 19th century, she recognized the need for the equivalent of today's "safe space" for women, and came up with the idea of merging a café and pastry shop, where ladies could socialize while sipping tea and munching on dainty cakes.

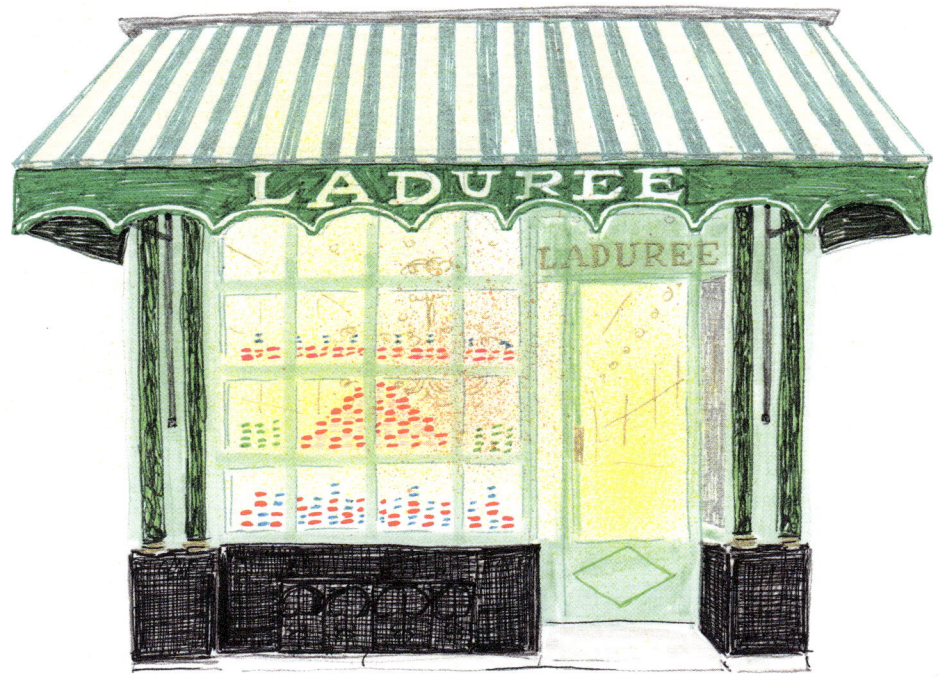

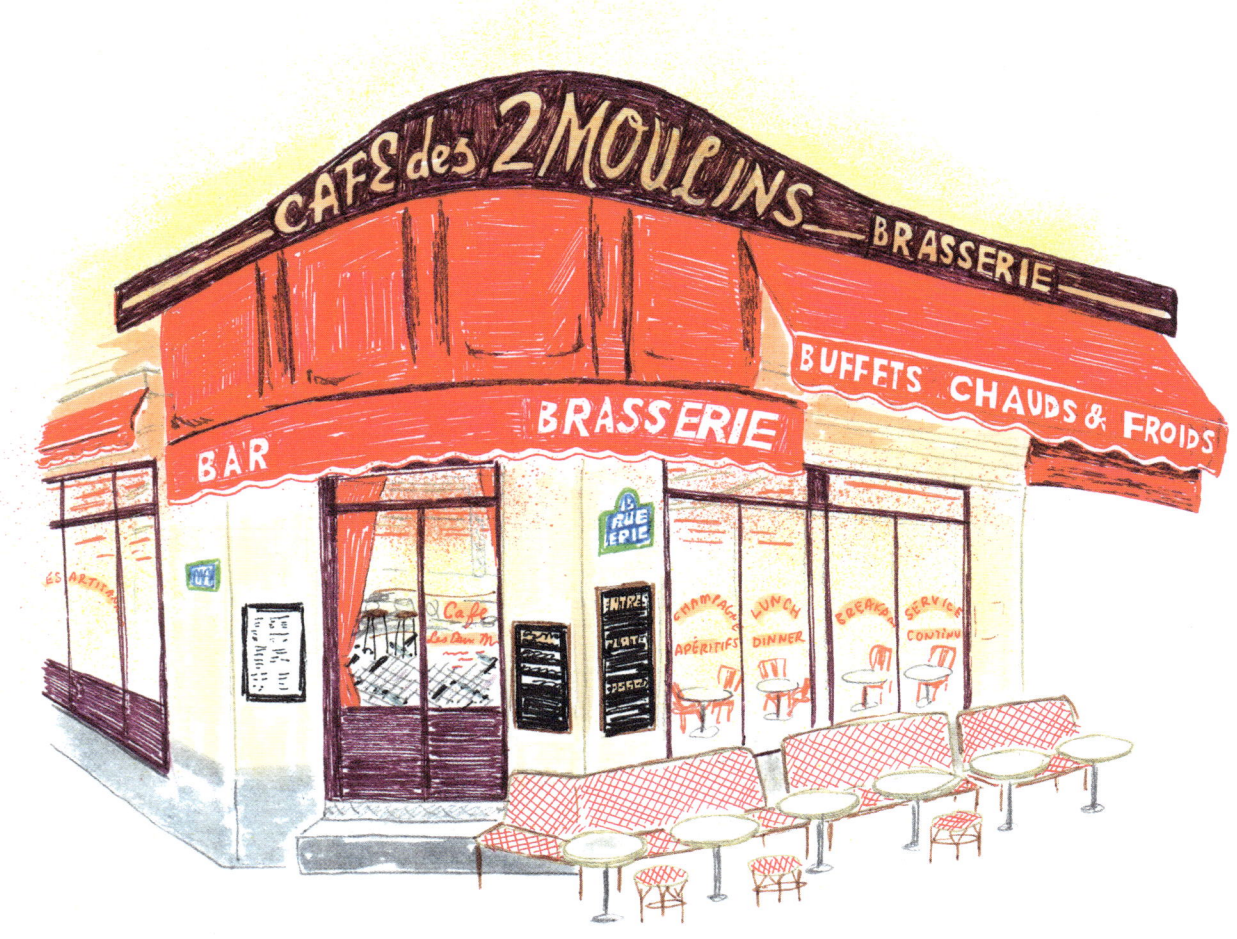

15 rue Lepic
18th arr.

Café des 2 Moulins

———

In 2001, a film about a shy, doe-eyed dreamer named Amélie Poulain, who worked as a waitress in the bohemian neighborhood of Montmartre, turned this nondescript café into an overnight tourist attraction.

(In English, Café des 2 Moulins means "Café of Two Windmills," and is a reference to the area's two landmark windmills, the Moulin Rouge (see p. 158) and Moulin de la Galette (see p. 143).)

In the critically acclaimed film directed by Jean-Pierre Jeunet, the café plays a pivotal role as the gathering place for an eccentric and colorful cast of characters, including Amélie herself. But be warned: fans of the film may be disappointed to discover that the real-life café bears little resemblance to the movie version, with the exception of the zinc bar. Georgette's tobacco counter has been removed, and aside from a framed movie poster and a small corner dedicated to the film, there is little of the vintage, old-Paris atmosphere depicted in the movie. Instead, the café is light, bright, airy, and modern.

That said, while it attracts its fair share of sightseers, the café is also a popular neighborhood spot for locals. Menu prices are reasonable for French dishes like leeks vinaigrette, croque-monsieur, beef tartare, and duck. And in a nod to the film, the dessert offerings include a "crème brulée d'Amélie."

Cire Trudon

———

The oldest wax factory and candlemaker still in operation in France today, Cire Trudon's heritage can be traced back to 1643, when Claude Trudon's beeswax candles illuminated the hallowed halls of the royal court and French churches. After being the preferred candlemaker of Marie Antoinette and Louis XIV, the factory became the official royal wax manufacturer under Louis XV. For the birth of his son, Napoleon commissioned a candle inlaid with three gold coins bearing his image.

Today, Cire Trudon's luxury candles are perfumed with scents like Moroccan mint tea, or leather and tobacco. One of its iconic fragrances, Tuileries, pays homage to Marie Antoinette, whose favorite flower was the rose. The brand is also famous for its wax busts shaped in the likenesses of Napoleon, Marie Antoinette, and Louis XIV. Cire Trudon's motto is: "The bees work for God and the King." There are four other locations in Paris, along with outposts around the globe.

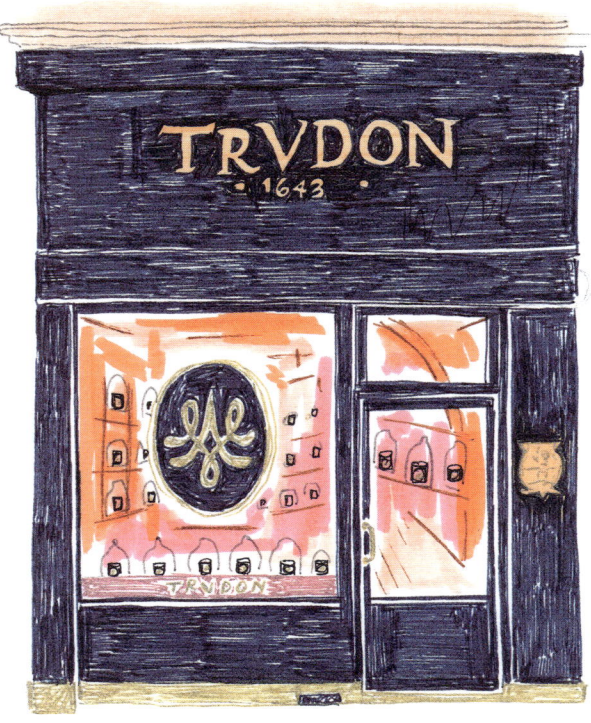

Le Louxor

It's understandable to do a double-take after stumbling upon what appears to be an Egyptian temple in the streets of Paris. Opened in 1921 with a capacity of 1,195 seats, the Louxor theater stands as a testament to the trends of the time, when Egyptian motifs—mosaic tiles, hieroglyphs, obelisks, and pyramids—were all the rage in art and design. Tragically, the man behind the colossal project, Henri Silberberg, died just a month after its inauguration, setting off a series of takeovers and makeovers.

While the theater enjoyed a good 30 years of success, the advent of television led to a decline in attendance. In the 1980s, attempts to revive it as various nightclubs failed, leading to closure and years of abandonment—until the city bought the building and reopened it in 2013, restoring its original decor. Today, the Louxor screens contemporary films and has special kids' programming.

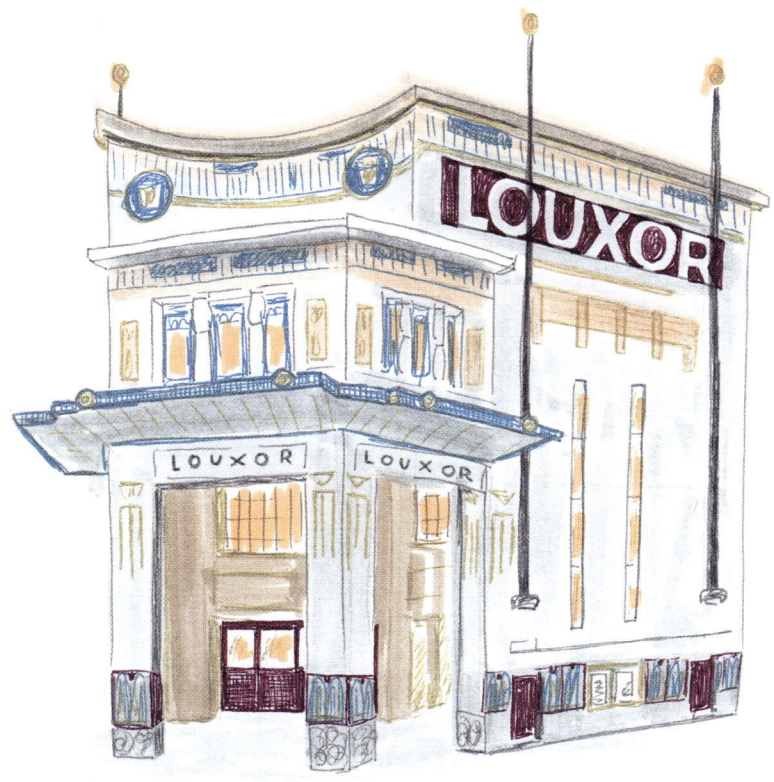

Au Petit Versailles du Marais

———

A visit to this historic bakery, which has been called one of the most beautiful in Paris, leaves a lasting impression not only for its sumptuous decor, but for its quality breads and pastries from one of France's top bakers, Christian Vabret.

Upon arrival, make sure to take note of the exterior's exquisite woodwork, as well as the decorative panels on either side of the main entrance that depict bucolic scenes of a young maiden and Frenchman working in a field of wheat. Once inside, tear your gaze away from the tempting baked goods and look upward toward the 19th-century glass ceiling tiles painted by Charles Anselm, worthy of an opera house or château.

A chandelier, Corinthian columns, ornamental moldings, wall-to-wall mirrors, and brass fixtures also elevate a routine baguette run into an unexpectedly luxurious experience.

Importantly, the breads and pastries live up to the majestic decor. Christian has been designated a Meilleur Ouvrier de France (MOF) since 1986, which honors the best craftspeople in the nation. He also runs cooking and baking schools in south-central France, along with pastry schools in China.

In 2019, the bakery opened a tea salon next door called Salon de Thé Marie-Antoinette, where guests can enjoy its pastries and cakes on-site. Christian's bakery in the 14th arrondissement, Académie du Pain, also has a sit-in area.

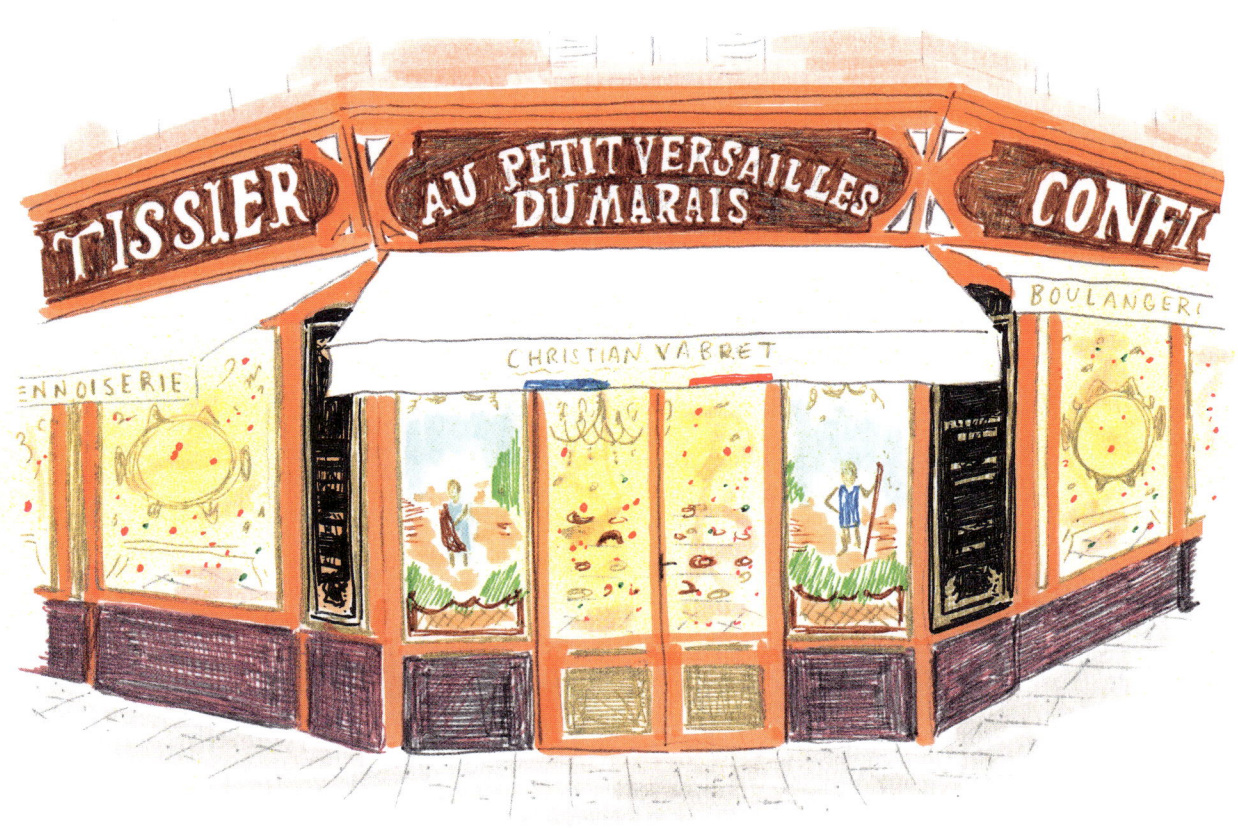

20 rue Bachaumont
2nd arr.

Nose

—

Beauty concept store Nose specializes in niche perfumes for anyone looking for a unique signature scent to claim as their own. Visitors can also get an "olfactory diagnosis" that offers personalized fragrance recommendations.

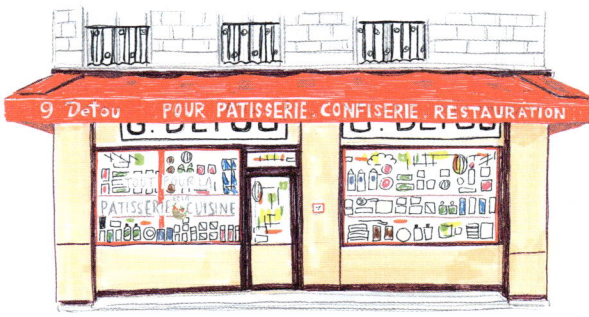

58 rue Tiquetonne
2nd arr.

G. Detou

—

In French, the name G. Detou is a play on words, and sounds like "I have everything." This fine food store stocks baking ingredients, nuts, jam, honey, oil, vinegar, candied and dried fruits, and everything in between.

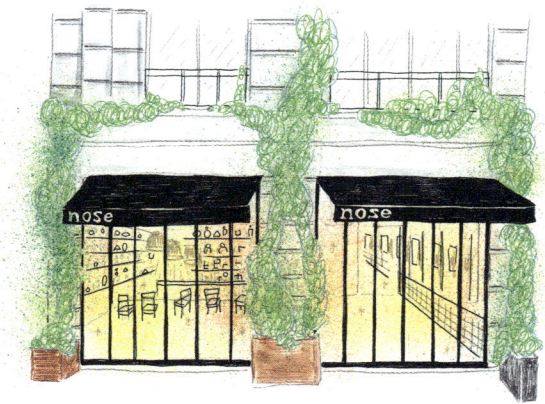

37 rue Saint-Ambroise
11th arr.

Les Mots à la Bouche

—

Opened in 1983, this bookshop is the oldest of its kind in Paris, stocked with 15,000 gay, lesbian, and queer-themed titles. After nearly four decades in the Marais, it moved to the 11th arrondissement in 2020.

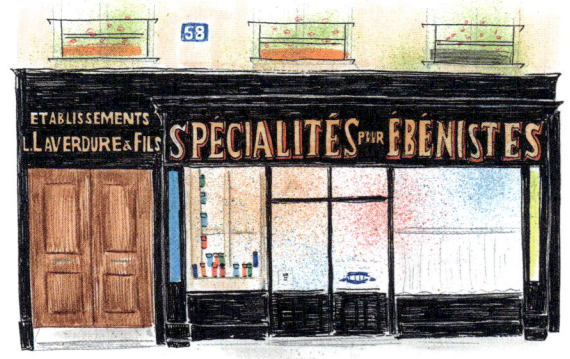

58 rue Traversière
12th arr.

Laverdure & Fils

—

Professional artisans have been coming to this art supply store since the 19th century knowing they'll find the varnish, glue, lacquer, or gold leaf they need for their project, whether it be a gilded frame or antique restoration.

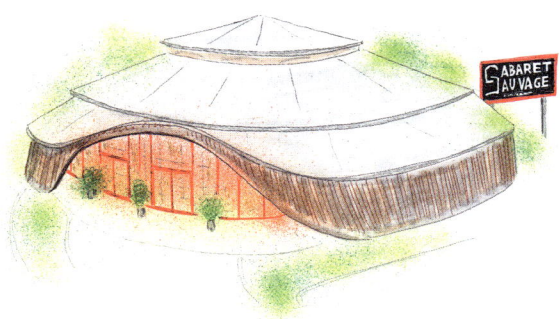

59 Bd Macdonald
19th arr.

Cabaret Sauvage

—

Located in Parc de la Villette, this concert hall opened in 1997 and is known for eclectic and international programming that includes everything from jazz to cabarets, circus acts, and international festivals.

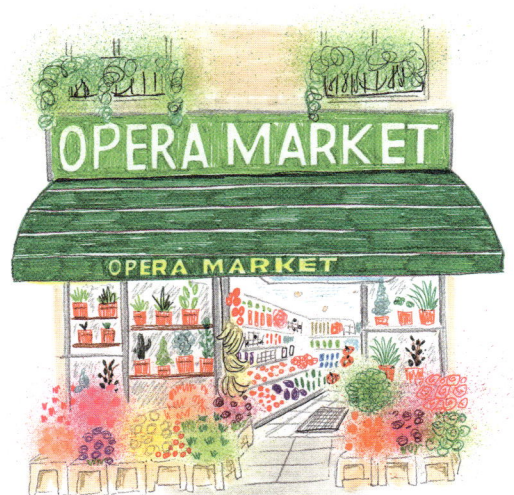

29 rue des Petits Champs
1st arr.

Opéra Market

—

This greengrocer in the Opéra neighborhood of Paris maximizes its small space to stock not just fruits and vegetables, but bouquets of fresh flowers, plants, and a wide selection of wines and bubbly.

13 rue de Crussol
11th arr.

Le Tagine

—

Moroccan restaurant Le Tagine opened in 1983 and is a favorite among some of Paris's top chefs. Specialties include tagines and couscous made with free-range chicken and lamb from the Pyrenees. There is also a natural wine list.

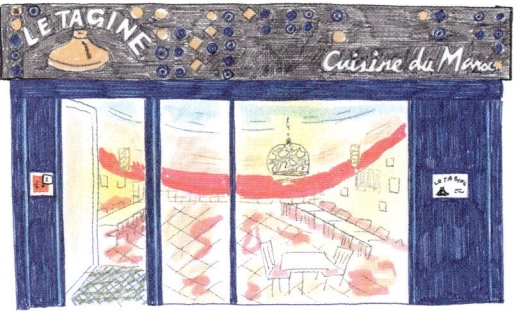

22 rue des Vinaigriers
10th arr.

Plan D – Dwich & Glace

—

This sandwich shop near the Canal Saint-Martin specializes in two things: gourmet vegan sandwiches on artisan sourdough bread, and plant-based soft serve sundaes for the neighborhood's lunch crowd.

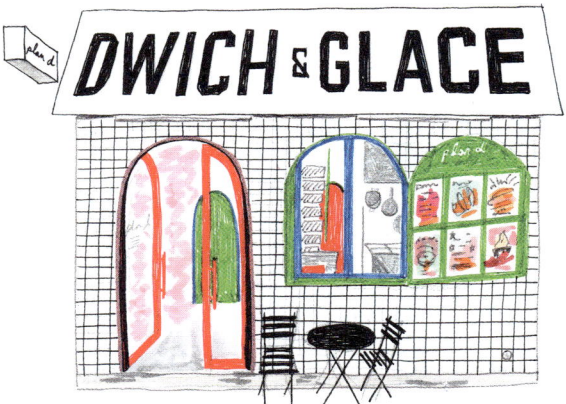

L'Ingénieur Chevallier

———

The exterior of this boutique is deceiving. Its sleek, modern, and minimalist façade belies a history that dates back to 1740, when Louis XV's appointed optician, François Trochon, was set up with his own spectacle shop. In 1796, his grandson, Jean Gabriel Augustin Chevallier, took over, earning a reputation as the best optician in Paris and fitting European royalty and Napoleon Bonaparte with their eyeglasses. As an engineer, he also made telescopes and microscopes.

Today, the brand has been revived by Franck Bonnet, a fourth-generation optician whose family's client roster has also included celebrities such as Yves Saint Laurent and Audrey Hepburn. Glasses are customized to ear, nose, eyebrow, and facial dimensions, then shaped and sanded by hand. Artisans also design and release a new frame at the store's workshop every month. A second address can be found on rue Vertbois.

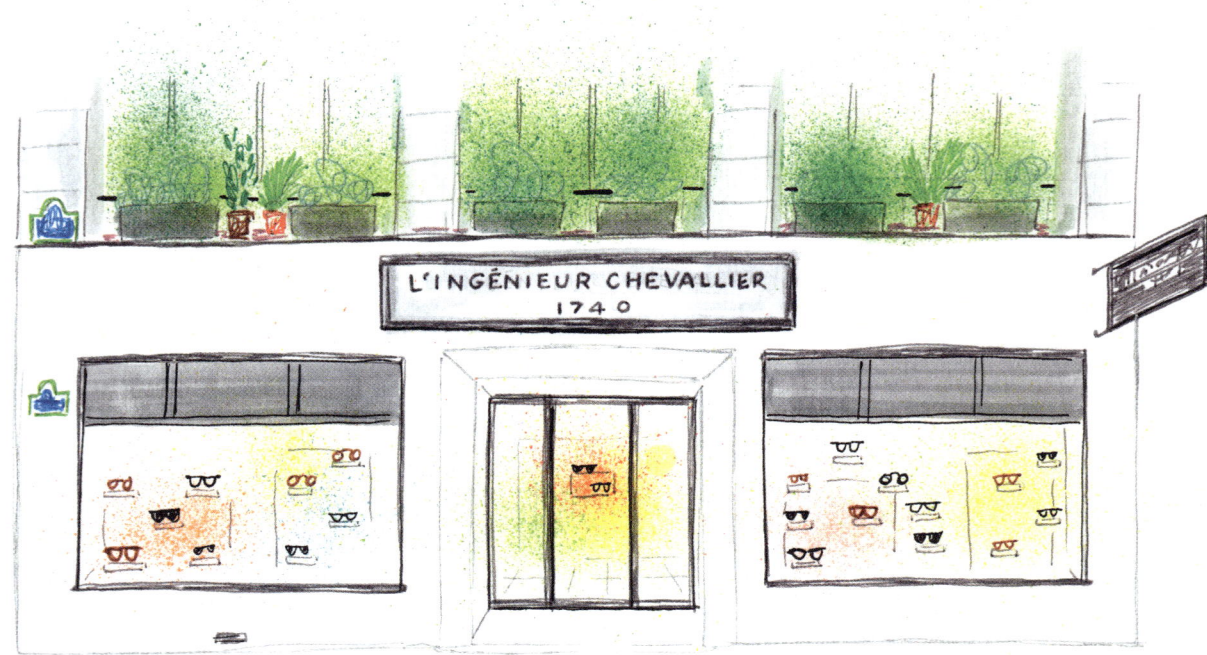

1000 & 1 Signes

This restaurant's name, as well as the trio of hands—palms facing outward—on its façade, may seem cryptic at first. But it all makes sense once you learn that 1001 & 1 Signes was Paris's first sign language eatery run by a deaf person. Sid Nouar, who was born deaf, was a teacher for 12 years, assisted by an interpreter in his classes. However, his childhood dream had always been to open his own restaurant. In 2018, he took a leap of faith and created a couscous restaurant in honor of his parents' Moroccan and Algerian origins.

To communicate with 1001 & 1 Signes' staff (most of whom were deaf), customers could point or try their hand at signing their order, thanks to illustrations on the menu. Sid says the aim was to break down clichés and build bridges. Though 1000 & 1 Signes has since closed, it succeeded in breaking barriers and making an impact.

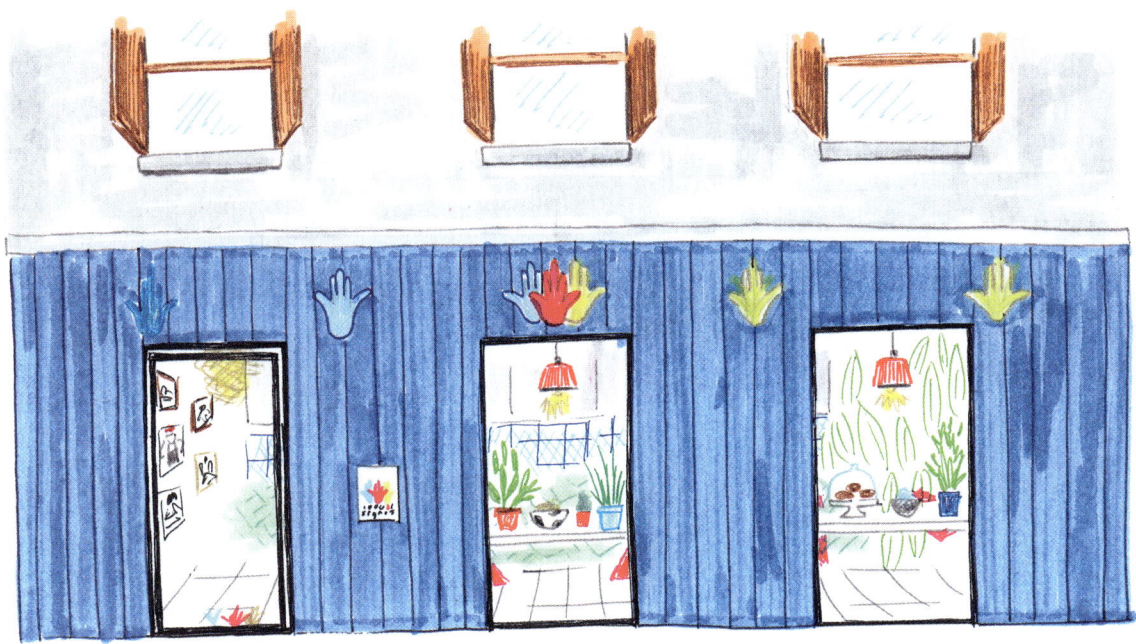

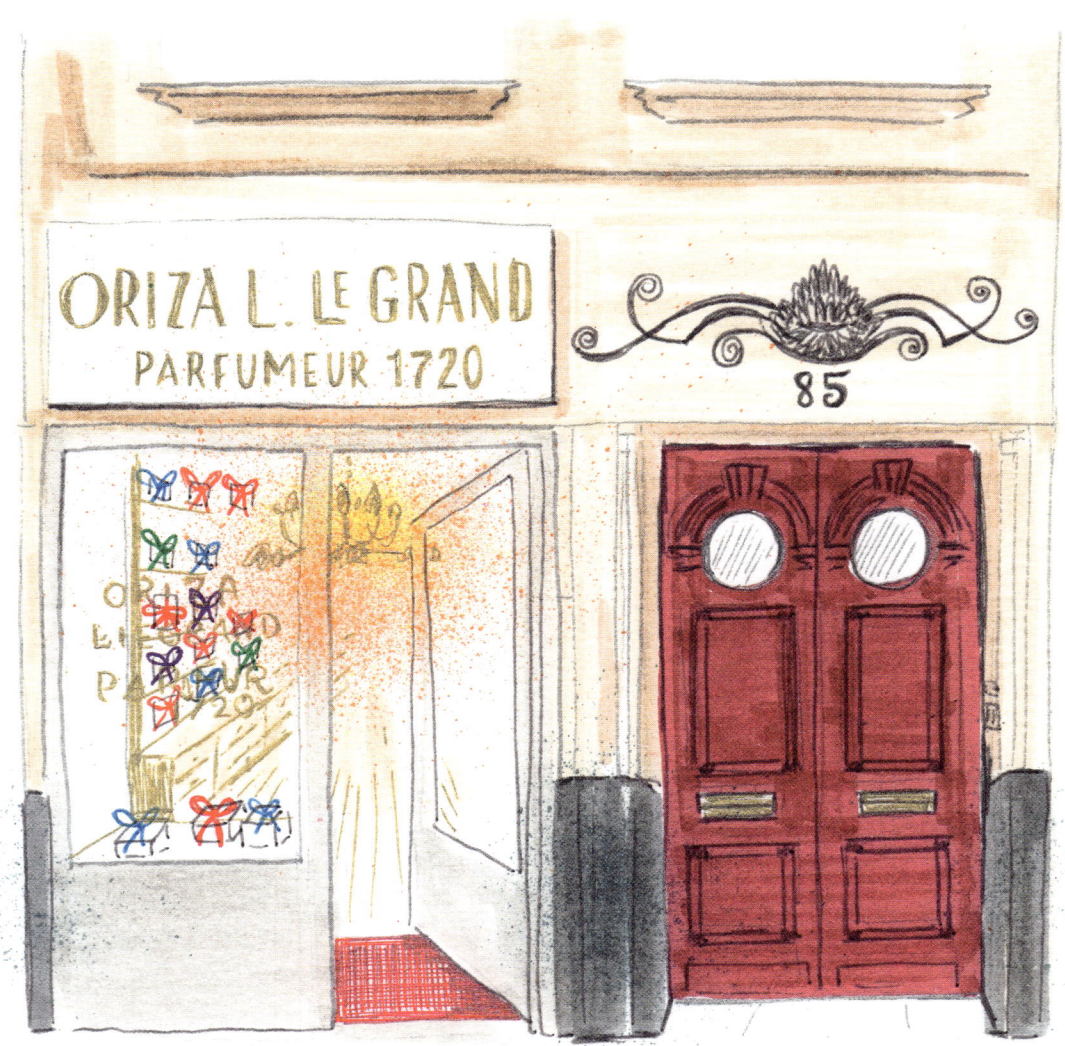

Oriza L. Legrand

Under the reign of Louis XV, who had an obsessive love of flowers and is said to have ordered that each room of his palace be sprayed with new fragrances every day, the Château de Versailles became known as the "perfumed court." One of its pivotal figures was the king's official perfumer, Fargeon Aîné, who founded Maison Oriza in 1720.

After supplying kings Louis XV and XVI and Marie Antoinette, the business survived the French Revolution, and went on to serve Napoleon and his wife Joséphine. Over the next two centuries, the brand would become the official supplier to the courts of Russia, Italy, and England, and would lay claim to creating the first solid perfume at its factory just outside Paris. In the late 1930s, Maison Oriza closed and faded into obscurity—until a pair of entrepreneurs, Franck Belaiche and Hugo Lambert, decided to resurrect it in 2012, after years of research and development.

Today, the boutique pays homage to the brand's history with a selection of room sprays, soaps, candles, *eaux de parfums*, and *eaux de colognes*, some of which replicate the scents of a bygone era.

The *eau de parfum* Oeillet Louis XV, for instance, brings the olfactory presence of the former king to life with a "powdery, peppery, silky, and spicy" scent that first hits the nose with berries and mandarin, before giving way to carnations, white orchids, cloves, pepper, and cedar wood.

Le Café des Chats

Fun fact: though clichés of Parisians often evoke images of small yappy dogs the size of designer handbags, the French capital's denizens are actually more into cats. Figures from 2023, for instance, show that the city's households own 250,000 cats versus 100,000 dogs. Which is why this cat café in the 11th arrondissement, the first of its kind in Paris, has been a huge success since opening in 2013.

Visitors here are the guests of a dozen cat hosts, such as Lancelot, Perceval, Frida, and Athena, who've been chosen for their characters—they get along with other cats and appreciate humans. They also happen to be irresistible. Refrain from falling in love with any one cat, though, as the feline creatures are not up for adoption and are permanent residents of the café. A full-service menu includes salads, sandwiches, steak, and dessert.

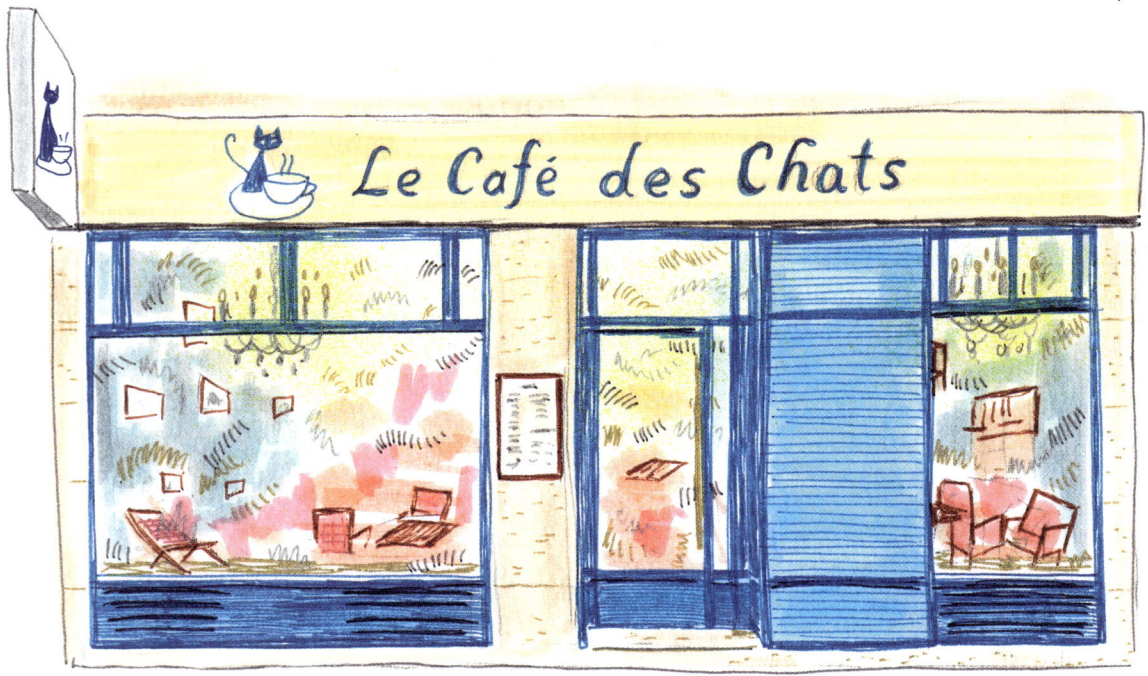

À la Folie

———

The motto at this LGBTQIA+-friendly venue is "open doors for open-minded people." With its fire-engine-red façade and industrial design, the building has been a striking presence at Parc de la Villette, on the northern edge of the city, since 2015. By day, the hybrid space might host bike repair workshops or kids' cooking classes. In the early evening, the program could include drag bingo or a "Dyke Menopause" aperitif, and attract diners for the restaurant's famous barbecue and poutine. But it's at night when À la Folie (which in English means "To madness") manifests its true destiny, transforming into an all-hours club. That's because founders Méziane Azaïche, Rémy Baiget, and Christopher Servajean have a strong background in Paris's nightlife scene, having worked at the Rex Club (see p. 31) and Cabaret Sauvage (see p. 59).

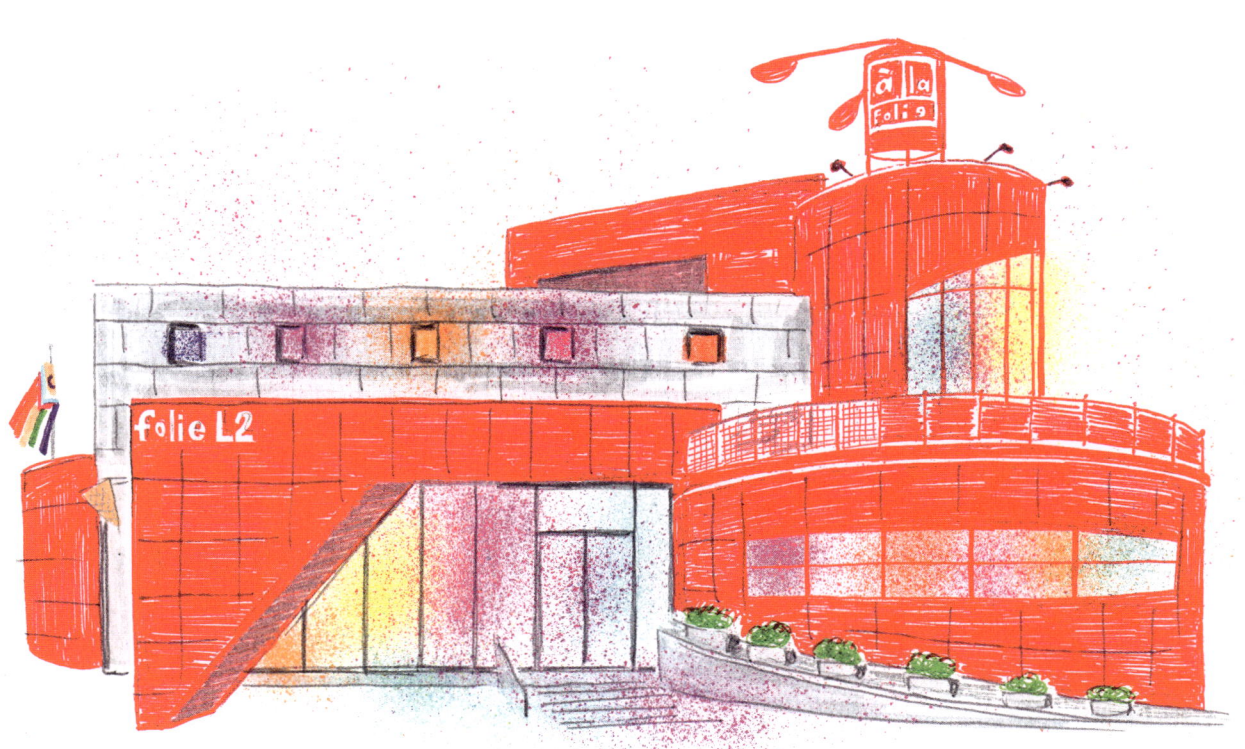

Chez Bob de Tunis

———

Bob Attal is known in Paris as the king of Tunisian sandwiches. Since 1982, his tiny hole-in-the-wall kosher Tunisian deli— it's 215 square feet and fits only two tables—has supplied the local Tunisian community with a taste of home. Part of his longevity in the business can be attributed to his loyal regulars, several of whom span three generations of the same family.

Shelves are lined with cans of El Manar tuna imported from Tunisia, along with preserved lemons, Tunisian beer, sodas, and faded black-and-white photos. Behind the makeshift counter, foil-lined trays are loaded with savory brik pastries, potato and meat croquettes (called *banatages*), and rolls of Bob's famous deep-fried fricassée bread, stuffed with tuna, hard-boiled eggs, chili peppers, and harissa.

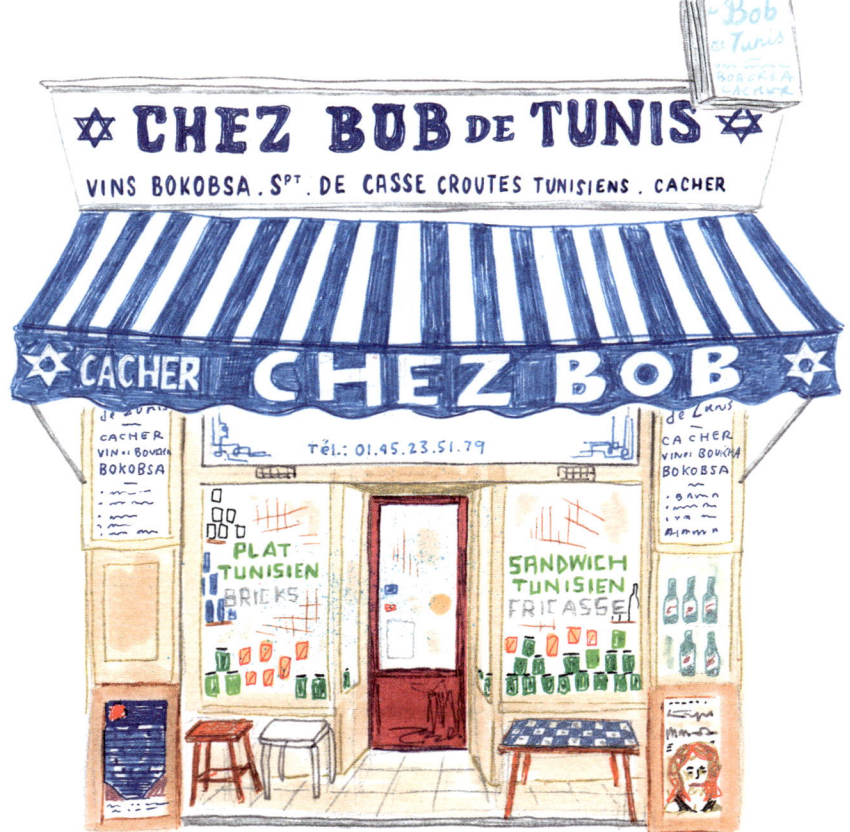

Librairie Jousseaume

———

Visitors to one of the most elegant covered passageways in Paris will no doubt be charmed by the historic and unmissable Librairie Jousseaume bookshop, which has remained largely unchanged since its opening in 1826. Inside, the time-weathered spines of antique books whisk visitors back to 19th-century France, as do the wood beams overhead and a beautifully preserved wooden spiral staircase that leads to the mezzanine. The shop's most illustrious customers have included writers Colette and Jean Cocteau.

The historic business remains a family affair, with François Jousseaume, great-grandson of the shop's namesake, managing it today. While it's best known for its rare and second-hand books, the store's 40,000 titles cover subjects like history, music, travel, and poetry, and also include a small selection of English-language books, prints, and engravings.

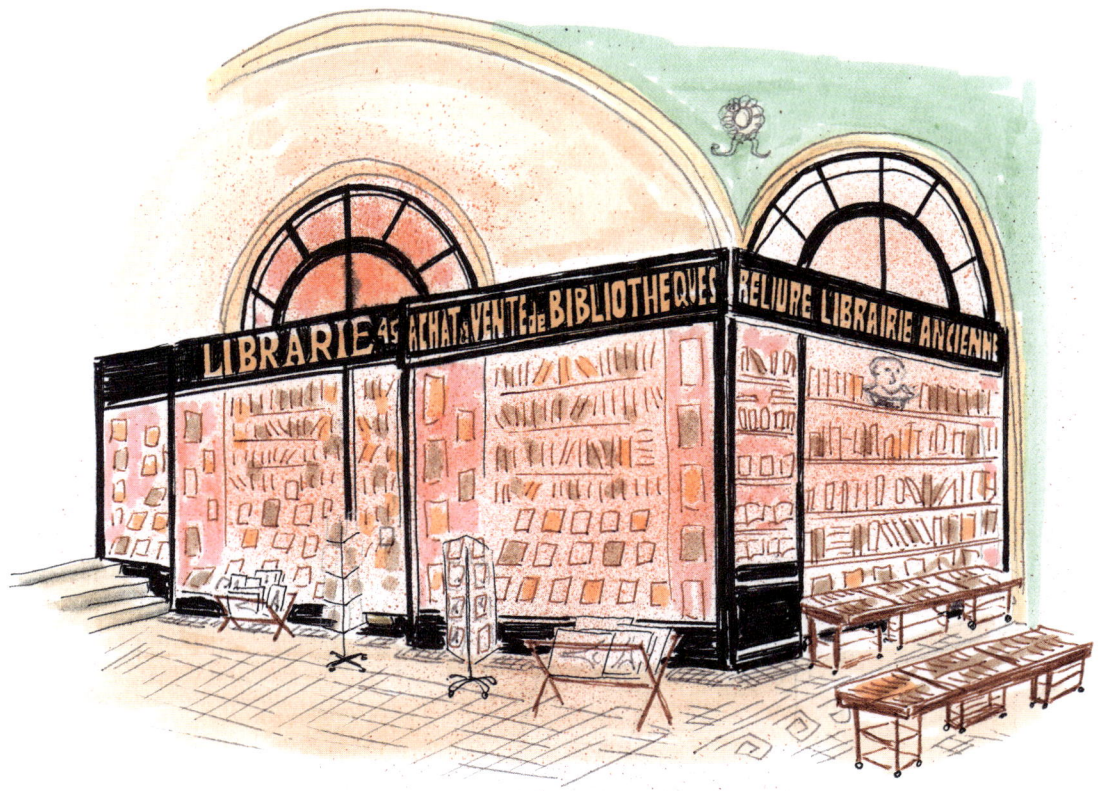

Officine Universelle Buly 1803

———

Not long after opening his first boutique in Paris in 1803, perfumer and cosmetologist Jean-Vincent Bully created one of the most sought-after beauty products in France and beyond, the "Aromatic and Antimephitic Vinegar." *Les Parisiennes* used it like a toner to achieve the rosy, fresh-faced complexion that was in vogue at the time. Bully's career was the inspiration for one of Honoré de Balzac's lesser-known novels, *César Birotteau*—which in turn inspired entrepreneurs Victoire de Taillac and Ramdane Touhami to revive the brand in 2014, nearly a hundred years after the last Bully boutique closed.

To evoke the ambience of old-world apothecaries, the shops (there are four locations in Paris, as well as outposts around the world) feature walnut wood, marble counters, and antique fixtures, while perfumes, body oils, and lotions are packaged in antique-looking flasks, vials, and glass jars.

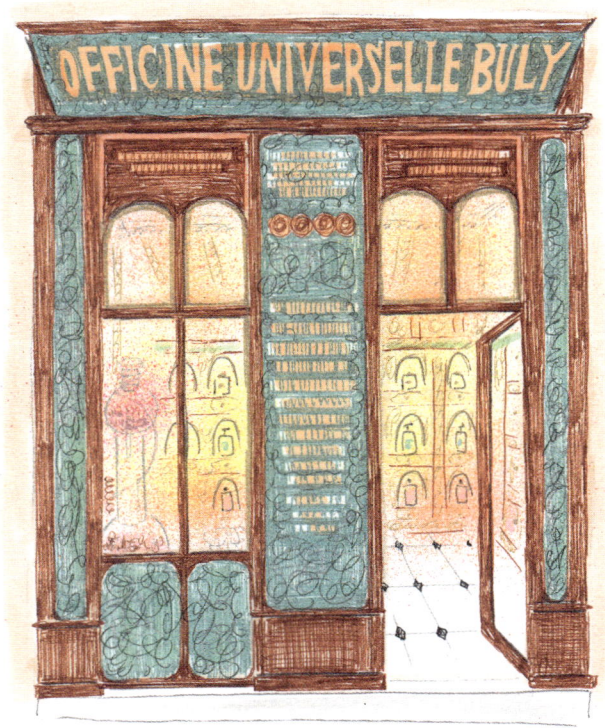

La Bonne Franquette

———

This restaurant's motto encapsulates the spirit of the French *bon vivant*: "Love, eat, drink, and sing." And its name, La Bonne Franquette, means "informal," "simple," "without fuss." It's this spirit that attracted painters like Paul Cézanne, Auguste Renoir, and local resident Vincent van Gogh to the humble bistro during the 19th century, when it was called Billards en Bois. It was renamed in 1925, and has been managed by the Fracheboud family since 1971.

Van Gogh immortalized the space in his 1886 painting *La Guinguette à Montmartre*, which now hangs in the Musée d'Orsay. The building itself dates back to the 16th century, and today anchors one of the highest intersections of Paris, where it faces another popular Instagram landmark, Le Consulat restaurant. It also offers an arresting view of Sacré-Coeur from its charming, narrow alleyway.

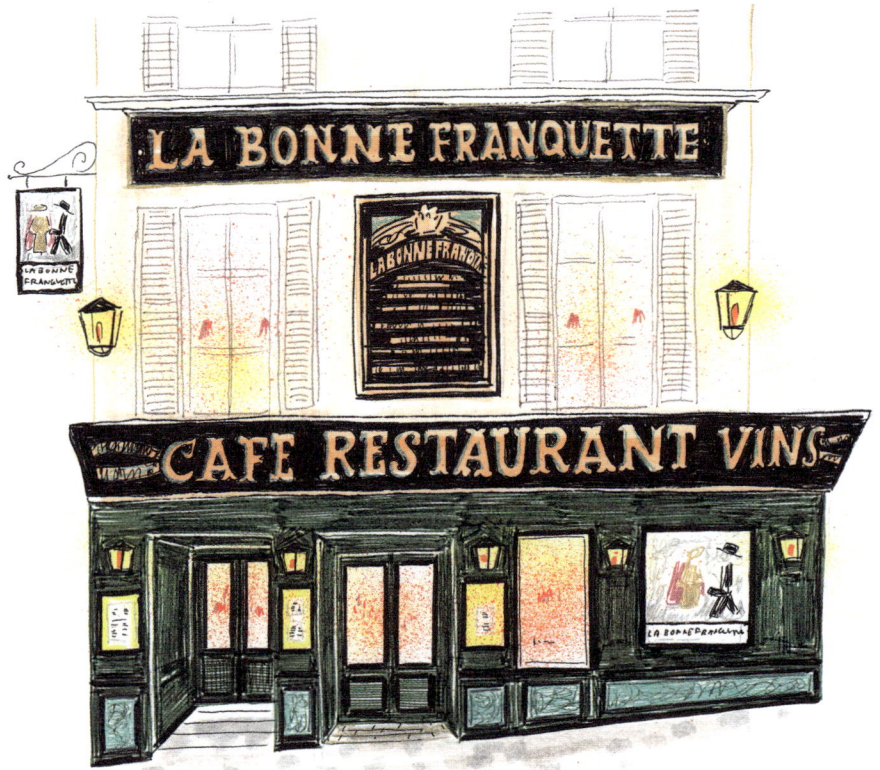

Musée des Arts Forains

———

It started as a personal hobby. Exhibition designer Jean Paul Favand was infatuated with fun fairs, and started collecting vintage artifacts in the 1970s. However, when his collection—which eventually included a full-sized carousel—outgrew his storage space, he decided to share his passion for fairgrounds in an interactive museum for children and adults alike.

At the Musée des Arts Forains, visitors are transported back to a nostalgic time of charismatic showmen in top hats, fortune tellers, illusionists, and puppeteers.

One of the museum's star attractions is the wooden carousel that dates back to 1900 and was designed not for children, but for adults. At the time, horseback-riding was an activity generally reserved for soldiers and aristocrats, and thus merry-go-rounds gave ordinary adults the rare chance to sit astride horses and feel like nobility. In place of beveled mirrors, carved panels, and silver plating for his illusions, Jean Paul uses video projections and digital tools to whisk visitors to Venice, India, or a ballroom circa 1925.

Unlike other museums where items are protected behind plexiglass or velvet ropes, visitors can ride, play, and touch exhibits as part of their guided tours. In fact, all visits must be reserved in advance and are led by tour guides, with the exception of the year-end Festival du Merveilleux, when the museum opens to the public. (Take note that tours are only in French.)

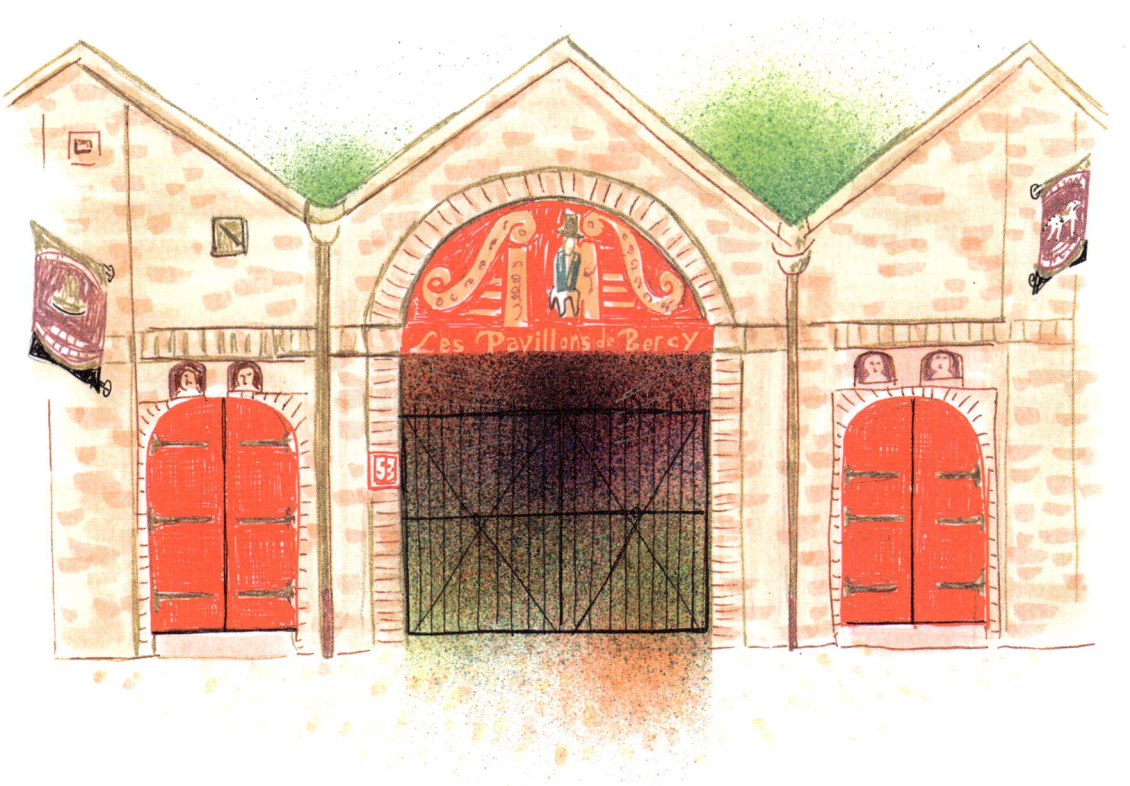

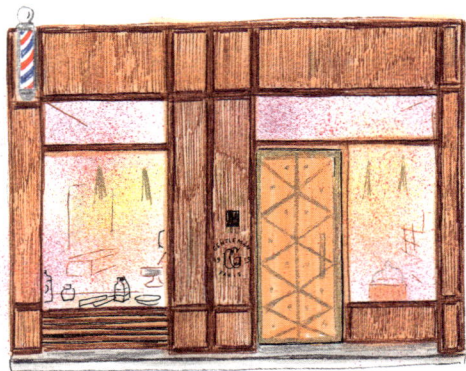

11 rue Jean Mermoz
8th arr.

Gentlemen 1919

—

This is the ultimate man cave. After a haircut and beard trim, clients can head to the back of the salon and access a hidden vintage-inspired speakeasy for a whiskey or cognac. There's also a cigar room.

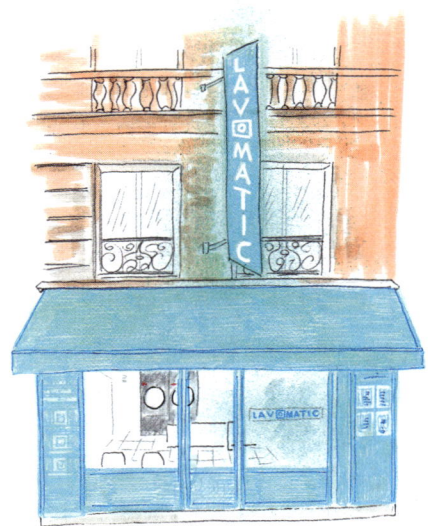

30 rue René Boulanger
10th arr.

Lavomatic

—

The lines outside this laundromat aren't because the washing machines deliver whiter whites: a fun speakeasy is hidden behind the back wall. To gain entrance, find the faux machine and press the button.

86 rue des Martyrs
18th arr.

L'Objet qui Parle

—

This tiny vintage thrift shop has been a treasure trove of eclectic flea market finds since 1998. Items are renewed regularly and may include desk lamps from the 1960s, apothecary bottles, and brass doorknockers.

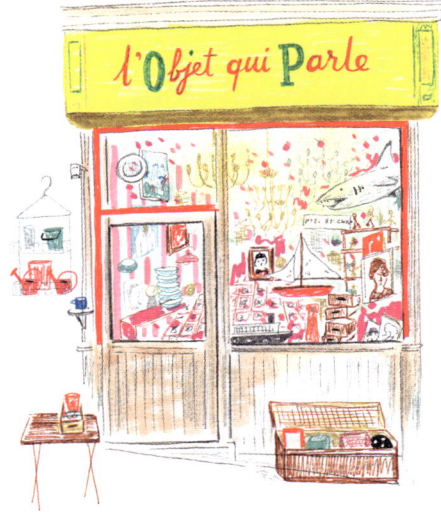

23 rue du Temple
4th arr.

Le Raidd

—

One of the most famous gay bars in Paris, Le Raidd is known for its buff go-go dancers and crowd-pleasing shower booth, where gents with six packs lather themselves in bubbles in view of voyeurs.

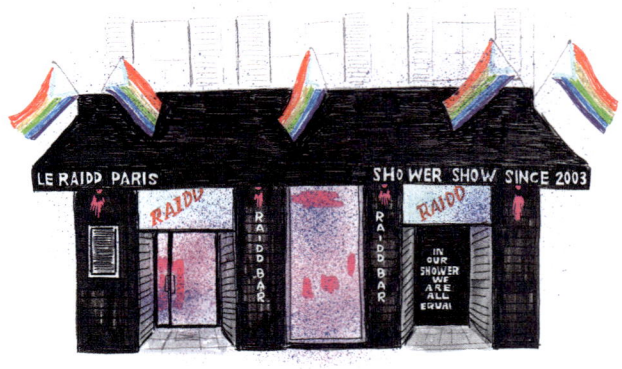

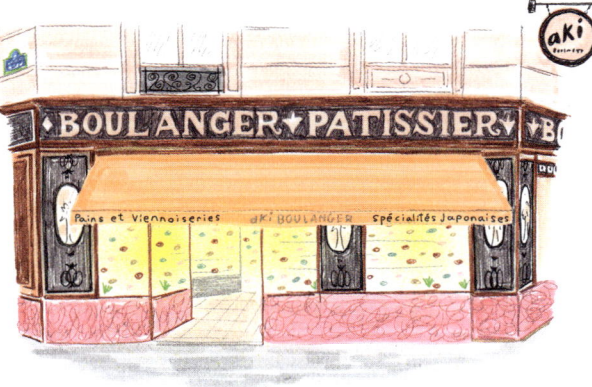

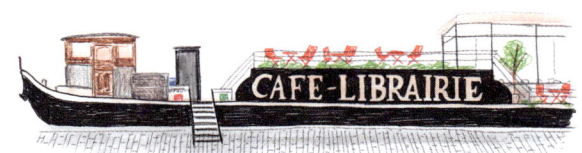

11 Quai de l'Oise
19th arr.

L'Eau et les Rêves

This boat anchored along the Bassin de la Villette in northern Paris is a floating restaurant, weekend brunch spot, and bookshop. Its name means Water and Dreams, and the deck is popular in warm weather.

16 rue Sainte-Anne
1st arr.

Aki Boulangerie

This Franco-Japanese bakery rarely empties, thanks to its selection of sweet and savory offerings like crispy cutlet bento boxes, generously stuffed onigiri, pillowy mochi, and green tea cakes. There are two other locations on the same street.

10 Bd Montmartre, 34 Pass. Jouffroy
9th arr.

Galerie Fayet

Located in the covered Jouffroy passageway, this boutique has been selling walking sticks and canes since 1909, including luxury specimens from the 18th and 19th centuries made from horn, silver, and precious stones.

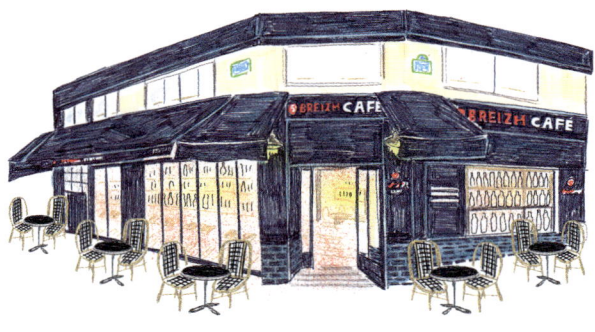

93 rue des Martyrs
18th arr.

Breizh Café

After opening his first crêperie in Tokyo in 1996, Breton Bertrand Larcher now runs a dozen cafés in Paris and beyond. Crêpes are made with organic buckwheat flour and toppings include country ham, smoked duck, and truffle cheese.

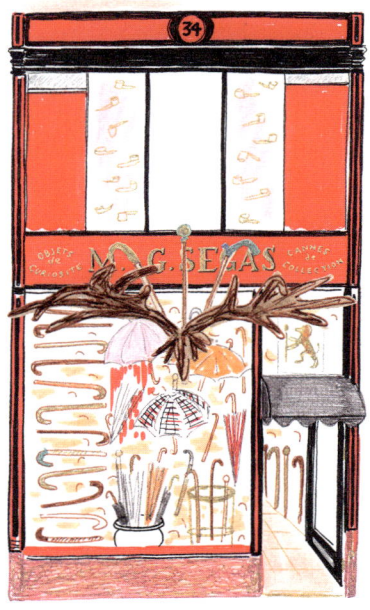

Ace Boucherie
& Traiteur

———

Every day at noon, the long but fast-moving line outside this charming butcher's shop fills the sidewalk and stretches around the corner. But it's not tenderloin or rump steak that people are waiting for. Local office workers with insider knowledge of the neighborhood's best-kept secrets have come to get a Korean takeout lunch.

In 2011, Kim Jin-shu took over the neighborhood butcher shop and continued preparing the typical French recipes that her predecessor had served and passed on to her. But with time, Jin-shu gradually began introducing thinly sliced Korean beef *bulgogi* and other assorted *banchan* (side dishes), which became a major hit with the lunchtime crowd. Often described as one of the best value-for-money deals in the area, regulars rave about the homemade taste of the *japchae*, spicy pork, fried chicken, and kimchi pancakes (*jeon*).

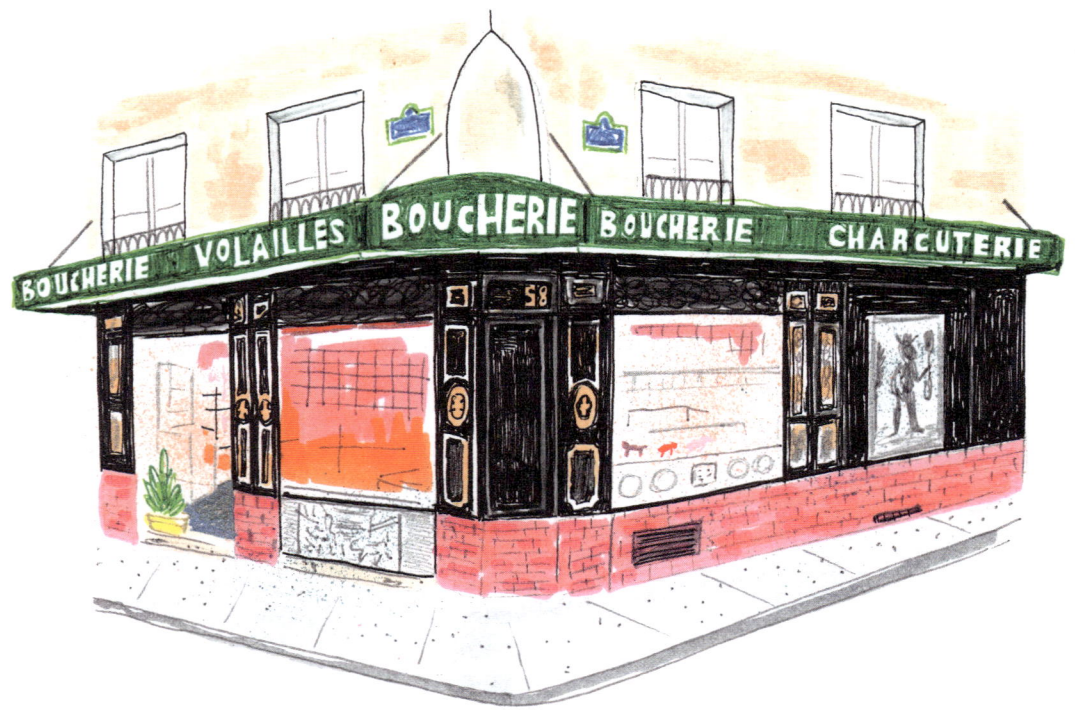

Le Grand Véfour

To eat at Le Grand Véfour is to dine with the ghosts of Victor Hugo, George Sand, Colette, and Napoleon Bonaparte. Located under the arcades at the Jardin du Palais Royal, the restaurant first opened in 1784 as Café de Chartres, making it one of the oldest eateries in the city. From the outset, it was frequented by Paris's high society (as the story goes, Hugo's favorite dish was vermicelli, mutton, and white beans). But it was under Jean Véfour, after whom the café is now named, that it was transformed into an opulent dining room, with its dramatic red velour banquettes and neoclassical glass paintings. Chef Guy Martin, who took over in 1991, renounced his Michelin stars in 2021 and pivoted from fine dining to a more casual "market dining" concept—and a (moderately) more affordable menu.

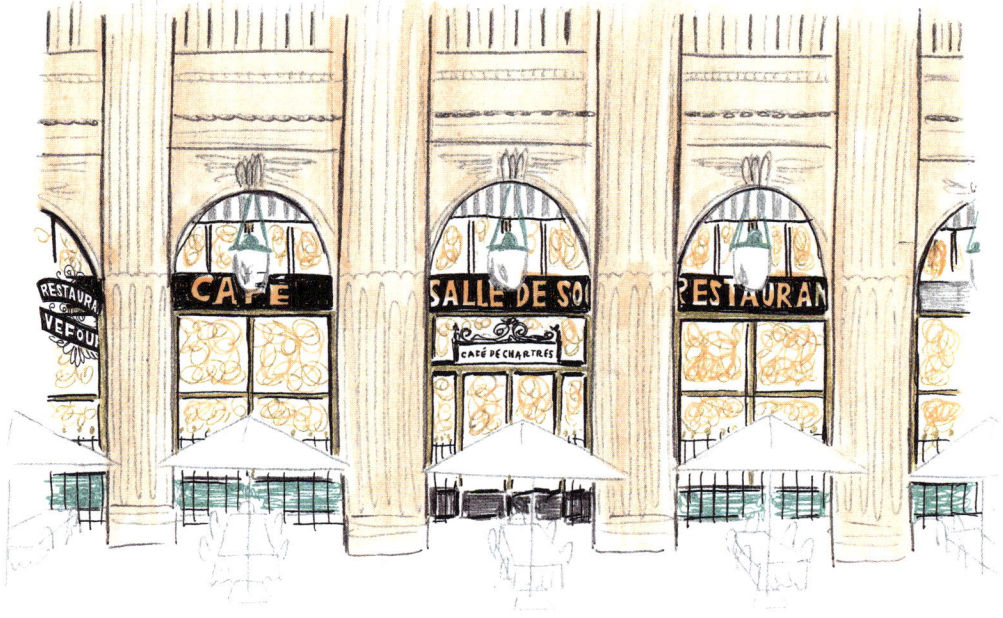

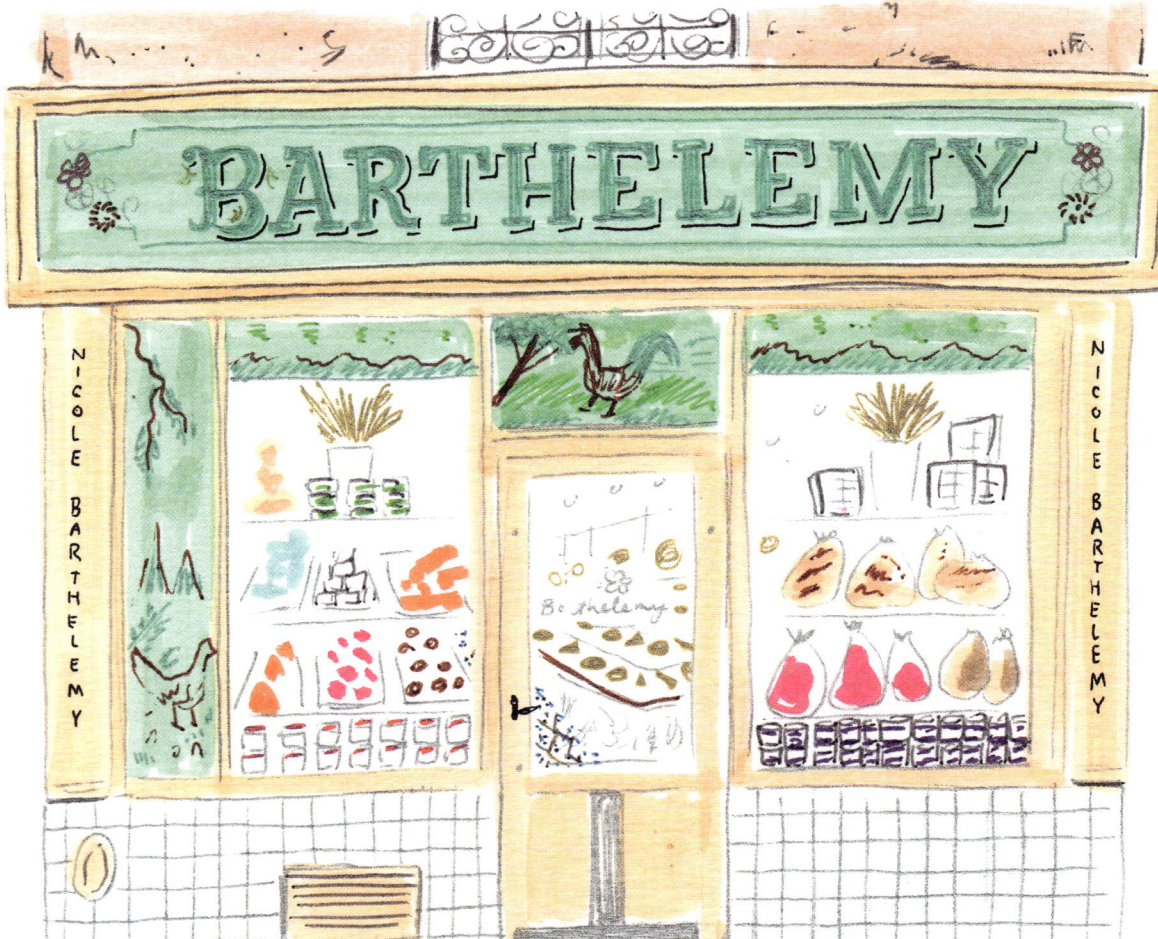

Barthélémy

This quaint cheese shop in the affluent seventh arrondissement has long been the official supplier of the Élysée Palace, feeding several French presidents since the 1970s.

Along with heads of state, Barthélémy is also a favorite of French legends Charlotte Gainsbourg and Catherine Deneuve, as well as American TV cook the Barefoot Contessa (aka Ina Garten), whose ringing endorsement of the store—which sits around the corner from her Paris apartment—has no doubt driven much foot traffic among US visitors over the years. "Too much cheese, too little time!" she wrote in an Instagram post in 2022.

Founded by Roland Barthélémy and taken over by his former wife Nicole, shelves groan with more than 200 types of cheeses, including standby bries and camemberts, along with goat and sheep's milk cheeses, all of which are aged on site in the shop's cellars. But Barthélémy's signature item is the Fontainebleau, a mild, light, airy cow's milk cheese that looks like whipped cream and contains 60 percent fat.

Interestingly, after working as the official cheese supplier to the country's leaders, Nicole transitioned into life as a civil servant herself, becoming a district councilor for the neighborhood arrondissement. In 2021, the shop passed to another reputable female cheesemonger, Claire Griffon.

Paradis Latin

———

Here's something unique to Paradis Latin, the oldest cabaret in Paris: in 2022, the theater came up with the novel idea to create a kid-friendly show called "Mon Premier Cabaret" ("My First Cabaret"). It features the same dreamy qualities of a burlesque show, but is G-rated compared to the theater's adult-only spectacle, "Bird of Paradise."

Meanwhile, Paradis Latin's origins stretch back to 1802, when it was commissioned as a theater by Napoleon Bonaparte when he was First Consul. In 1870, it burnt to the ground and was left abandoned until 1889, when Gustave Eiffel himself undertook its reconstruction. Over the next few decades, the center of Parisian nighttime entertainment shifted from the Left Bank to the Right, leading to its closure. But since 1977, when it reopened under the prince of the city's nightlife, Jean-Marie Rivière, the venue has enjoyed a long stretch of success.

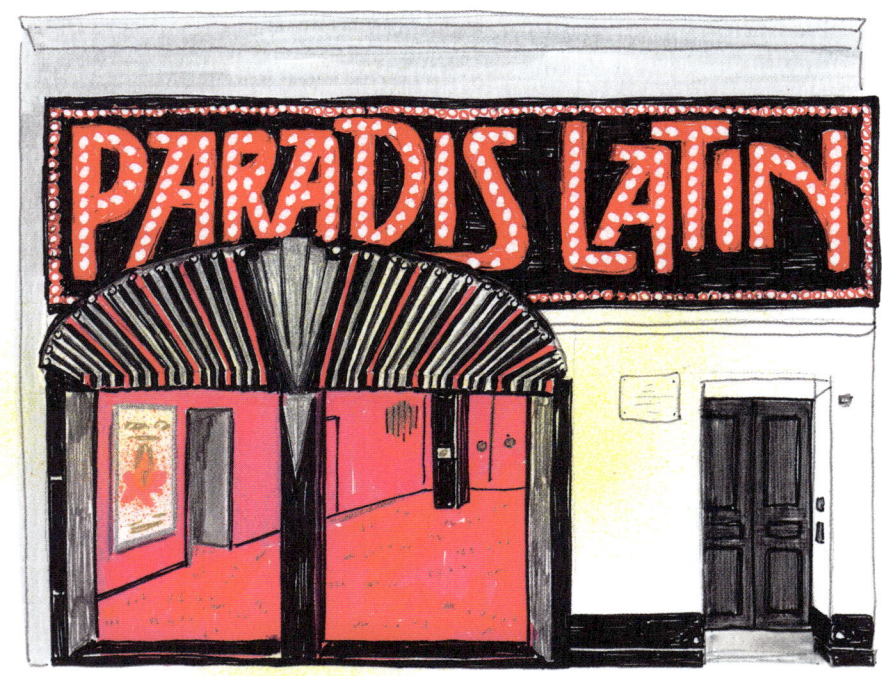

Du Pain et des Idées

It could be argued that this picturesque bakery was one of the earliest stars of social media in the 2010s, when photo-sharing platforms like Instagram began to create overnight sensations. The shop has also benefited from its location in Canal Saint-Martin, a gentrified neighborhood that got a major popularity boost after its appearance in the 2001 film *Amélie*. Unlike other viral hits that fizzle out, though, Du Pain et des Idées continues to attract long lines of both tourists and locals for its historic, photogenic architecture—painted glass ceilings, beveled mirrors—and its quality breads and pastries made by award-winning pastry chef Christophe Vasseur. The bakery's specialties include *pain des amis* (a rustic loaf with a lightly smoked crust, which he's trademarked), apple turnovers, and chocolate-pistachio "*escargot*" pastries, all of which are made with organic ingredients.

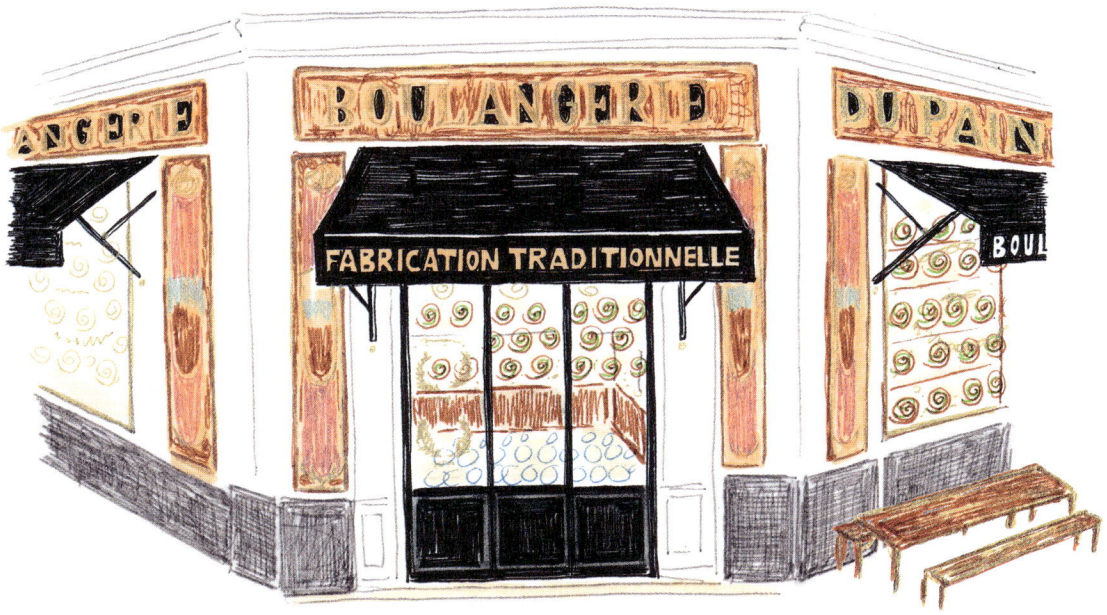

Au Rocher de Cancale

Rue Montorgueil is densely packed with fetching shopfronts, be they cheesemongers, bakeries, or fruit and vegetable stands. But Au Rocher de Cancale, opened in 1804, is arguably the most arresting building on the street, with its pastel-blue façade and gold-accented neo-Renaissance architecture. As popular as it is today, the corner café held even more significance during its golden years, when French writer Honoré de Balzac sought inspiration there for *La Comédie humaine*, his collection of stories and essays depicting 19th-century French society. At that time, the café was also a hotspot for fresh oysters, when they were all the rage among the bourgeoisie and were slurped down on the street. Today, the menu remains classically French (*escargots*, foie gras, and *entrecôte de boeuf*).

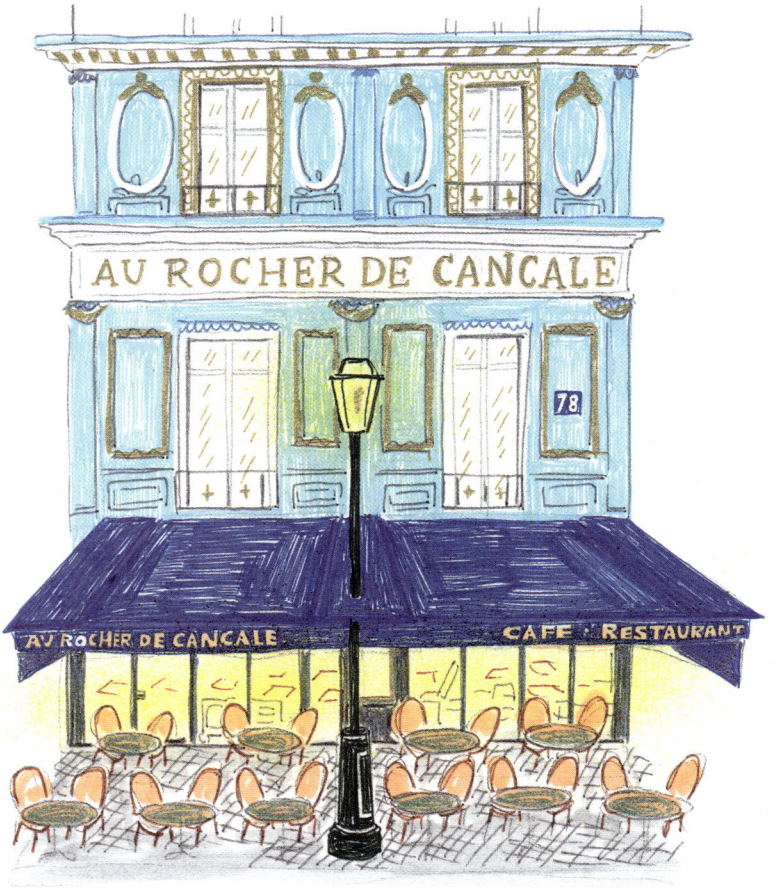

BMK Folie-Bamako

—

In the mid- to late 2010s, Paris saw an exciting wave of trendy African restaurants pop up around town. They were helmed by hip, young, savvy entrepreneurs—the children of African immigrants from former French colonies such as Cameroon, Ivory Coast, Mali, Senegal, or the French West Indies. Two of the most popular restaurants to lead this charge were BMK Paris-Bamako, which opened in 2017, and BMK Folie-Bamako, which opened in 2020. Brothers Fousseyni and Abdoulaye Djikine said they wanted to shatter French stereotypes about African cuisine—that it's heavy and greasy—and give younger members of the African diaspora a taste of their childhoods. While both spots are popular and dynamic, BMK Folie-Bamako's menu features smoky *mafé*, a rich, comforting peanut stew made with roasted peanuts and chicken that will leave an indelible impression.

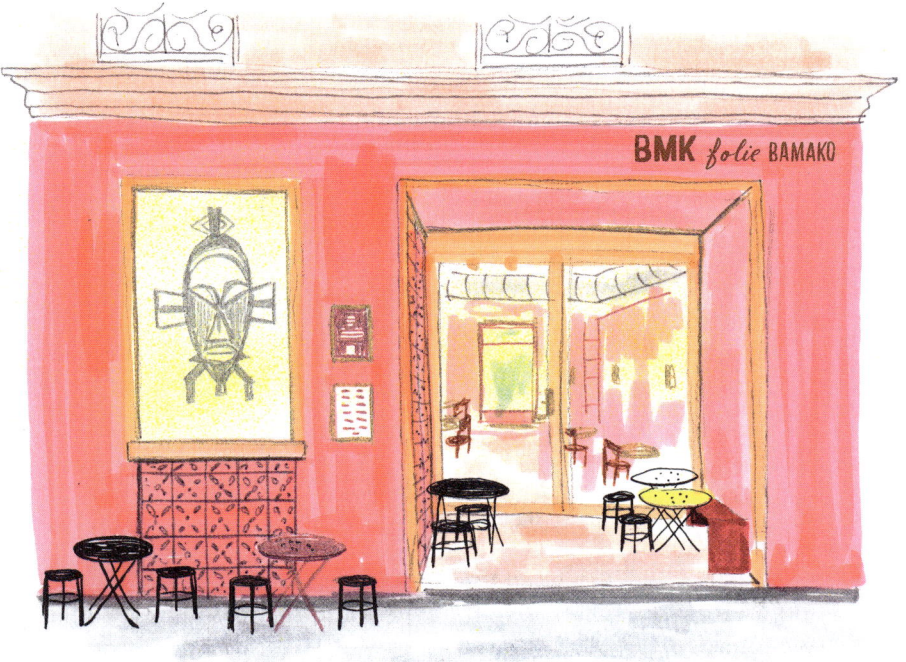

Tang Frères

—

When brothers Bou and Bounmy Rattanavan opened their first Chinese grocery store in Paris's 13th-arrondissement Chinatown in 1981, little did they know that it would set the foundation for a mini-empire that would come to include no fewer than 10 Asian supermarkets and eateries across France decades later. Built in a former 21,530-square-foot garage owned by national rail company SNCF, the first Tang Frères is the flagship that still draws large crowds every weekend. It's a one-stop shop for any Asian food needs: Chinese, but also Vietnamese, Korean, Japanese, Taiwanese, Singaporean, Malaysian, and Filipino ingredients, all in one place. Locals also come here for the wide selection of fresh and affordable fruits and vegetables. Tang Frères supplies many Chinese restaurants across France.

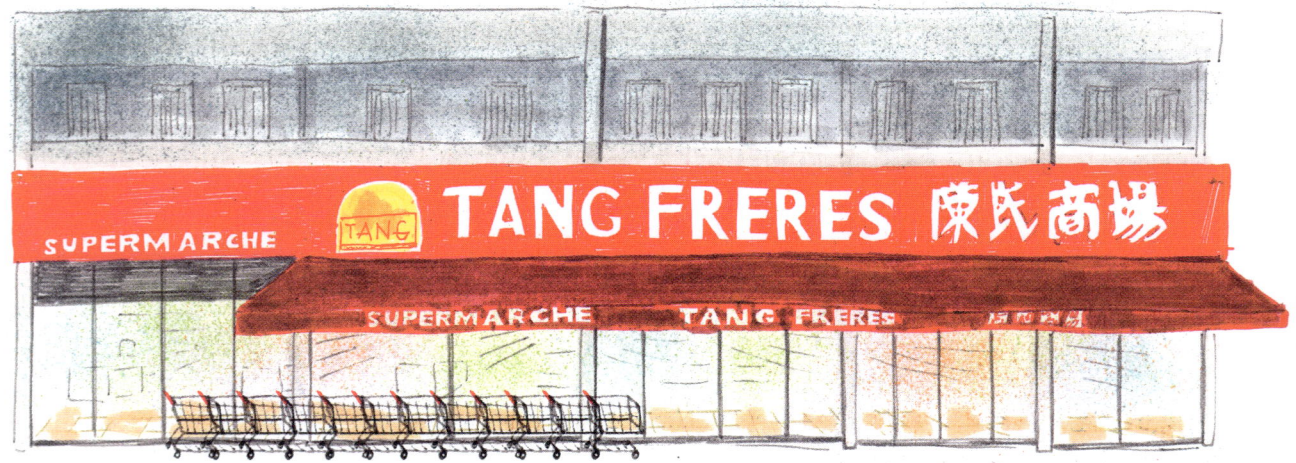

Sunset Sunside

A night at Sunset Sunside jazz club can yield all sorts of surprises for music lovers. For instance, Sting was once sitting in the audience when he joined players onstage and gave a surprise mini-concert, much to the delight of the room. And legendary trumpeter Wynton Marsalis once accompanied fellow musicians in an impromptu all-night jam session after being recognized while sipping cognac at his table.

Opened in 1982, the club is divided into two parts: at Sunside, in what used to be a restaurant on the ground floor, the music is acoustic jazz, while the basement venue, Sunset, plays electric. The club has hosted greats like Miles Davis, Herbie Hancock, and Chet Baker. Its success led to the opening of more jazz clubs nearby, making the Châtelet area a dream for lovers of the genre (other popular spots include Le Duc des Lombards and Le Baiser Salé).

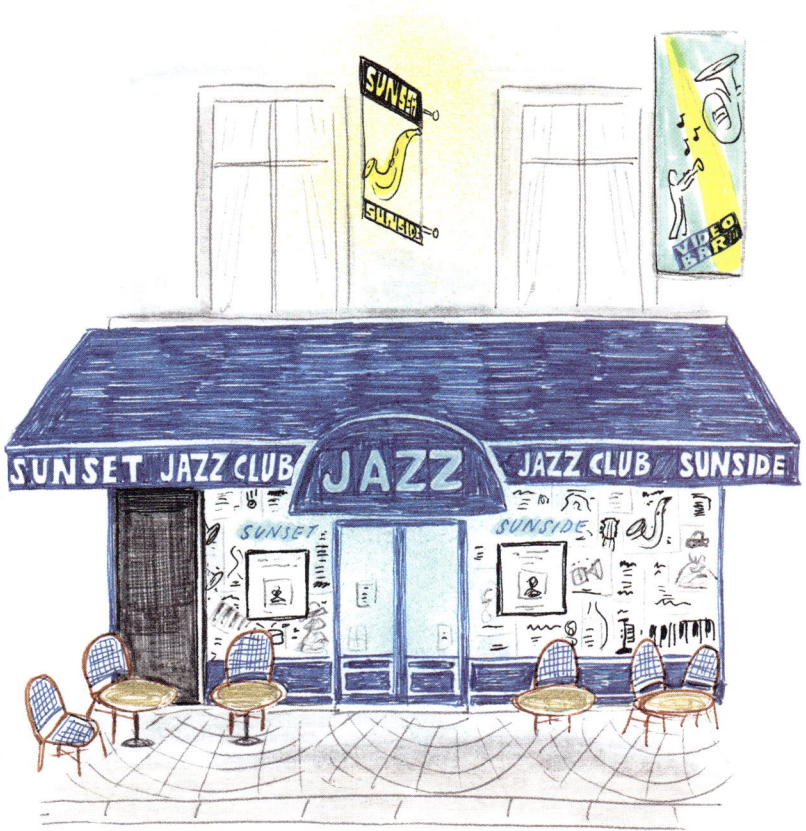

Charvet

———

Opened in 1838, this high-end haberdashery at Place Vendôme stakes a claim as the world's first shop dedicated to men's shirt-making.

Its lineage can be traced back to Napoleon Bonaparte: founder Joseph-Christophe Charvet's father supervised his wardrobe, while his cousin was a linen keeper who oversaw the making of imperial shirts.

Over nearly two centuries, the store's reputation as a creator of bespoke shirts has attracted an impressive client list that includes royalty, artists, and heads of state. Marcel Proust, Charles Baudelaire, Winston Churchill, Edward VIII, Yves Saint Laurent, and John F. Kennedy have been among its devoted customers. Today, it's steered by brother-sister duo Jean-Claude and Anne-Marie Colban, whose father Denis Colban was an importer of fine English fabrics and took over from the Charvet family in 1965.

On the fifth floor, a master tailor traces out patterns on premium cotton, wool, or cashmere before sending the materials to their workshop in Saint-Gaultier in west-central France for assembly. The sixth floor houses a silk atelier, where seamsters put the finishing touches on neckties, scarves, and pajamas by hand and come up with hundreds of new patterns every year.

Along with their shirts, some of Charvet's signature and trendsetting looks include a classic interwoven stripe on its silk jacquard ties, silk knot cufflinks, Parisian paisley prints, and exuberant silk dressing gowns.

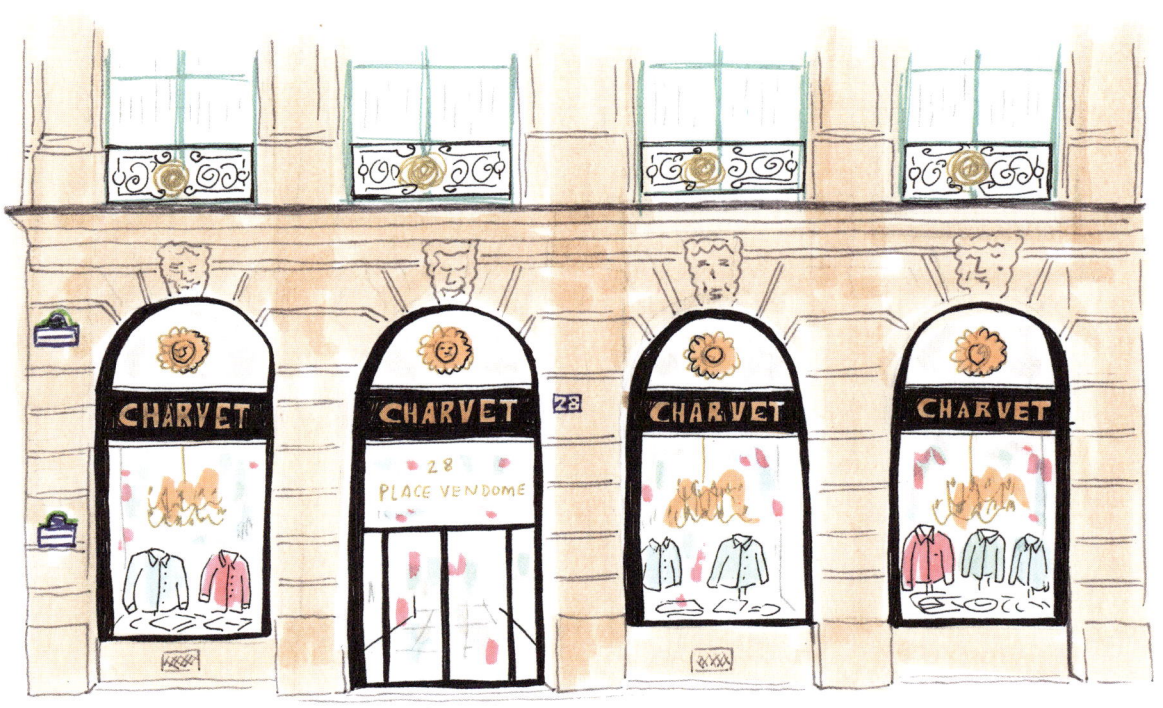

Paris Jazz Corner

——

A magical place for jazz lovers, this music store stocks vinyl from across all related genres, and from around the world—but its strength is indie artists and collectors' records.

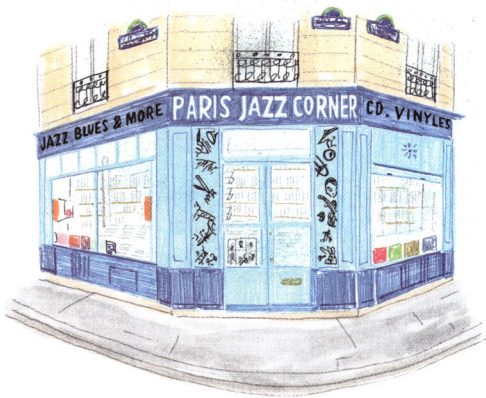

10 rue Tholozé
18th arr.

Studio 28

——

When this theater opened in 1928, it was the first avant-garde cinema in Paris. Today, the independent movie house continues to screen a mix of arthouse and contemporary films. It was also featured in the movie *Amélie*.

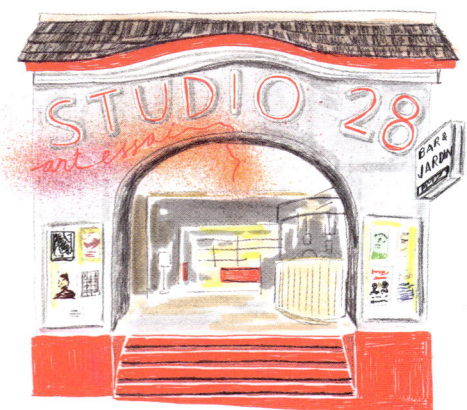

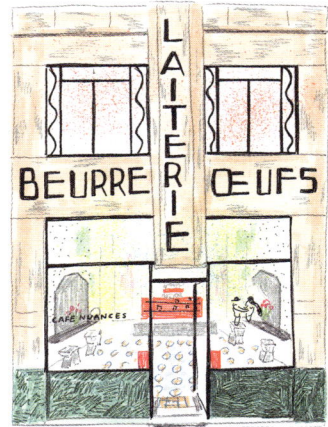

25 rue Danielle Casanova
1st arr.

Café Nuances

——

Inside this former creamery (the signage reads "creamery, butter, and eggs") is a craft coffee shop that opened in 2021. Café Nuances' beans are roasted in Paris, and go by evocative names like "coffee and cigarettes" and "slow dance." There are two other locations in the city.

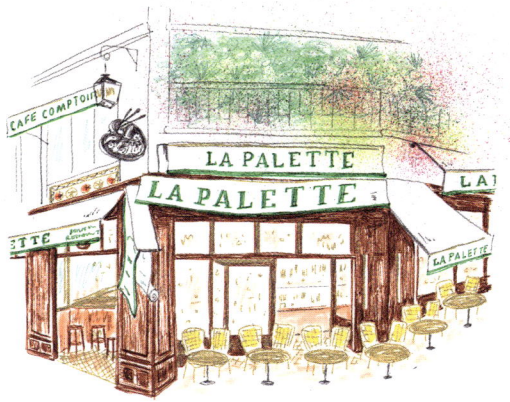

43 rue de Seine
6th arr.

La Palette

——

Located near a school of fine arts in a neighborhood densely packed with private galleries, this historic bistro was traditionally frequented by artist types (past patrons include Jim Morrison and Pablo Picasso).

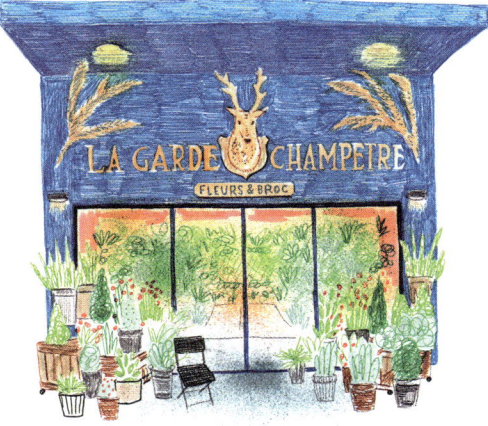

41–47 rue des Martyrs
9th arr.

La Garde Champêtre

—

This striking flower shop—unmissable, with its deer head trophy and midnight-blue façade—sells bouquets of fresh and dried flowers sourced from France and elsewhere in Europe, along with a selection of antiques from around the country.

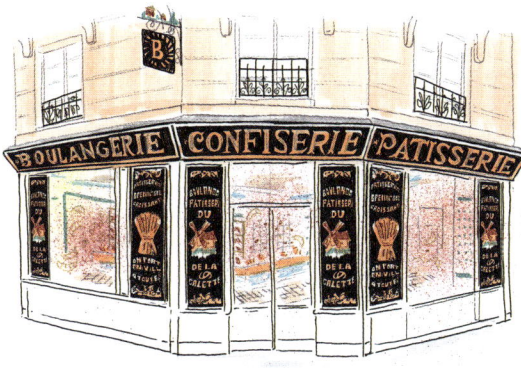

48 rue Caulaincourt
18th arr.

Boris Lumé Boulangerie

—

Aside from being a historic monument and serving up exquisite Franco-Japanese pastries, this bakery is known for its star turn in the children's animated series *Miraculous: Tales of Ladybug & Cat Noir*, and the film *Julie & Julia*. There's a second location in the 18th arrondissement.

46 Pass. Jouffroy
9th arr.

Hôtel Chopin

—

Located at the end of the long, covered Jouffroy passageway is one of the oldest hotels in Paris. Since its opening in 1846, a receptionist has staffed the front desk 24/7—because the front door has no lock.

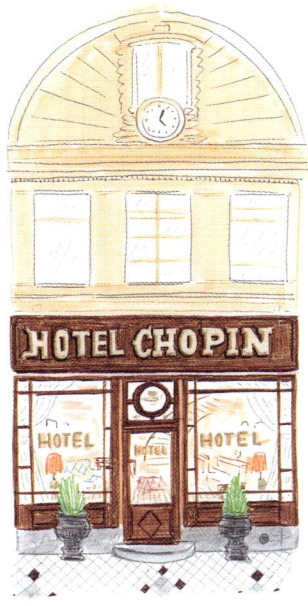

6 rue Hallé
14th arr.

Magasin Sennelier

—

Founded by chemist Gustave Sennelier, this shop has been producing materials for professional artists since 1887. The brand's flagship product is its oil pastels, developed at the request of Pablo Picasso in 1948. There are two other locations in Paris.

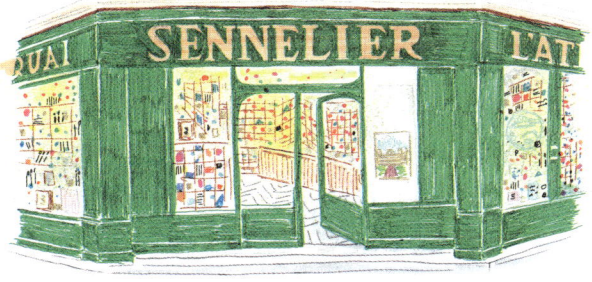

Fulgurances—L'Adresse

———

When Fulgurances opened in 2015, it injected a new, exciting energy into the sometimes stuffy world of French fine dining by giving young, aspiring chefs a place to shine. Described as an incubator for talent, it offers up-and-comers—often second-in-command sous-chefs—the chance to slip out from under the shadows of their bosses and steer their own restaurants for a six-month residency. It also provides open-minded, adventurous diners with fresh experiences. Former alumni include chefs who've worked in some of the best restaurants in the world, including Atelier Crenn in San Francisco, Kadeau and Noma in Copenhagen, and Martín Berasategui in Spain, but also Septime, Astrance, and Agapé in Paris. Chefs are given staff, space, and carte blanche to create three-course meals. *Prix fixe* prices are reasonable, considering that customers could be sampling meals from the future Alain Ducasse. Fulgurances—Laundromat replicates the experience in Brooklyn, New York.

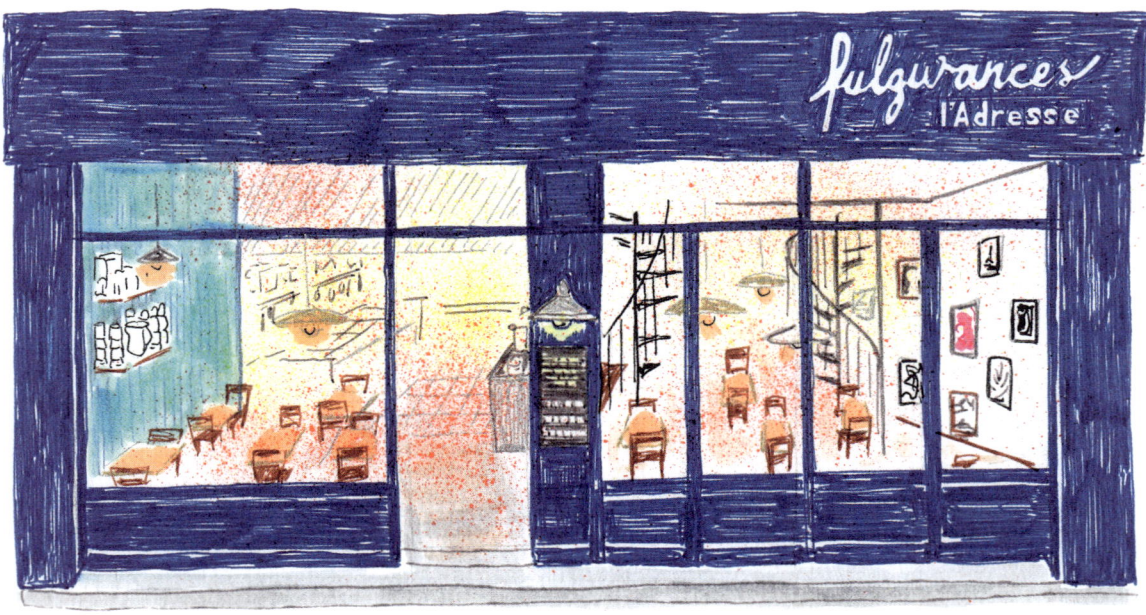

Bofinger

———

Located a few steps from the Place de la Bastille, Bofinger is the oldest Alsatian brasserie in Paris, and was the first to introduce the city's denizens to the concept of draft beer. Its beloved signature sauerkraut dish is topped with no fewer than six types of pork: shank of salted pork, white sausage, cumin sausage, Strasbourg sausage, and smoked pork belly. For pescatarians, the menu includes oyster and seafood platters, mussels, lobster ravioli, and sole *meunière*.

Opened in 1864 by an Alsatian native, Frédéric Bofinger, the restaurant has been listed as a historic monument for its 19th- and 20th-century architecture. In 2021, it reopened following a restoration project that preserved its best features, much to the relief of its regulars, including its stained-glass dome ceiling and wrought-iron staircase.

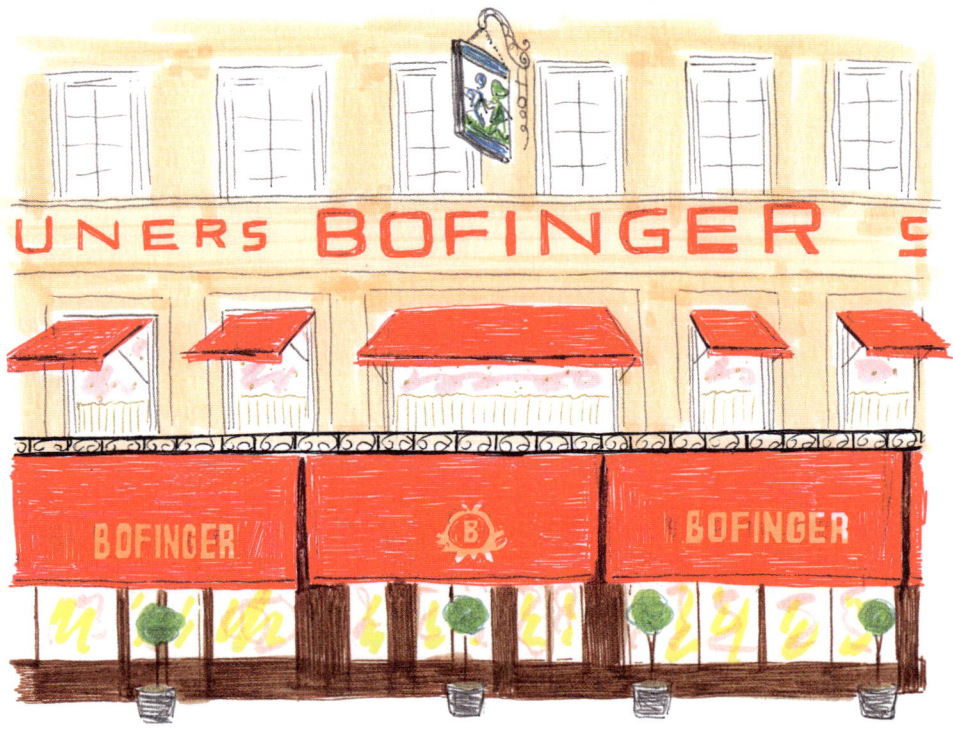

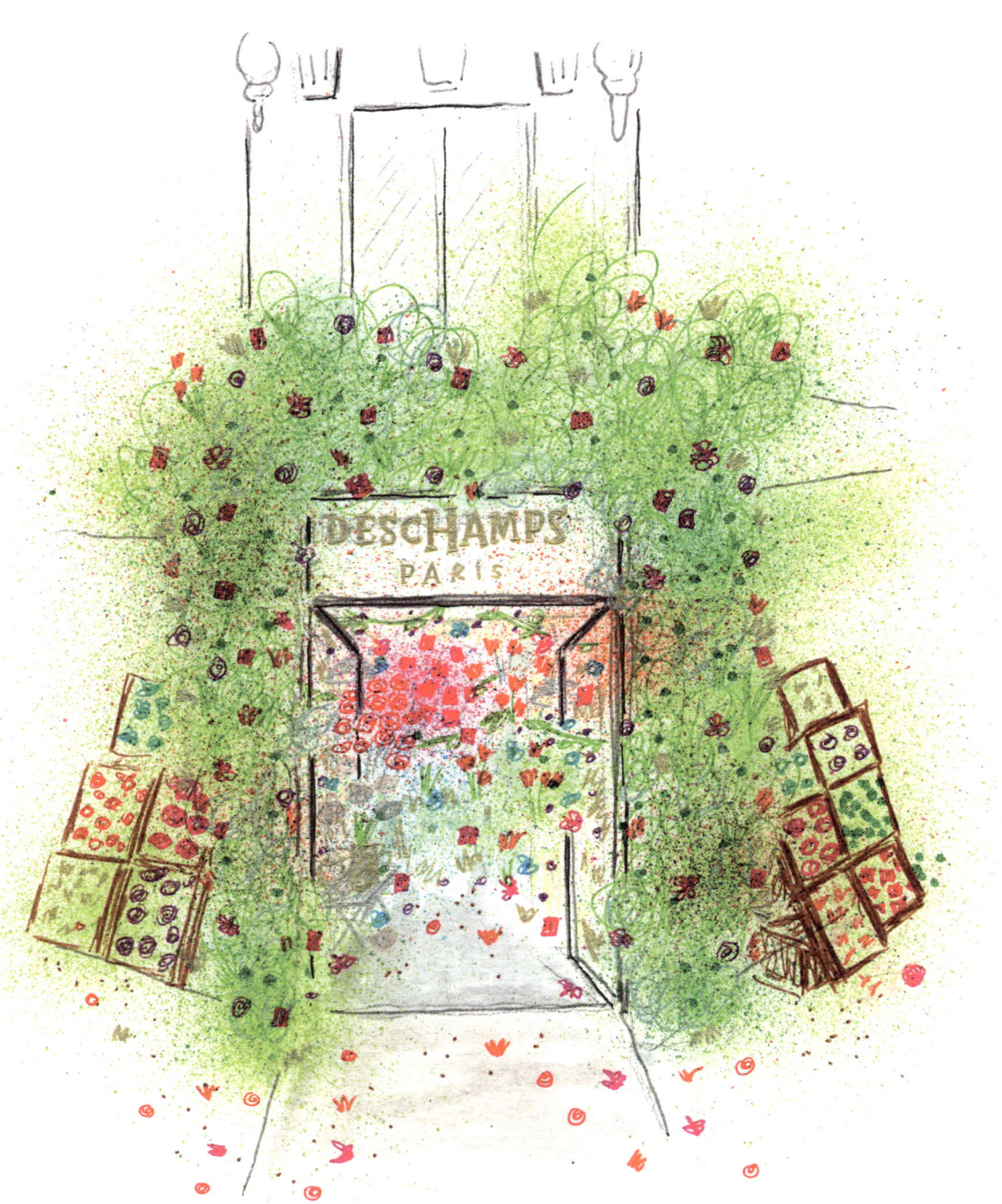

18 Av. Niel

17th arr.

Deschamps

———

Visitors to Paris will no doubt be struck by the curious number of cafés and storefronts exploding in extravagant florals. Many of these displays, if not most, come from this flower shop in the affluent 17th arrondissement, which has been embellishing storefronts, façades, and outdoor terraces with artificial floral arrangements since 2015, transforming the urban streetscape.

Owner Luc Deschamps, who comes from a family of florists, was inspired to create blossoming installations after a trip to New York, where he discovered a shopfront covered in artificial wisteria vines.

His first project in Paris, the façade of Maison Sauvage in Saint-Germain-des-Prés, was an instant success, with photos of the café going viral on social media and requests pouring in from other restaurateurs and shop owners to do the same for them.

Along with outdoor installations, Luc is a highly sought-after florist to the stars (like Naomi Campbell), as well as for luxury brands and hotels, fashion shows, wedding receptions, and special soirées. The boutique is also known for its sophisticated and elegant floral arrangements, including signature hat box bouquets, *paillon* (or natural straw) vase bouquets, and Petits Pots Deschamps—affordable fresh flowers in vintage glass jars.

Bouillon Chartier Grands Boulevards

Be advised: a meal at this historic *bouillon* restaurant will be loud, busy, and maybe even rushed. There's a frenzied kind of energy here, where servers zip to and fro, orders are scrawled by pen on paper table coverings, and dishes of deviled eggs, sauerkraut and sausages, and duck confit are slapdash affairs. In short, little has changed since the *bouillon*'s opening in 1896, when the Chartier brothers opened a fast casual dining spot where locals on tight budgets could fill their bellies with French comfort foods. Today, the tradition continues for those seeking cheap, modest fare and an authentic *bouillon* experience in a beautifully preserved Belle Époque setting of high ceilings, globe lights, framed mirrors, and brass railings. Since 2019, two more locations have opened at Montparnasse and Gare de l'Est.

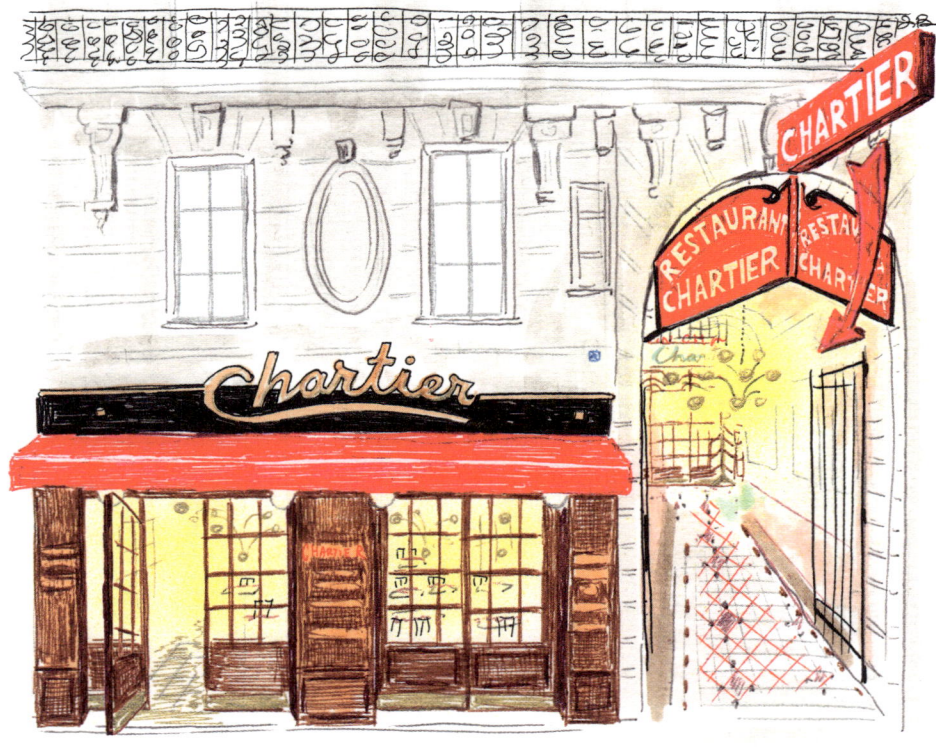

Debauve & Gallais

———

The regal façade of this historic boutique is befitting of its heritage as the official chocolate supplier to France's royals. It all started in 1779 when Marie Antoinette, who suffered from severe headaches, complained about the taste of her medicine. Her pharmacist, Sulpice Debauve, came up with the idea of masking the flavor by mixing it with cocoa butter to create chocolate medallions. The concoction delighted the queen, and birthed the invention of the first "chewable" chocolate. Marie Antoinette named the chocolates *pistoles* (coins), launching the chemist into the unexpected role of chocolatier to the royal court.

In 1800, Debauve opened a shop on rue des Saints-Pères, where he was later joined by his nephew Antoine Gallais. Their most iconic product remains the Pistoles de Marie-Antoinette, which come in flavors like orange blossom and Bourbon vanilla. There's a second location in the 2nd arrondissement.

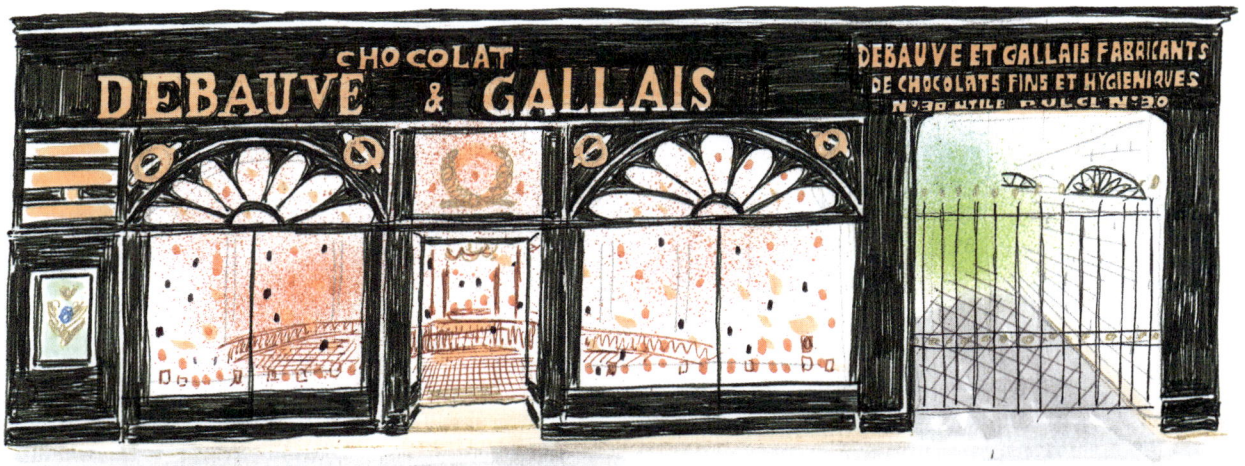

Harry's New York Bar

——

This watering hole is a longtime Paris institution: it's said to be the birthplace of the Bloody Mary, and is where George Gershwin composed the music for *An American in Paris*. Its lengthy, imaginative cocktail list (the bar also claims to have invented the Sidecar, Blue Lagoon, and White Lady) and distinctly New York vibe have attracted stars like Rita Hayworth, Humphrey Bogart, Ian Fleming, and Daft Punk over the years.

Harry's opened in 1911, when enterprising New Yorker Tod Sloan evaded Prohibition in the US by dismantling the mahogany woodwork and stained-glass windows of his bar on 7th Avenue—and rebuilt it all in Paris. In 1923, the bar's new owner, Scottish bartender Harry MacElhone, added his name to the sign. Don't miss the piano bar downstairs, where live jazz is performed after 10 p.m.

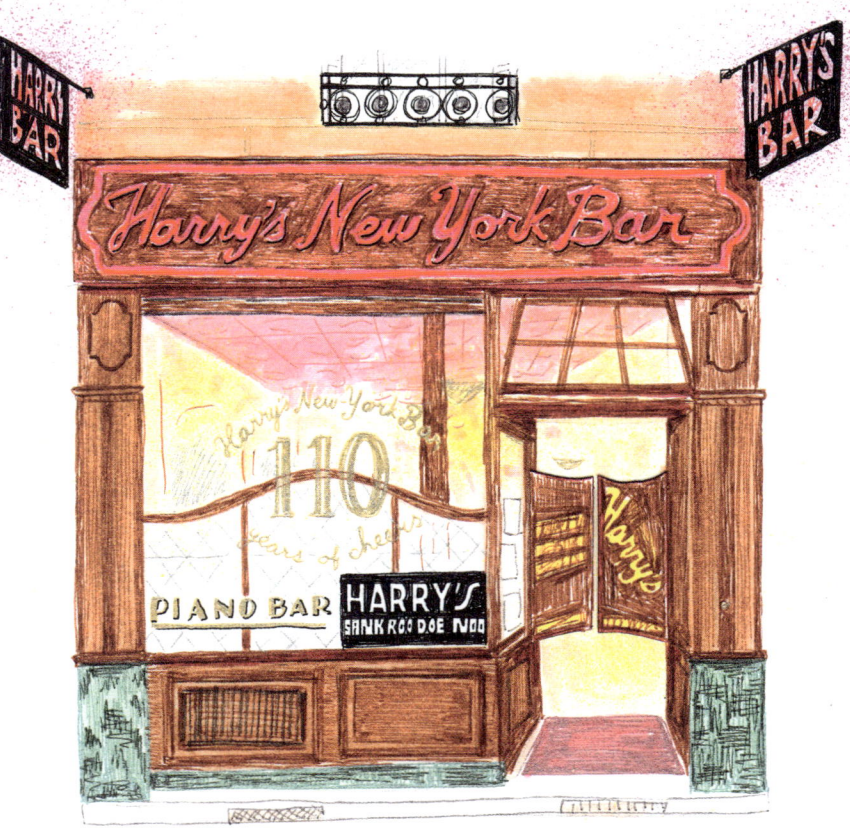

Brasserie Martin

Take a moment to look up and appreciate the custom-made window above this restaurant's neon sign, and chuckle at how its specialty, spit-roast chicken, is rendered holy thanks to the stained-glass treatment normally reserved for churches. This paradox can also be found inside, where the ambience is playful and casual, but the food is honest, sincere, and no-nonsense.

Brasserie Martin is one of four Paris brasseries from the restaurant group Nouvelle Garde, whose self-proclaimed M.O. is to "defend the art of French living" and its culinary heritage. The team works directly with 50 local suppliers and everything is homemade, including the pâté and terrine, which are crafted in the charcuterie lab downstairs. But the stars here are the rotisserie chicken, pork, and guinea fowl, which cook on spits that turn from morning to night and are served with fries, potato gratin, and cabbage.

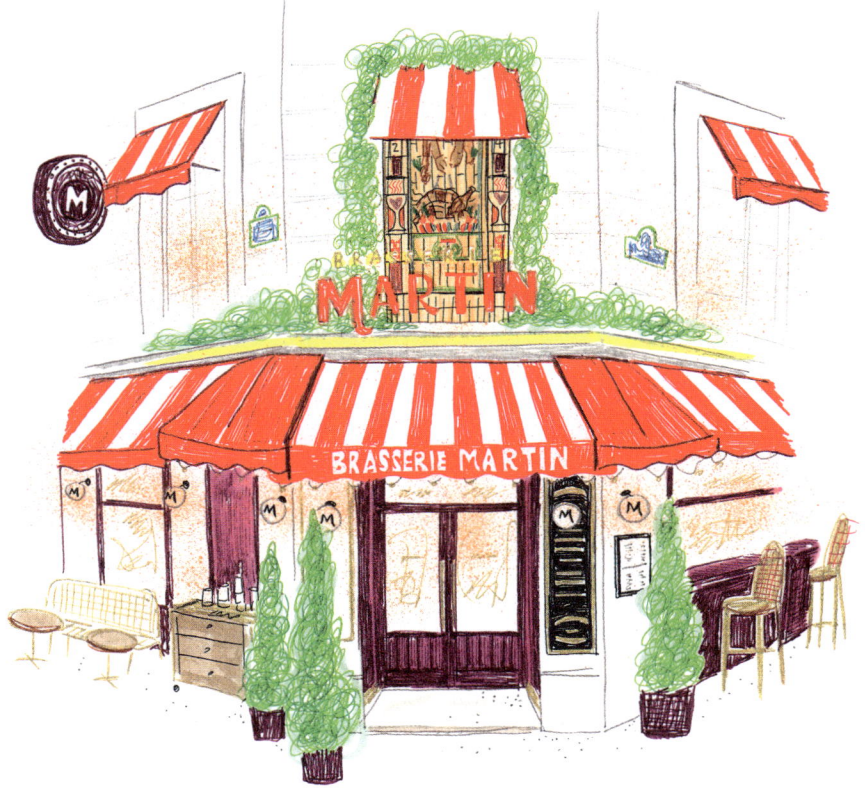

Maison Boissier

Loyal customers of this historic confectionery shop admit to being suckers for both its candy and its packaging. Inside dainty, collectible, pocket-sized pink, blue, and gold tins lie sweet spheres of rose, peach, or mint-flavored candy evocative of the bonbons Parisian theater-goers consumed in the 19th century. Cylindrical boxes bearing images of lovely young maidens contain powdery, pastel-colored "pearl" candies that follow vintage recipes. The store's candied chestnuts are also famous.

Founded in 1827 by Bélisaire Boissier, Maison Boissier became the confectioner to the stars, satisfying the sweet tooths of the Parisian bourgeoisie and writers like Victor Hugo, Alexandre Dumas, and Émile Zola. After going out of business near the end of the 20th century, two entrepreneurs resurrected the brand in 2000, with two locations on rue du Bac and another on rue de Passy.

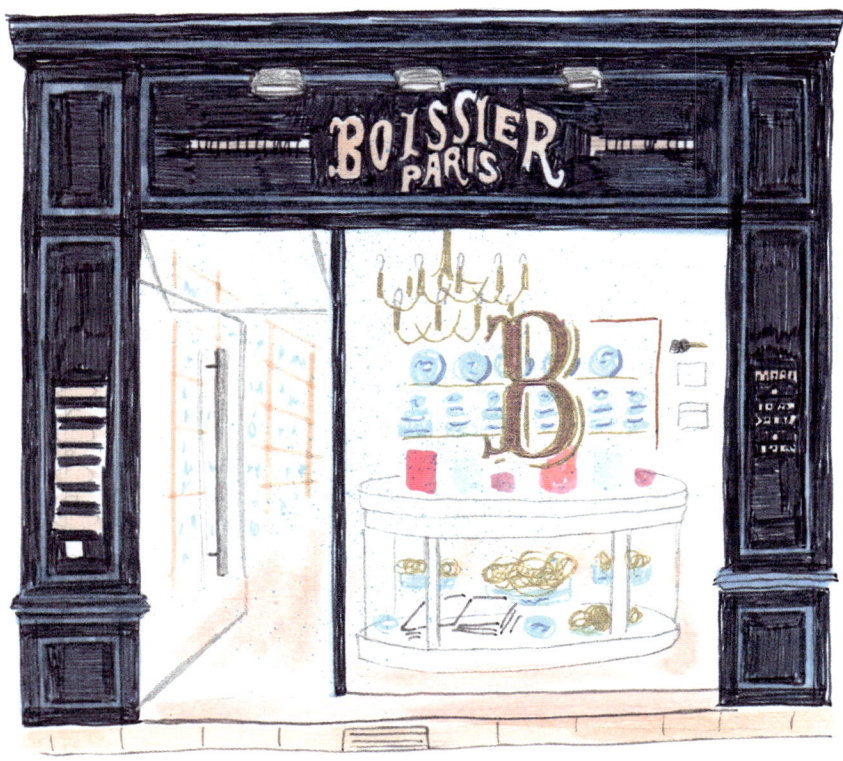

La Maison Rose

—

With its bubble-gum-pink façade, green shutters, and picturesque location atop a sloping hill in the Montmartre area, La Maison Rose (The Pink House) is one of the most photographed spots in the neighborhood. It was one of the house's earlier 20th-century owners, painter Ramon Pichot, and his wife, Germaine, who painted it pink, inspired by the colorful houses they saw during a trip to Spain. Before turning it into a neighborhood restaurant for their artist friends, the couple welcomed pals like Pablo Picasso and Salvador Dalí into their home and art studio. At one point, La Maison Rose went through an identity crisis and was painted white, but the folly was remedied and it was returned to pink. Today it's run by Béatrice Miolano, the granddaughter of one of the house's previous owners (also named Béatrice Miolano), and serves a French-Italian menu.

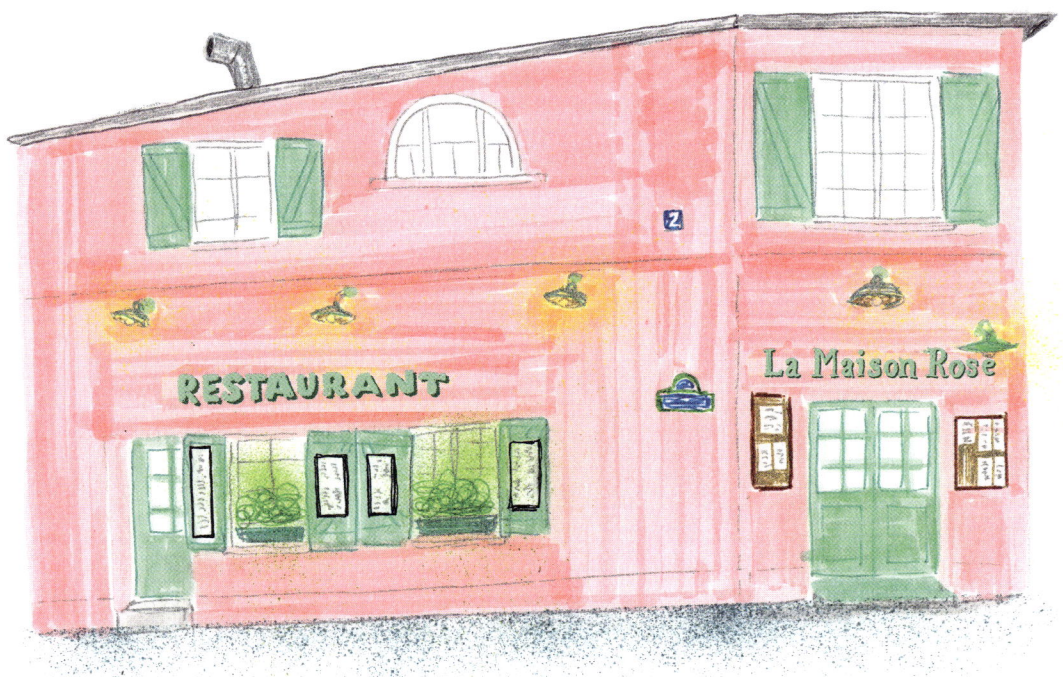

Lapérouse

——

The House of Pleasures: that's what this 18th-century restaurant was known as when it used to host Paris's most powerful men and their courtesans for scandalous soirées dripping with wine and diamonds. Legend even has it that a secret underground passageway connected the Senate to the establishment, allowing senators to join their mistresses on the down-low.

The history of Lapérouse dates back to 1766, when it opened as a small wine cellar along the Seine. Its owner, the king's personal beverage maker, also turned the servants' rooms into private salons, not knowing then that they would go on to become dens of pleasure about a hundred years later. During the Belle Époque, the restaurant was one of the hottest spots in town, attracting everyone from Victor Hugo to Marcel Proust and George Sand.

Alongside lively intellectual debates, the closed-door salons hosted men and their paramours, who famously used the mirrors to authenticate their gifts of precious gems (scratch marks that can still be seen today are supposedly etchings made by ladies of the night).

In the 20th century, Lapérouse earned a reputation as a serious dining destination and became one of the first restaurants in Paris to earn all three Michelin stars in 1933. After losing its stars, it became obsolete and forgotten, until it was resurrected in 2019 and reopened as *the* place to see and be seen. Celebrity guests have since included Kendall Jenner, Nicole Kidman, and Zoë Kravitz.

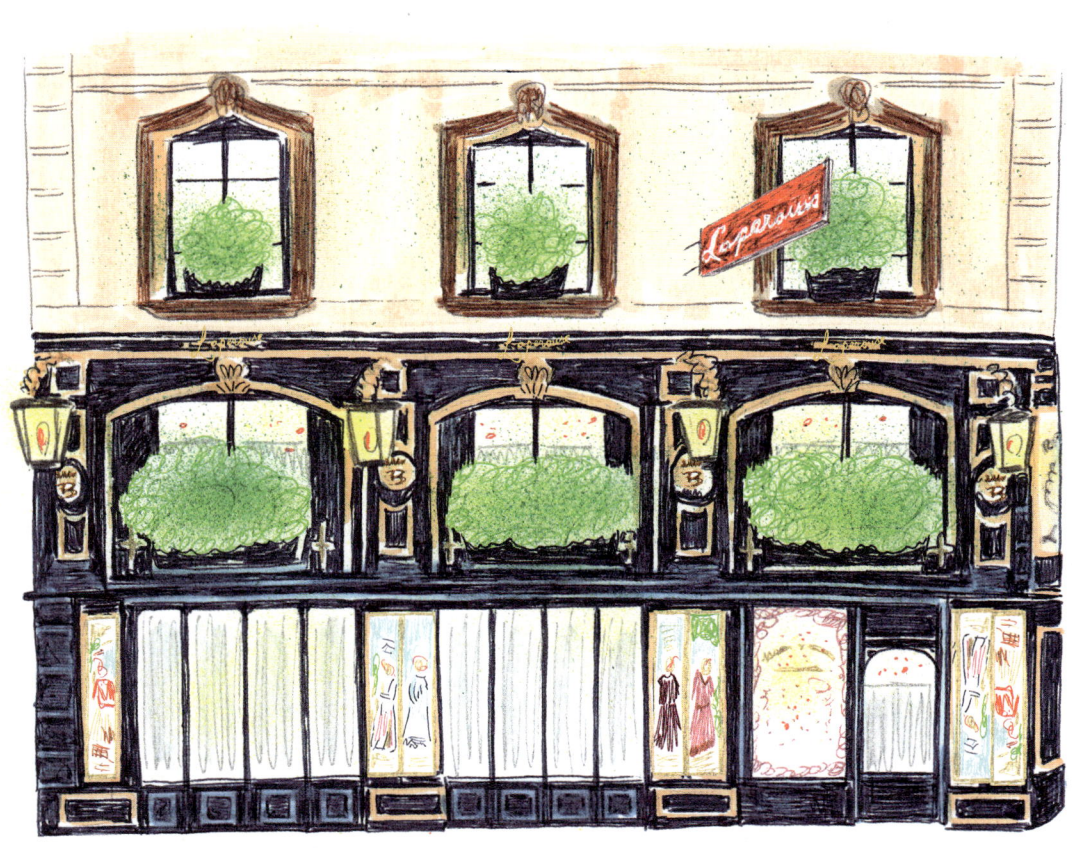

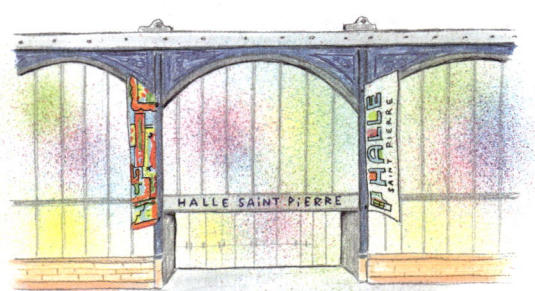

2 rue Ronsard
18th arr.

Halle Saint-Pierre

—

A must-see during a visit to Montmartre is this former covered market built in 1868 opposite the Butte Montmartre gardens. A glass roof creates a luminous space that houses a museum, gallery, auditorium, and photogenic bookshop.

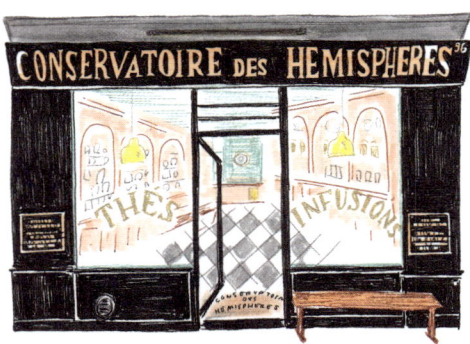

96 rue du Bac
7th arr.

Conservatoire des Hémisphères

—

At this shop, tea is elevated to an art form akin to winemaking: terms like "terroir" and "grand cru" are used to describe its tea leaves. Inside, teas are stored in handsome oak cabinets reminiscent of an apothecary. There's a second location in the 16th arrondissement.

10 Bd Montmartre
9th arr.

Musée Grévin

—

France's answer to Madame Tussauds, this wax museum has been bringing kings, queens, celebrities, and athletes to life since 1882. Its collection of 2,000 personalities ranges from Napoleon Bonaparte and Louis XIV to Lady Gaga and Ryan Gosling.

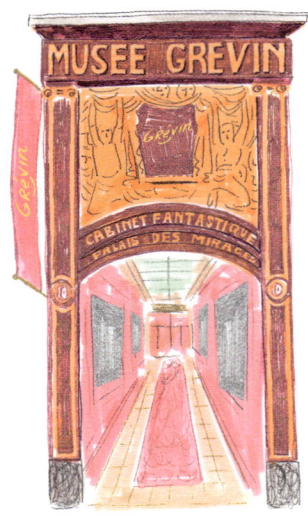

74 rue de la Folie Méricourt
11th arr.

Melt

—

After discovering Texas barbecue during a visit to the US, two French friends opened this slow-cooked BBQ spot, which serves brisket, pulled pork, and ribs with the help of American pitmasters. There are two other restaurants, as well as two delis, in Paris.

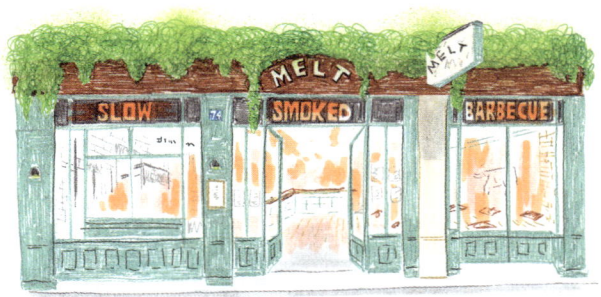

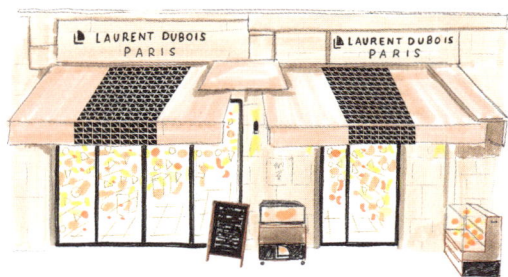

97–99 rue Saint-Antoine
4th arr.

Fromagerie Laurent Dubois

———

One of France's top master cheesemakers, Laurent Dubois has been producing award-winning raw milk cheeses since 1996. His creations are one-of-a-kind, and include Roquefort layered with quince paste, and Neufchâtel topped with morello cherries. There are three other locations in the city.

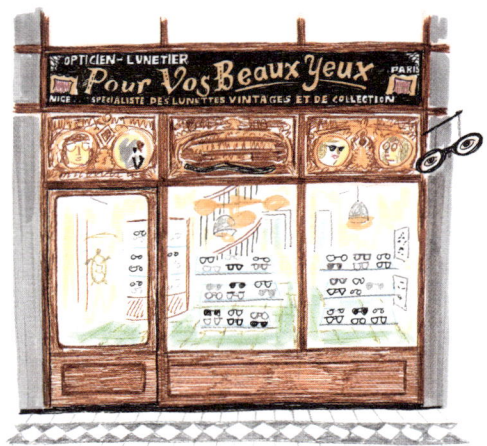

10 Pass. du Grand Cerf
2nd arr.

Pour Vos Beaux Yeux

———

Located in a covered passageway, this 19th-century eyewear store specializes in vintage designer frames that have never been worn, dating from 1900 to 1980. Brands include Persol, Ray-Ban Wayfarer, Sol-Amor and Matsuda.

33 rue Rambuteau
4th arr.

Legay Choc

This bakery in Paris's queer neighborhood rose to fame for its "zizi"-shaped (that is, penis-shaped) breads and pastries. Named "magic baguettes," the anatomically correct baked goods are available in a range of sizes.

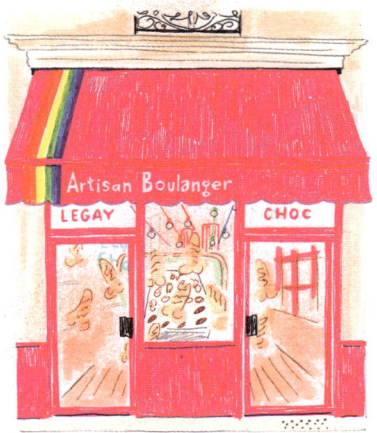

34 rue des Rosiers
4th arr.

L'As du Fallafel

———

The most famous falafel restaurant in Paris started out as an Israeli grocery store in 1979 before introducing locals to the wonders of pita stuffed with tender eggplant and falafel balls. Lenny Kravitz is famously a fan.

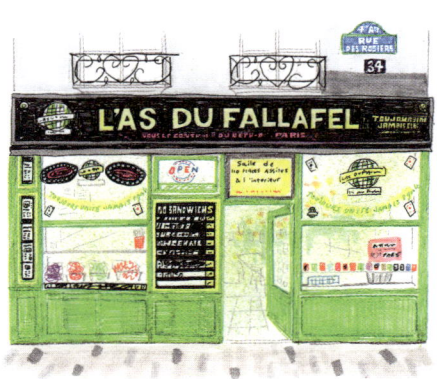

Mosugo

———

As the first Black chef in Paris to earn a Michelin star for his fine dining restaurant MoSuke in 2021, the 2022 opening of Mory Sacko's casual fried chicken sandwich shop next door caused a round of fresh buzz (especially for those who had been on the waiting list for a table at MoSuke for months).

The menu at Mosugo is a mashup of African street foods and flavors, alongside fried chicken sandwiches, with a touch of French and Japanese influences. What does that look like? A fried chicken burger topped with Alsatian pretzel bread and miso mayo, with a side of fried plantains and Cajun spices. A second Mosugo can be found at Galeries Lafayette Le Gourmet department store in the 9th arrondissement.

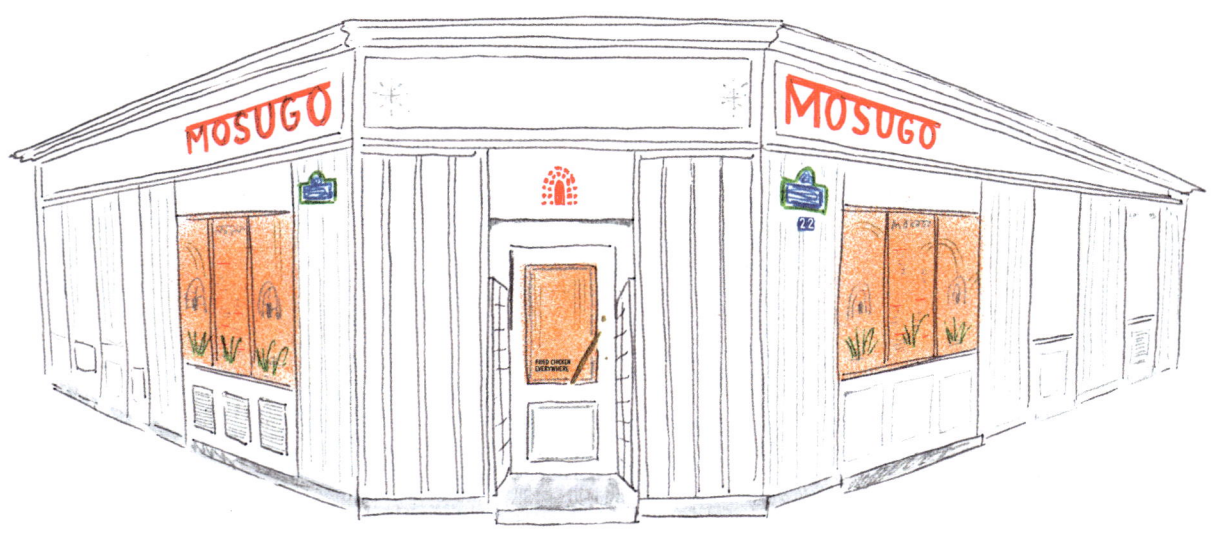

Manga Story

———

The French are voracious fans of Japanese manga. So voracious, in fact, that for years, France has been the second-largest consumer of manga after Japan. And for many readers, Manga Story has been the place to go to get the latest issue of their favorite series, be it *Dragon Ball*, *One Piece*, or *Naruto*.

The transformation of the neighborhood along Boulevard Voltaire is also testament to the nation's obsession with manga. For decades, the area was saturated with video game retailers, until they were gradually supplanted by more and more manga and figurine shops. Opened in 2012, the walls and shelves of Manga Story are lined with the latest bags, T-shirts, toys, and games from beloved manga series and storylines. Its sister shop Tsume Store, right next door, is an official purveyor of Tsume Art, a Luxembourg-based brand that creates high-end collectible figurines.

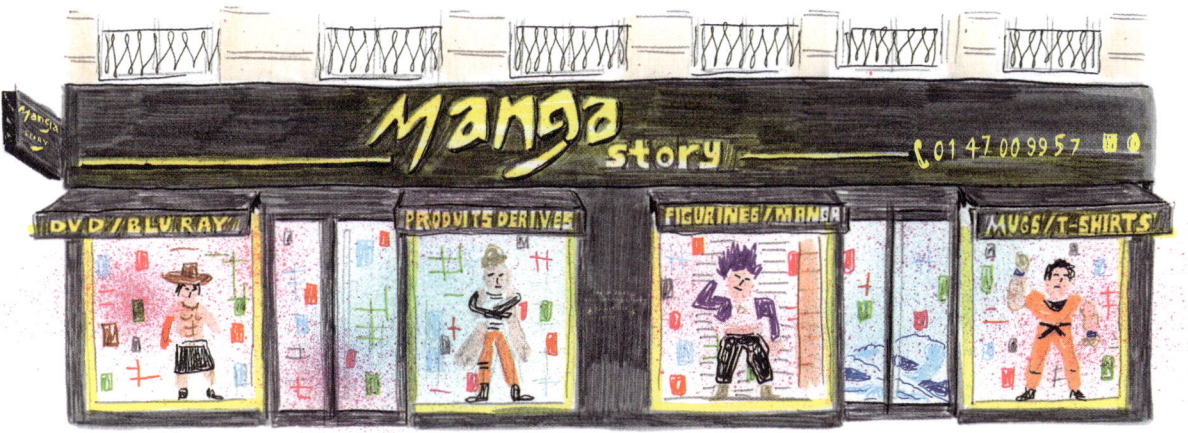

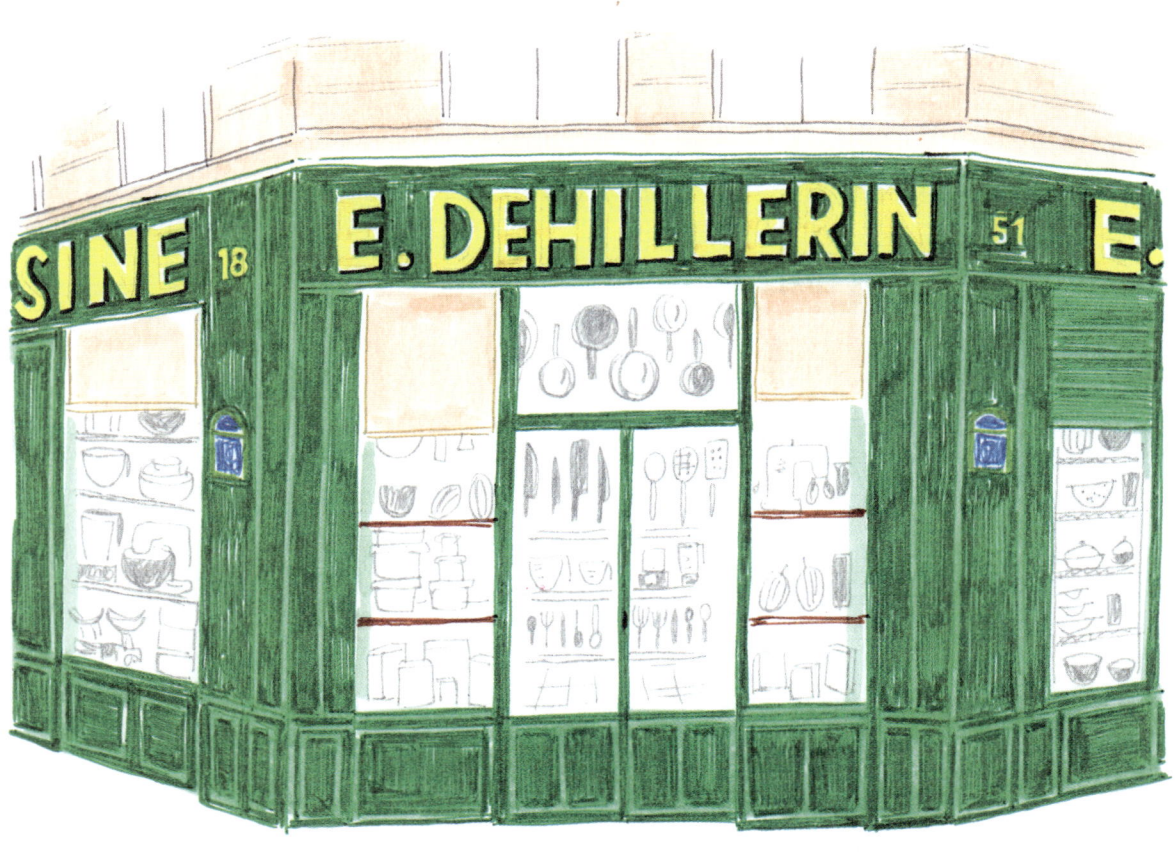

E. Dehillerin

Professional chefs and avid home cooks are likely familiar with the name E. Dehillerin, given its international reputation as one of the best and most historic kitchen supply stores in Paris. Its story starts in the early 19th century, when Eugène de Hillerin opened a small hardware and kitchenware store near Les Halles. At that time the area was home to a massive wholesale market, attracting chefs and restaurateurs—who also became the shop's faithful clients. In 1820, he moved the business and opened a bigger space at the corner of rue Coquillière and rue du Louvre, where fourth-generation owners Éric and Édouard continue the family legacy today.

Along with supplying the French President's official residence Élysée Palace, top restaurants, and hotels around the city, the brand was the cookware of choice onboard the most famous ocean liner in history.

During an excavation of the *Titanic* wreckage carried out in the 1990s, scientists recovered a *bain-marie* (or double boiler) from E. Dehillerin, which went on to be displayed in a *Titanic* exhibit in Cherbourg, France, in 2015. Word of E. Dehillerin's reputation also traveled across the Atlantic thanks in large part to Julia Child. "I was thunderstruck," she wrote of her first visit to the shop in her 2006 memoir *My Life in France*.

The store is best known for its copper pots and pans and its specialized French cookware, like molds for madeleines and canelés, copper fish-braising kettles, and cast-iron dishware for snails.

Pierre Hermé

———

Pierre Hermé has been called the "Picasso of pastry" and a "pastry provocateur" for modernizing the world of macarons with inventive, whimsical flavors. A fourth-generation pastry chef from Alsace, Pierre moved to Paris at the age of 14 to work under one of the best pastry chefs of his time, Gaston Lenôtre, founder of an eponymous French pastry chain. After cutting his teeth there and at Ladurée, Pierre opened his first boutique in Tokyo in 1998, followed by one in Paris in 2001, and now has dozens of boutiques and distributors around the globe. The range of flavors has included everything from *foie gras*, to strawberry and wasabi, to arugula, mint, green apple, and cucumber. But it's his signature Ispahan macaron—an elegant and delicately sweet rose, lychee, and raspberry flavor—that is the showstopper. The shop's cakes and pastries are flavored like its own macarons.

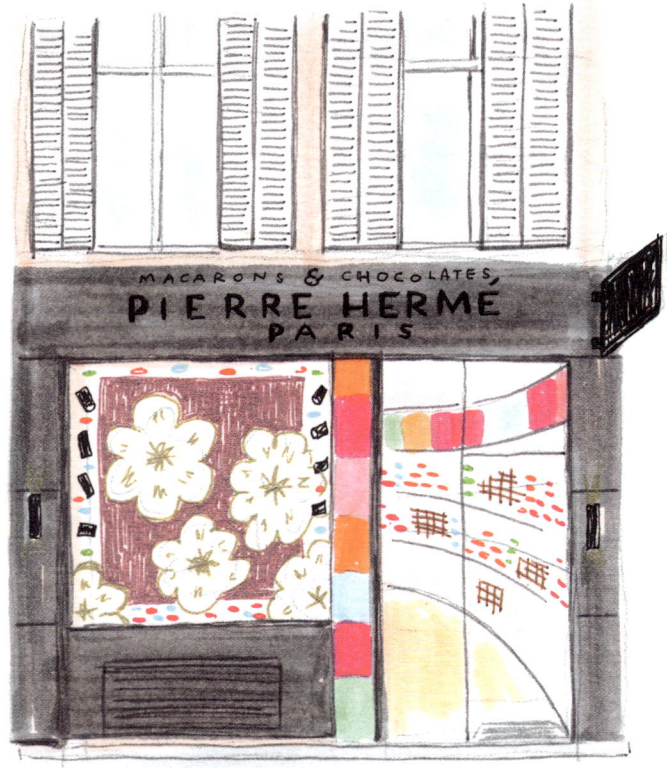

Dior Paris 30 Montaigne

In 1946, Christian Dior moved into this corner mansion on the posh Avenue Montaigne, where he launched his luxury fashion brand and birthed game-changing ideas that dramatically transformed the female silhouette. His iconic 1947 collection "New Look" debuted to the press in the salons of 30 Montaigne, featuring raised busts, cinched waists, rounded shoulders, and voluminous skirts.

In 2022, after nearly three years of renovations, the house launched a new chapter in its storied history, converting nearly 150,000 square feet of former offices (which were relocated to the Champs-Élysées) into a boutique, restaurant, café, rose garden, and museum. Along with exhibiting hundreds of Dior's most exquisite dresses, La Galerie Dior opens up the couturier's workshop, studio, and offices to the public. Visitors can learn about the brand's history, impact on high fashion, and evolution under its successors.

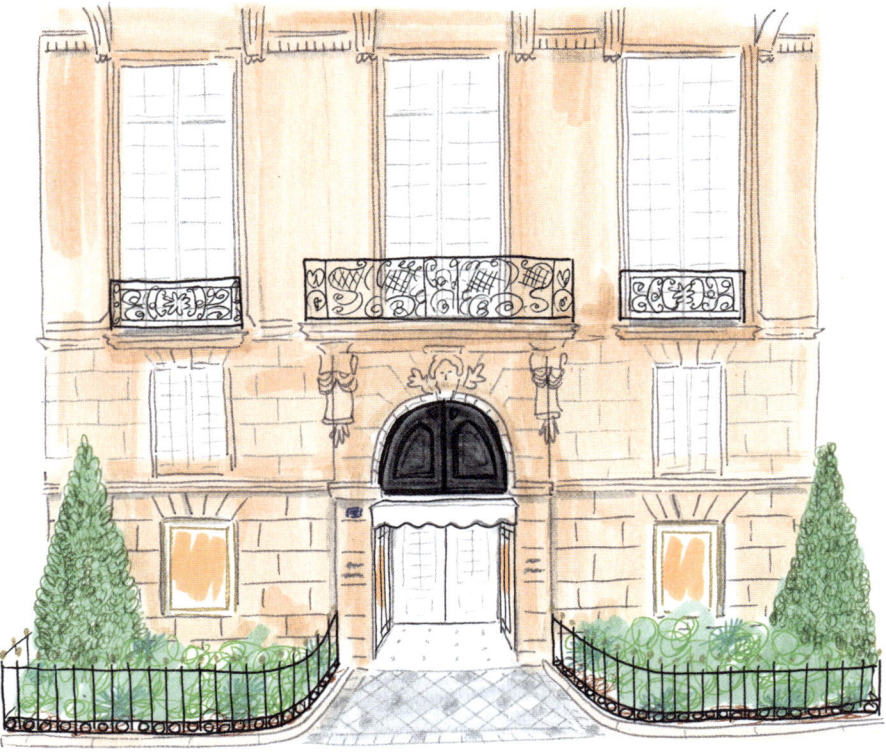

Combat

———

While working as a lawyer in New York, French native Margot Lecarpentier fell in love with the world of mixology, abandoned her legal career, and returned to Paris, where she opened this bar in 2017 alongside friend Elena Schmitt. They gave their business a name with double meaning: Combat was the old nickname of the neighborhood on the edge of Belleville's Chinatown where they set up shop, and also embodied the spirit of the strong all-female team they'd assembled entering a male-dominated field. The aim was to give the artsy, multicultural, working-class neighborhood an inclusive and artisan cocktail bar. The result is an airy, unpretentious space brightened by cheerful yellow backsplash and hanging vegetation, as well as complex and inventive flavor pairings. The Combat Margarita, for example, contains tequila, sake, chamomile, curaçao, lime, and CBD.

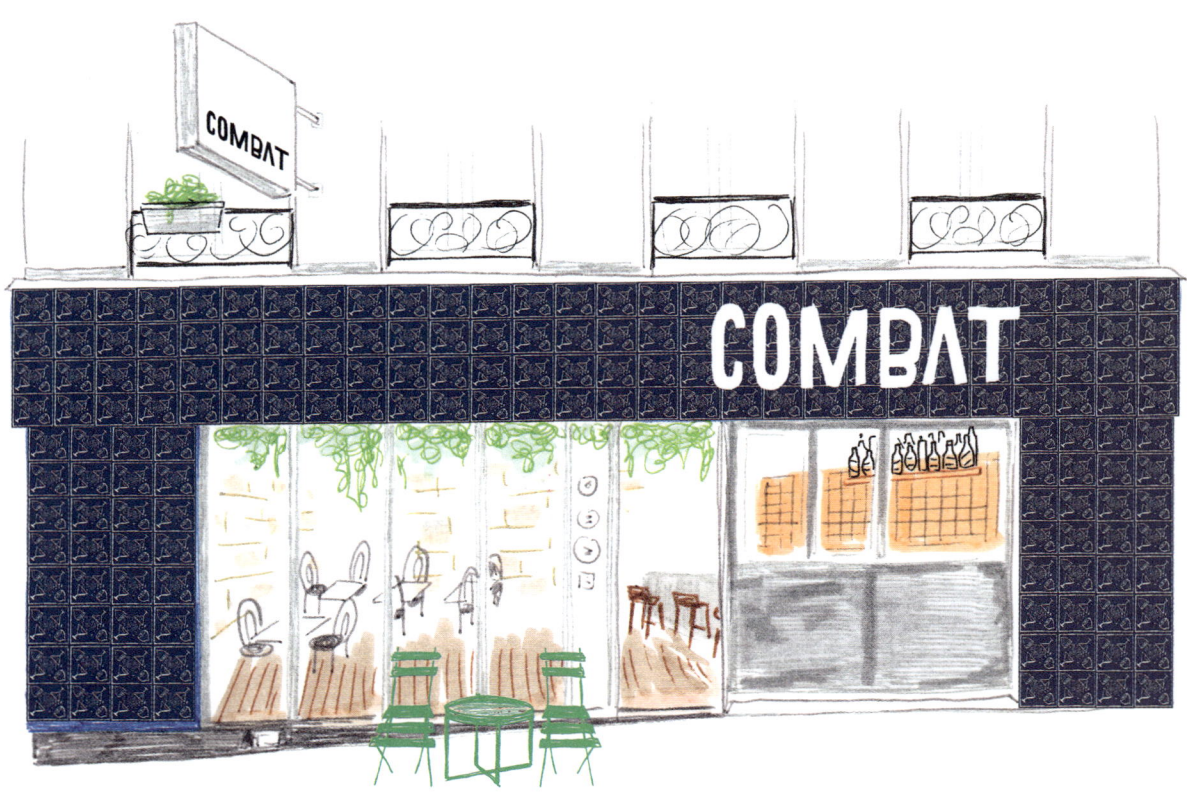

Deyrolle

——

Behind the doors of this Paris institution lies a weird and wonderful world where exotic animals—including zebras, tigers, lions, and polar bears—have been restored to lifelike effect in a space that is part natural history museum, part boutique, part science lab. Founded in 1831 by Jean-Baptiste Deyrolle and his son Achille, both passionate about entomology and the natural world, Maison Deyrolle is a cabinet of curiosities that has become internationally renowned for the craftsmanship of its taxidermy.

Surrealist artists like André Breton and Salvador Dalí, and more recently Damien Hirst, Wes Anderson, and Nan Goldin, have all sought inspiration in the shop, which has been a fixture of rue du Bac since 1888. Rest assured, though, that the animals here are all donations from zoos, parks, or circuses, and died of natural causes.

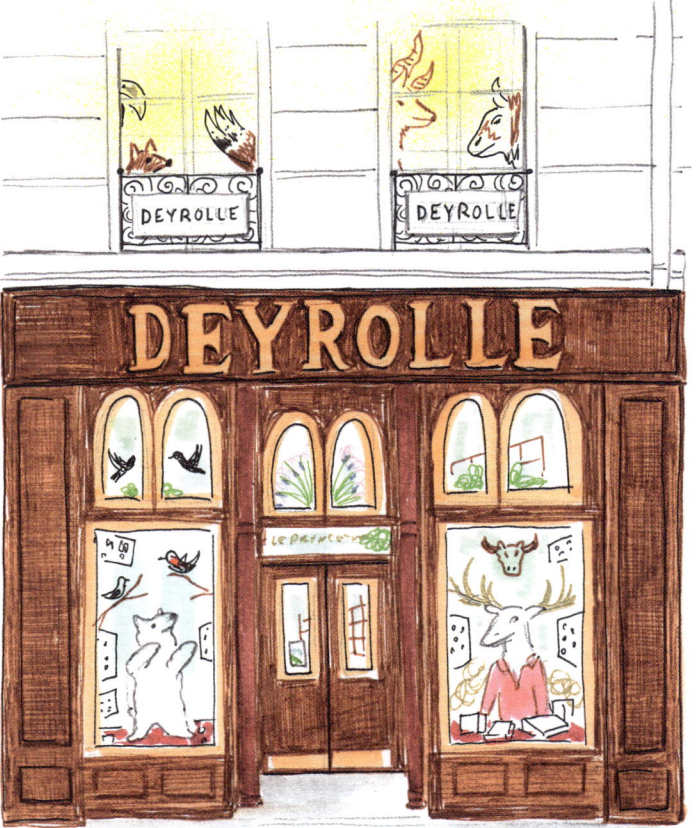

Les Sales Voleurs

Despite appearances—faux ATM machines, a blasted doorway that looks like the aftermath of a break-in, and a room full of safety deposit boxes—this surprising spot is a thrift store where secondhand clothes are a real, ahem, steal. The concept at Les Sales Voleurs, which translates to "Dirty Thieves," is simple: all items are sold at the same price depending on the day of the week, and decrease on a sliding scale. At the time of writing, prices start at a few euros on Fridays, before bottoming out at under one euro on Thursdays. In line with the bargain basement pricing, though, expect to do some serious rummaging through bins. Efforts could be rewarded with finds from YSL, Christian Dior, Maje, and The Kooples.

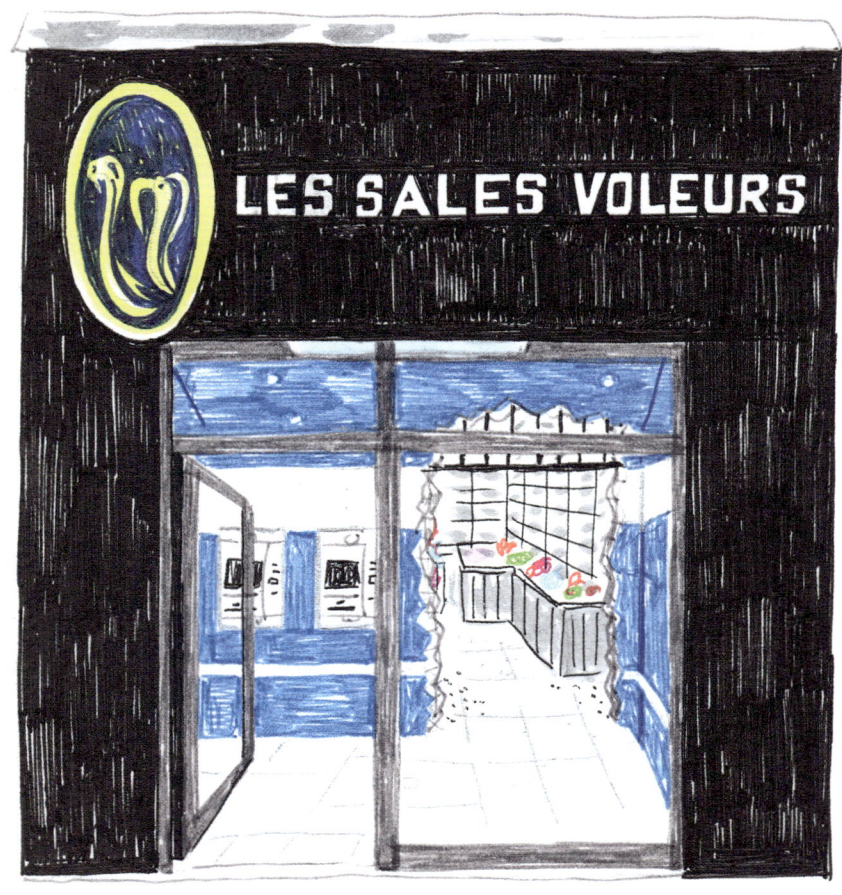

La Taverne de Zhao

Today, Paris's Asian street food scene has exploded. But Zhao Baoyan was one of the earliest trailblazers to bring new and flavorful regional Chinese dishes to the mainstream "bobo" Parisian—slang for "bourgeois-bohème," middle-class urbanites left of the political spectrum. Cleverly, he opened his first Taverne de Zhao in the 10th arrondissement in 2011, one of the most "bobo" neighborhoods in the city. The first restaurant was small and cramped; hardly the sleek, modern ambience of his four newer locations. But word got around of their *rou jia mo*—Chinese flatbread stuffed with savory meat—and their stews in earthenware pots, making Taverne de Zhao a local institution. More eateries followed, where they came up with their signature dish, biang biang noodles: chewy, hand-pulled, wide noodles typical of Xi'an in central-west China that are nearly seven feet long and come with slow-cooked pork or braised beef.

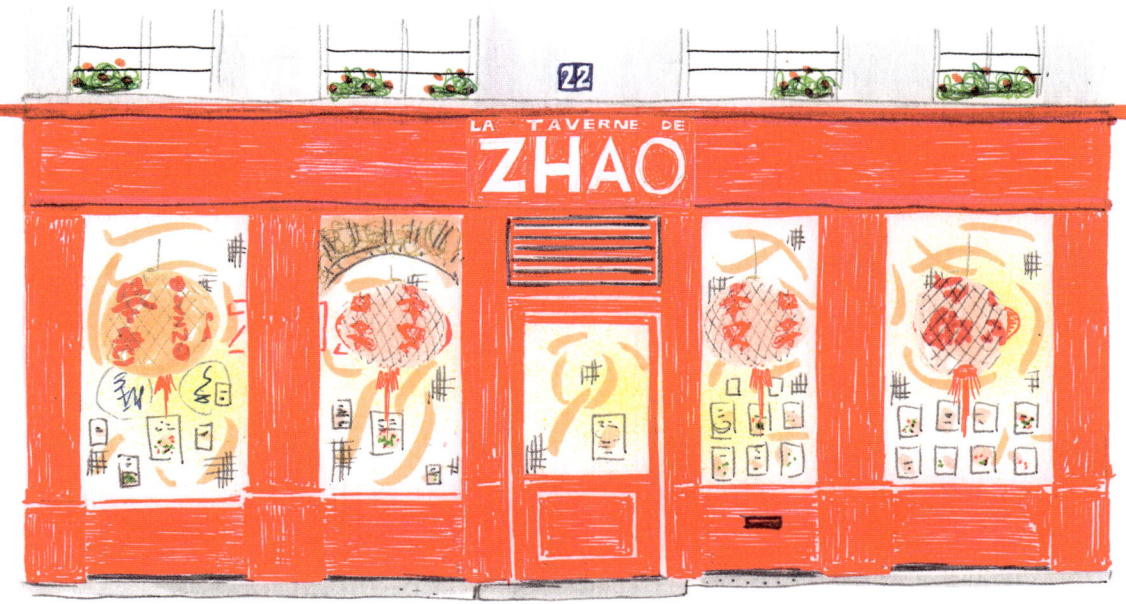

29 rue de la Parcheminerie

5th arr.

The Abbey Bookshop

———

True bibliophiles are aware that, along with the historic Shakespeare and Company (see p. 27), Paris's Latin Quarter boasts another jewel of an English-language bookstore that lies hidden like a delightful secret, shared only by those in the know. On a narrow side street named after its origins as the home of prosperous parchment merchants in the Middle Ages (*parcheminerie* means "parchment maker"), the Abbey Bookshop was opened by Toronto expat Brian Spence in 1989, who brought Canadian authors to France's reading circles.

The charm of this store lies in its unapologetic chaos.

Narrow aisles require visitors to shuffle sideways when passing each other, books sit packed tightly together, and orphaned titles are stashed in grocery bags and random plastic bins. Books are piled high in Jenga-like towers off the shop floor, yet miraculously seem to be topple-free. And while it seems cluttered at first glance, it becomes clear that the chaos is of the organized kind. When asked for a specific title, Brian can often find it with little trouble.

In warmer weather, he often sets up a stand outside the shop and offers free coffee or tea to visitors and passersby, as well as an open-air bookstore with crates and baskets filled with second-hand books for perusal. Along with Canadian authors, visitors can find English translations of French classics, and multiple copies of Ernest Hemingway's *A Moveable Feast*.

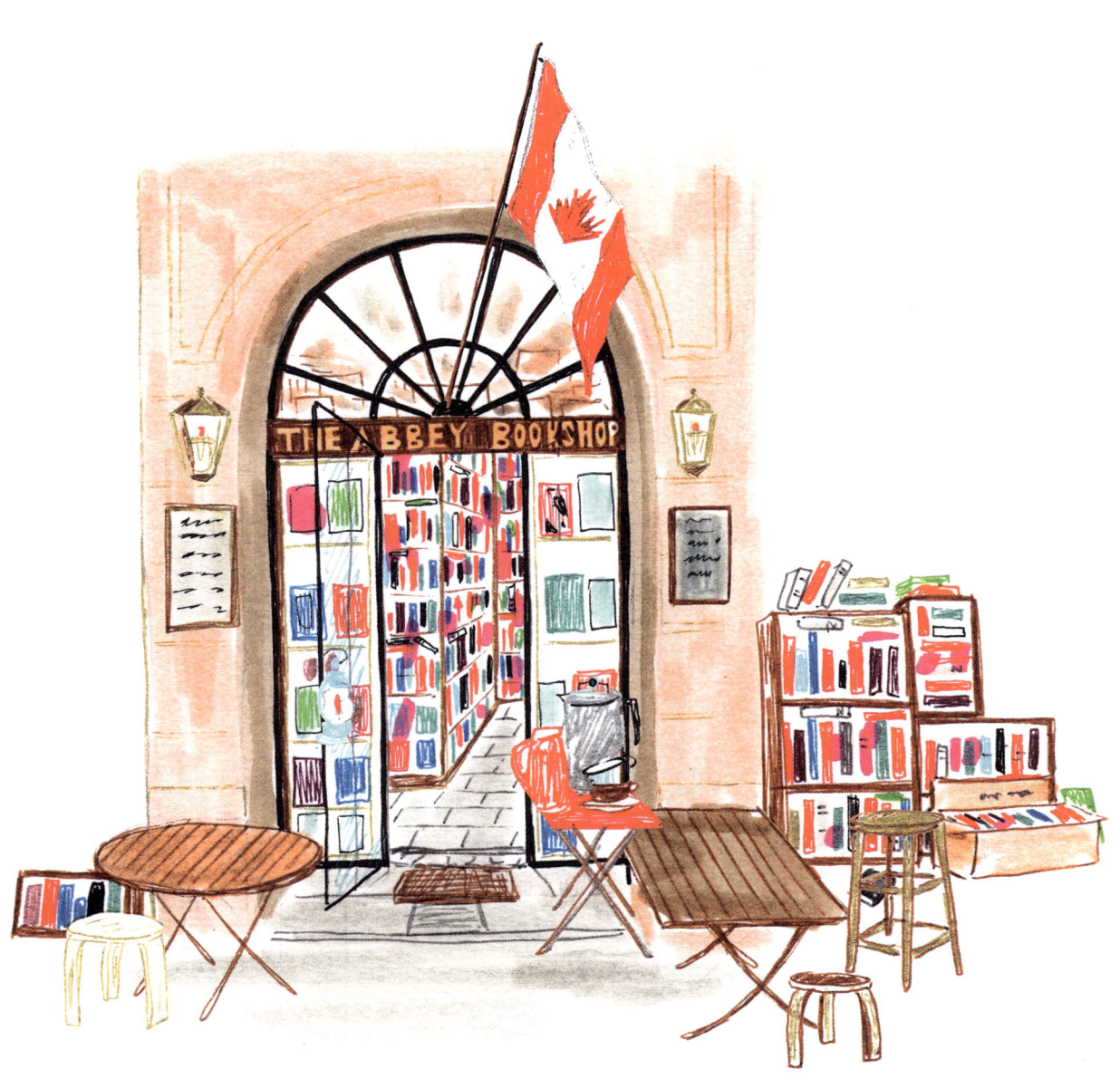

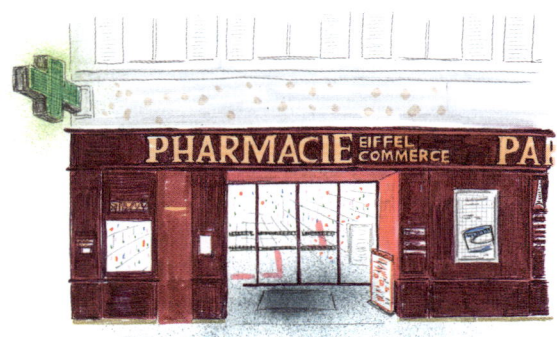

13–15–17 rue du Commerce
15th arr.

Pharmacie Eiffel

———

The CityPharma pharmacy on rue du Four gets a lot of social media love, but this pharmacy in the 15th arrondissement also boasts year-round deals and a huge selection of French beauty products, in a bigger, more customer-friendly space.

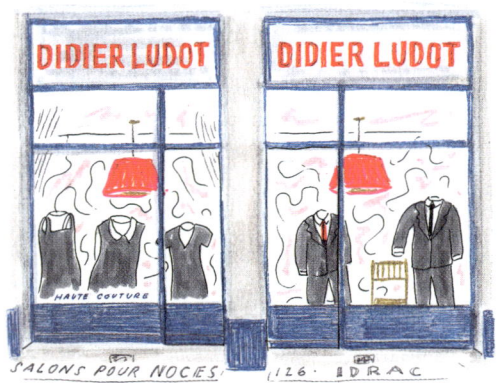

24 Gal de Montpensier
1st arr.

Didier Ludot

———

Located under the arcades of the Jardin du Palais Royal, this shop belongs to one of the largest collectors of vintage *haute couture* dresses in France. Alongside Balenciaga evening gowns, expect Chanel suits and Dior cocktail dresses.

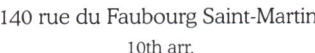

140 rue du Faubourg Saint-Martin
10th arr.

Vendredi Soir

———

This restaurant's name—Friday Night—is a nod to Friday-evening Shabbat dinners. Only here, diners can tuck into home-cooked Jewish feasts every day of the week. The menu features dishes like latkes, chopped liver, and couscous.

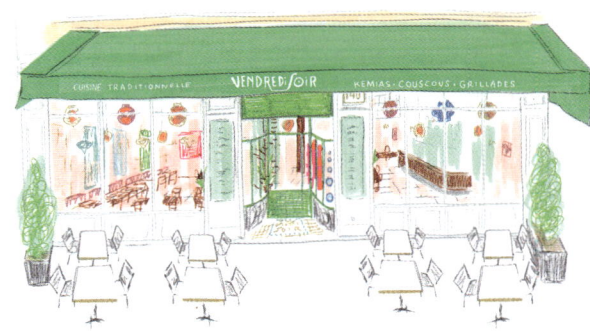

44 rue de Lourmel
15th arr.

Manna

———

Manna, which means "to meet," has long been upheld as one of the most authentic and tastiest Korean restaurants in Paris. Along with *bibimbap* standbys, it also serves delicacies like blood sausage and raw marinated crab.

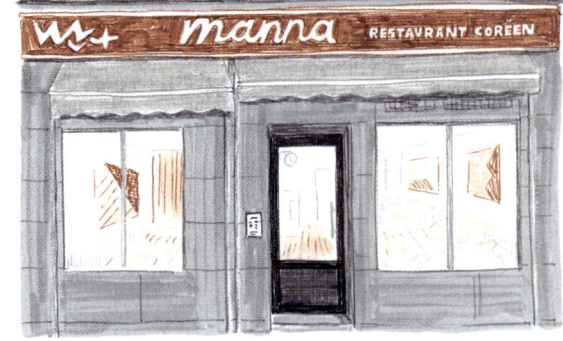

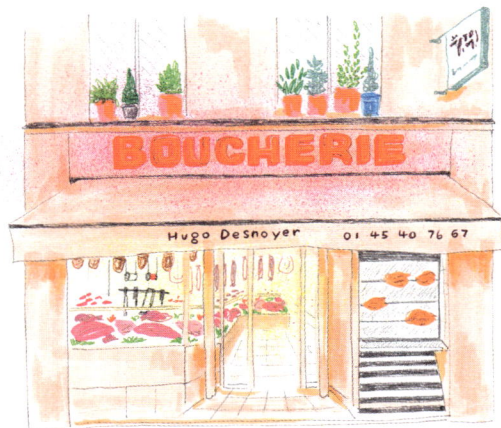

Boucherie Hugo Desnoyer

45 rue Boulard
14th arr.

Butcher to the stars Hugo Desnoyer is famous for his high-quality French meats, like Limousin beef and pork from Gascony; he also supplies top chefs and the Élysée Palace. Hugo advocates for eating less—but quality, sustainably raised—beef. There's a shop/restaurant in the 16th arrondissement as well.

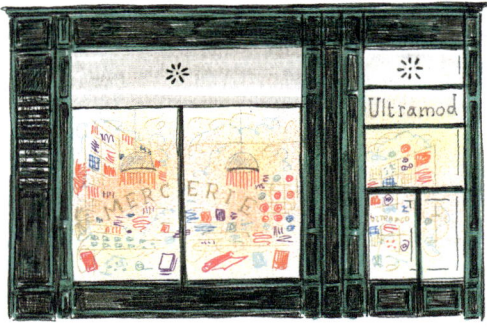

Ultramod Mercerie Paris

4 rue de Choiseul
2nd arr.

This sewing shop has changed very little since it first opened in 1920 across the street from its sister hat store. Here, original wooden dressers hold vintage buttons and trimmings, as well as silk, satin, and velvet ribbons.

24 rue Vignon
9th arr.

La Maison du Miel

Since 1898, this shop has specialized in honey produced in different regions across France. Shelves are lined with chestnut-, lavender-, fir-, and sage-infused varieties, along with beeswax candles and soaps. The façade is a historic monument.

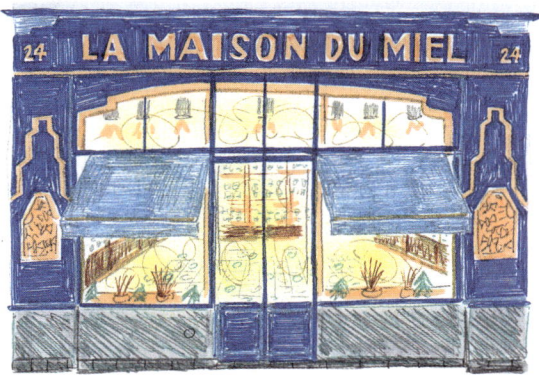

176–178 rue Saint-Martin
3rd arr.

La Mutinerie

A feminist bar run by and for lesbians, queer, bisexual, and trans people, La Mutinerie is a community space that promotes queer art and culture. It hosts everything from writing workshops to drag shows, concerts, political activism events, yoga, and self-defense classes.

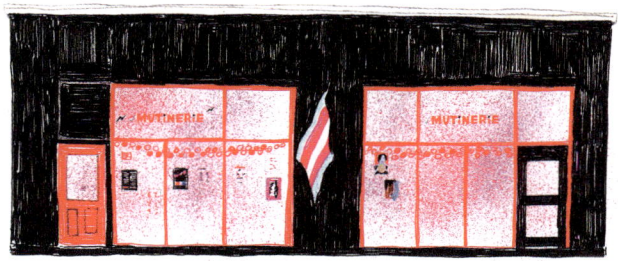

Maxim's

———

Soirées at Maxim's over the years have been legendary, and there's no shortage of black-and-white photographic evidence to prove it. Paparazzi shots from the 1950s through the '80s capture personalities like Elizabeth Taylor and Richard Burton, Jacqueline Kennedy Onassis, Salvador Dalí, Mick Jagger, Grace Kelly, and Sophia Loren entering, dining at, or exiting the restaurant, which in its golden years was the hottest late-night party destination in Paris. Located near Place de la Concorde, Maxim's opened in 1893, and at its peak held three Michelin stars in the 1950s. It hosted a long list of A-list celebrities until it gradually fell out of fashion, and was mostly rented out for private parties in the 2000s. The restaurant reopened in 2023 following a major refurbishment that restored its Belle Époque luster. Live bands and crooners serenade diners with jazz every night.

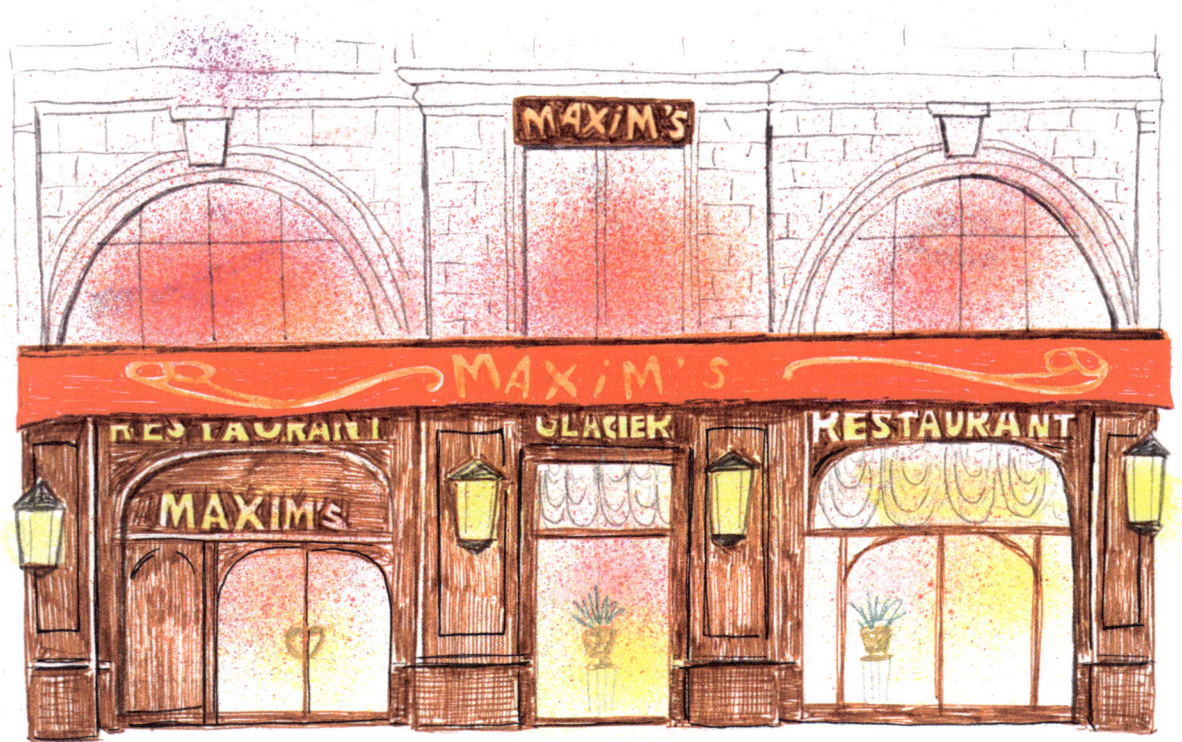

Marin Montagut

———

Born into a family of antique dealers and painters in Toulouse, illustrator Marin Montagut first began translating his love for his adopted city of Paris into goods for the home via colorful maps and charismatic prints, earning him a loyal following. One of the most common descriptors for his first interior decor boutique, which opened in 2020, is "cabinet of curiosities." Marin is now known for turning iconic Parisian insignia—metro signs; the green Senate chairs at the Luxembourg Garden; the Eiffel Tower—into an assortment of charming objects. Mouth-blown glassware is emblazoned with words like "Amour" and "Maman," and glass decanters are patterned with cute hearts and cherries. His whimsical watercolor drawings are also printed on silk scarves, cushions, and notebooks, and he has collaborated with shops and restaurants, including Le Bon Marché (see p. 154), Café de Flore (see p. 10), Maison Kitsuné, and the Ritz Paris.

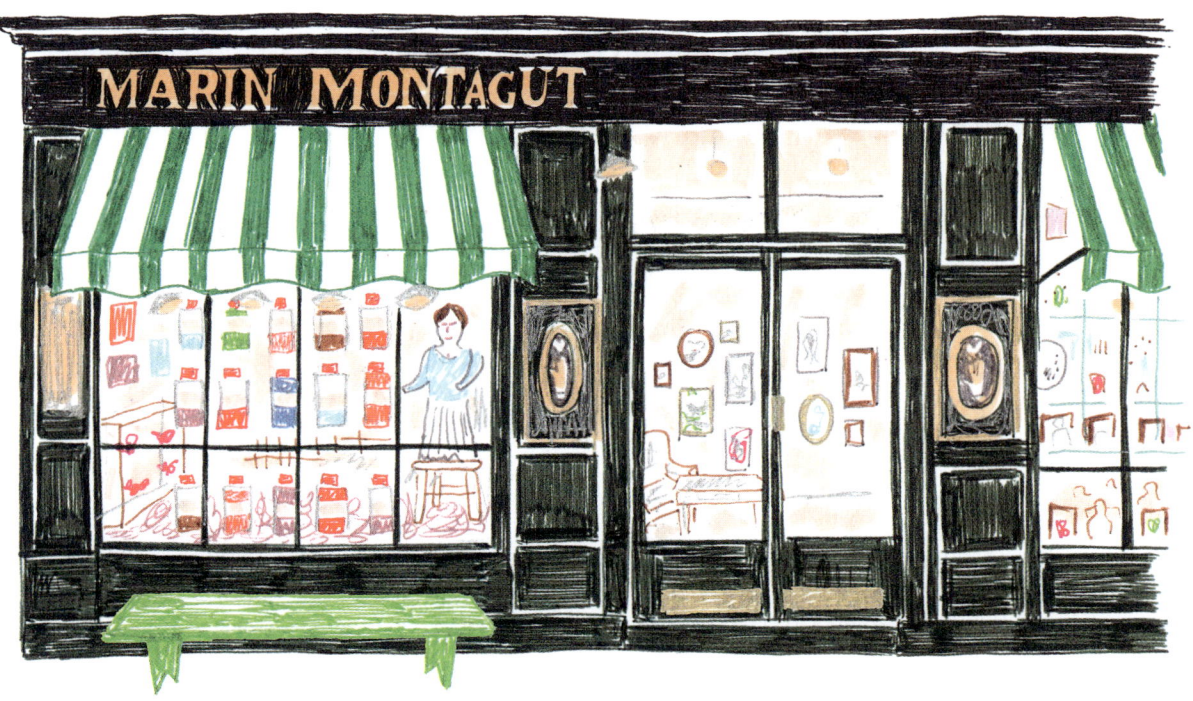

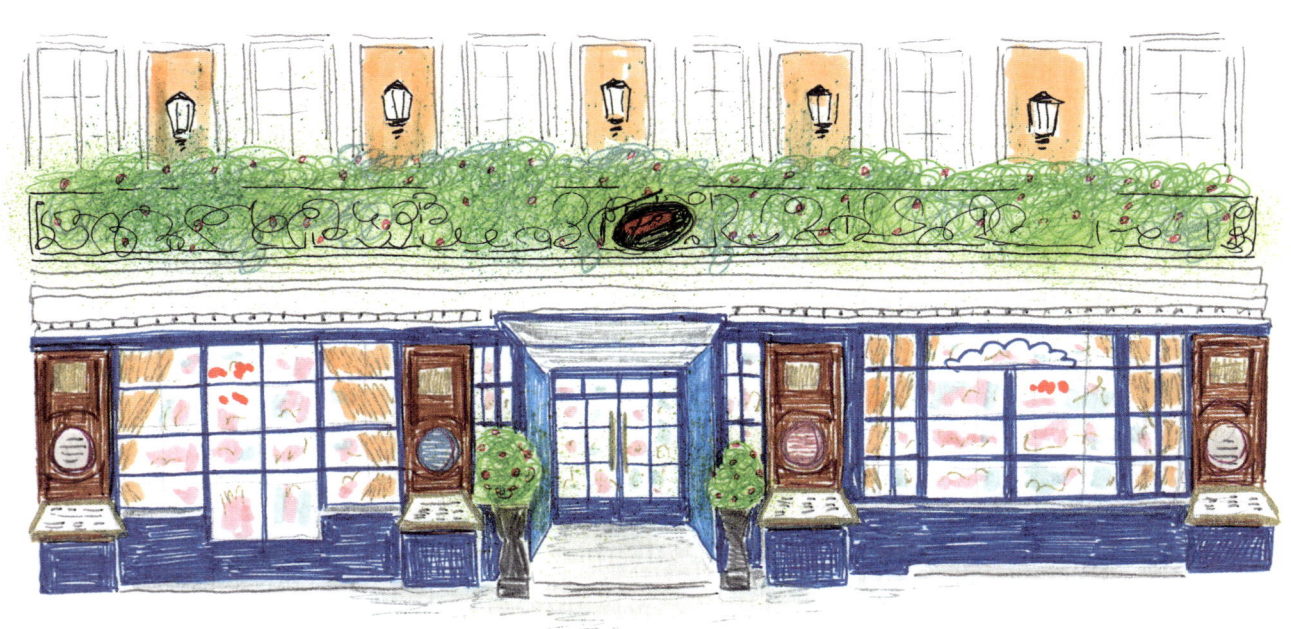

Le Procope

Opened in 1686 by a Sicilian transplant to Paris, Le Procope claims to be the oldest café in the city. In its heyday, it was also one of the capital's most important literary salons, where the country's brightest philosophers, writers, and intellectuals gathered for lively debates. These included Voltaire, Jean-Jacques Rousseau, and the creator of the French encyclopedia, Denis Diderot (it's said that he wrote a few entries within its walls).

Benjamin Franklin was also a patron, and legend has it that he came up with a few ideas for the US Constitution during one of his many visits.

Le Procope was also a popular gathering place for leading figures of the French Revolution. A quote from journalist and lawyer Camille Desmoulins, who played an important role in the storming of the Bastille, adorns one of its walls: "This café is not decorated like the others with mirrors, gilding and busts, but it is adorned with the memory of Great Men …".

Today, the space is a bustling restaurant and café that serves up French classics like *escargots*, sole *meunière*, beef tartare, and *coq au vin*. In 2023, the venue opened a new coffee and ice cream lounge in homage to its origins as Paris's first purveyor of the exotic elixir coffee, which was brought over from the Ottoman Empire. Before leaving, make sure to check out historic memorabilia from some of the café's most illustrious guests, including a hat allegedly worn by Napoleon and the writing desk used by Voltaire.

Libertino

———

The French love their pizza. In fact, by some market estimates, outside Italy, France is the second biggest consumer of pizza in the world after the US. But it would be no exaggeration to say that the arrival of the Big Mamma Group, launched by entrepreneurial twentysomethings Victor Lugger and Tigrane Seydoux, transformed the landscape of Italian pizzerias in Paris with the frenzied opening of nine bars and restaurants since 2015. The premise: hip, lively trattorias where everything is made with fresh ingredients shipped thrice weekly from Italy, served by a staff made up mostly of young Italians (the average age of employees is 24). At Libertino, the top floor has Garden of Eden vibes, while the downstairs area is a disco bar. Neapolitan flour and wood-fired ovens give the pizzas their characteristic thin, chewy crusts. Other locations include London and Milan.

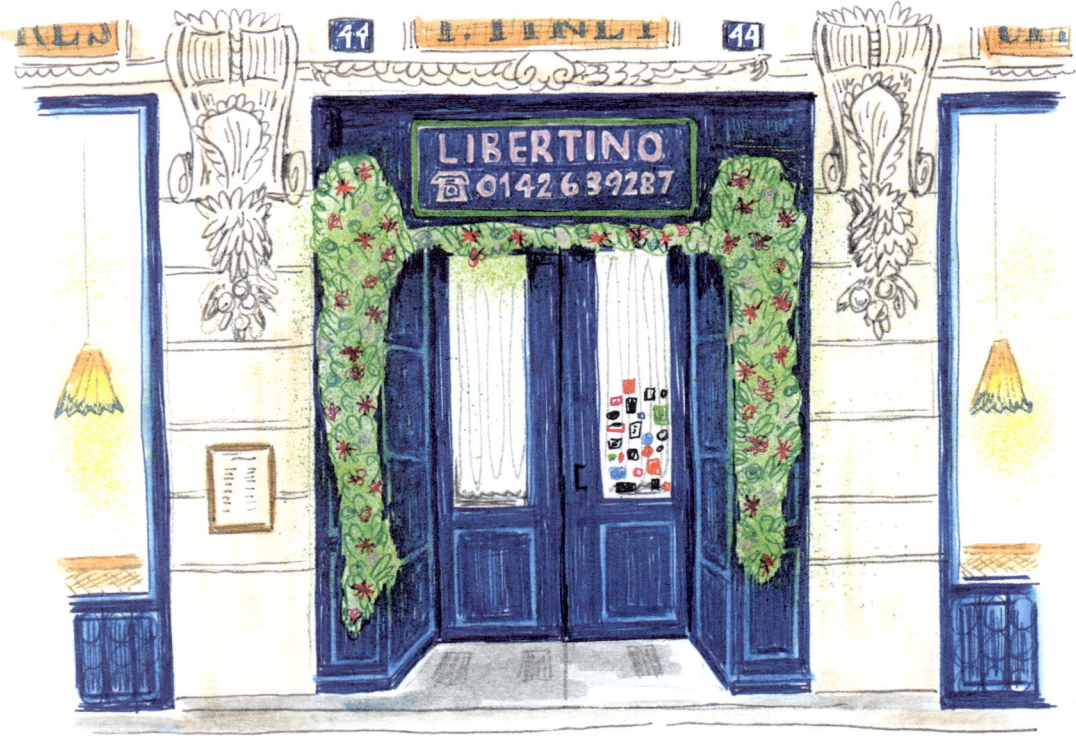

Qasti Shawarma & Grill

The backstory of this shawarma canteen is both moving and inspiring. At the age of 24, Alan Geaam fled the civil war in Lebanon and arrived in Paris in 1999 as an undocumented immigrant with the equivalent of €30 in his pocket. He slept on the streets, worked on construction sites, and washed dishes at a Lebanese eatery. It was here that he got his first break: when the restaurant's chef cut himself, Alan, who grew up watching his mother in the kitchen and had cooked in the military, stepped in, and did so well he was asked to take over. That experience led to more kitchen stints and, 18 years later, his Michelin-starred restaurant Alan Geaam. For those who can't afford a Michelin meal, though, Qasti Shawarma & Grill is a casual spot that embodies Alan's childhood food memories of Lebanon.

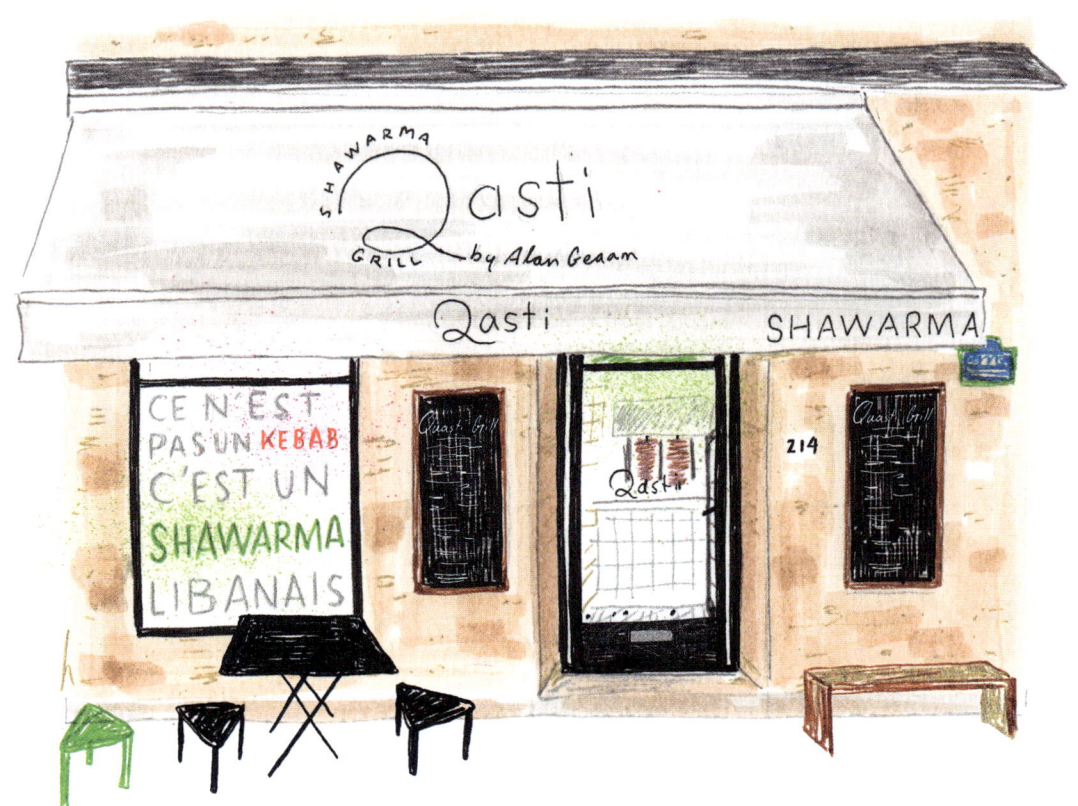

Le Pavillon des Canaux

———

Le Pavillon des Canaux is easily one of the most surprising and quirky venues in the 19th arrondissement, where visitors can eat their lunch in a bathtub, nurse their beer in a bedroom, or sip on their espresso in a salon. Opened in 2015 by Sinny & Ooko, a company that specializes in creating cultural spaces in unusual places, this abandoned building once housed the lockkeeper of the Canal de l'Ourcq, when locks were operated manually. While the ground floor houses a bar, the upstairs is laid out like a private home, with themed pink and green bedrooms, a red salon, a retro kitchen, and a bathroom, all whimsically decorated in thrifted finds. A hybrid inclusive and feminist space, Le Pavillon hosts workshops, exhibits, concerts, and DJ sets, and its restaurant is mostly vegetarian. The glass terrace also offers visitors front-row seats to the canal.

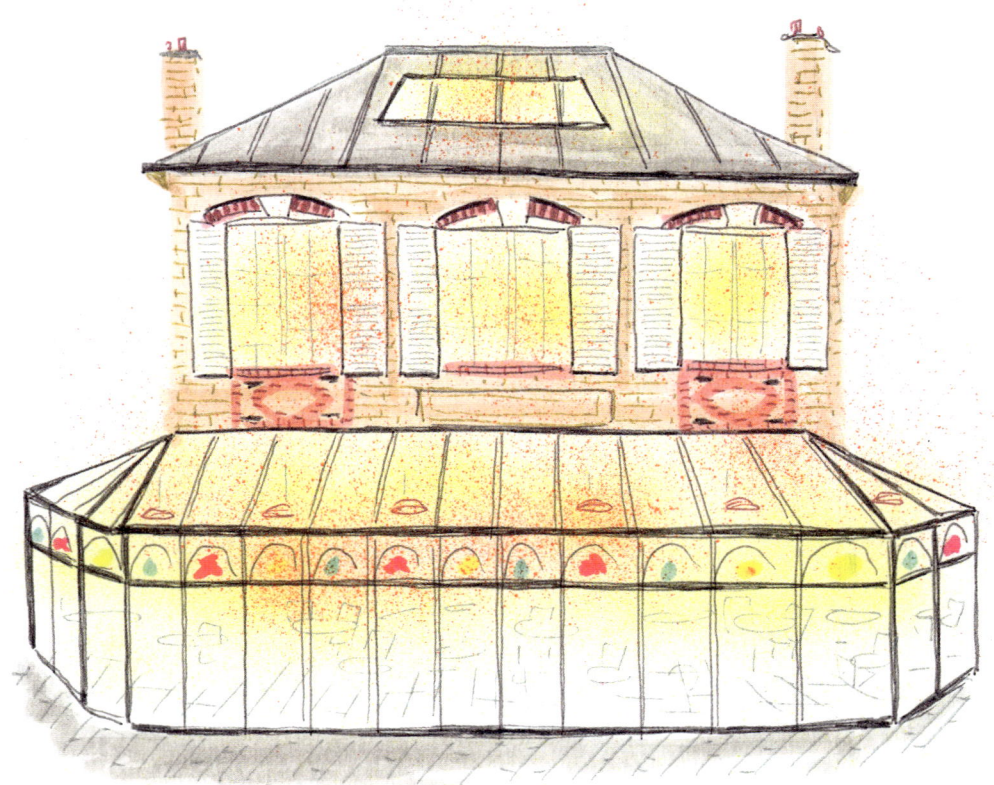

Le Select

If Le Dôme (see p. 28) was the first literary café in Montparnasse, Le Select, which opened in 1923, was the first to stay open all night. At the time, the neighborhood was popular among Paris's intellectual and literary elite, including Ernest Hemingway, Pablo Picasso, Henri Cartier-Bresson, and F. Scott Fitzgerald. Today, that tradition continues among locals. In a fascinating 2019 article for *Le Monde*, a journalist reported on conversations he'd overheard there in recent years. A filmmaker was seen pitching a studio exec at one table, and politicians and their aides were power lunching at another. The café is also popular among journalists for conducting interviews, and with editors for meeting their writers. While the food is classically French—duck confit, beef tartare, and French onion soup—the drinks menu features a long selection of whiskies, bourbons, and cocktails.

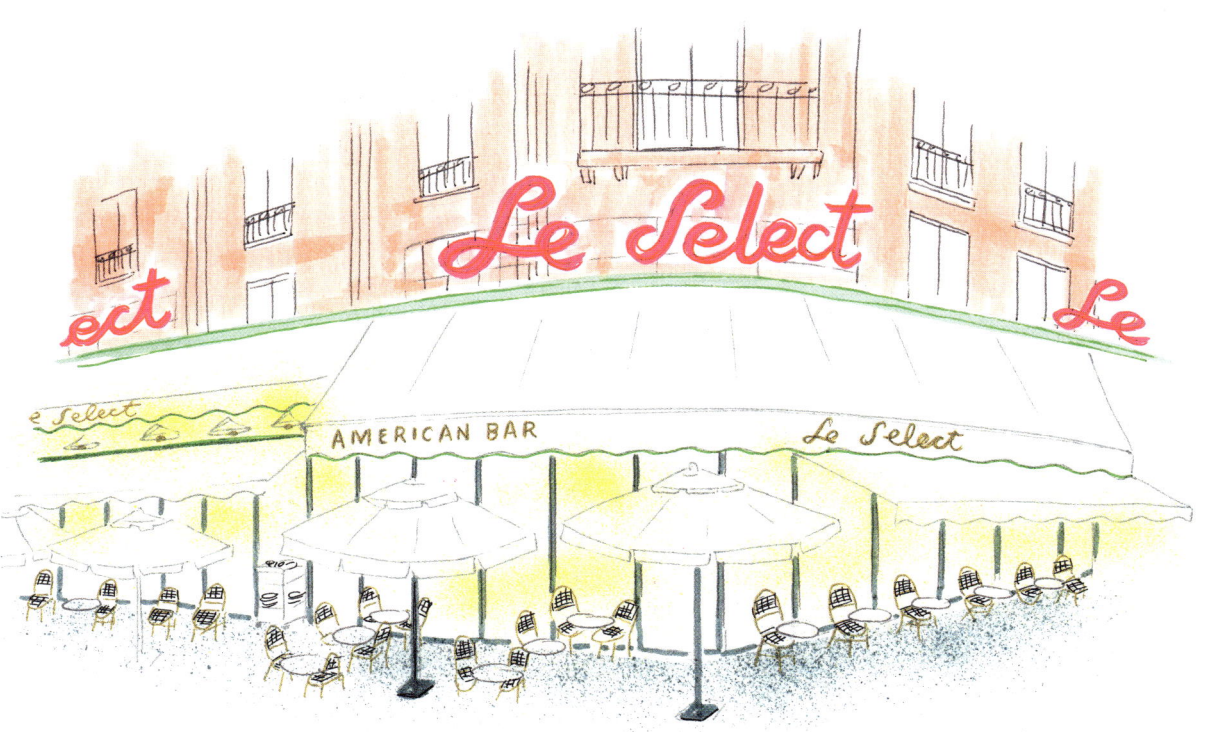

Born Bad Record Shop

———

Since 1999, this indie music shop has been the place of record, so to speak, for fans of rock and roll, metal, punk, cold wave, new wave, garage rock, and everything in between. Owner Mark Adolf, drummer of the post-punk band Frustration, gives special attention to vinyl and LPs from French rock groups, independent labels, and small bands. If names like Bad Brains, Police Control, and Drunk Meat mean something to you, this place is one to check out.

In an interview with *Le Figaro*, Mark recommended the music of Fotomatic from Toulouse, a mix of garage and punk, and Al-Qasar, a French-American-Egyptian group that mixes garage and psychedelic music, sung in Arabic. (Worth noting: Born Bad—the record shop—is often confused with the label Born Bad Records, founded by Jean-Baptiste Guillot, alias JB Wizz, in 2006.)

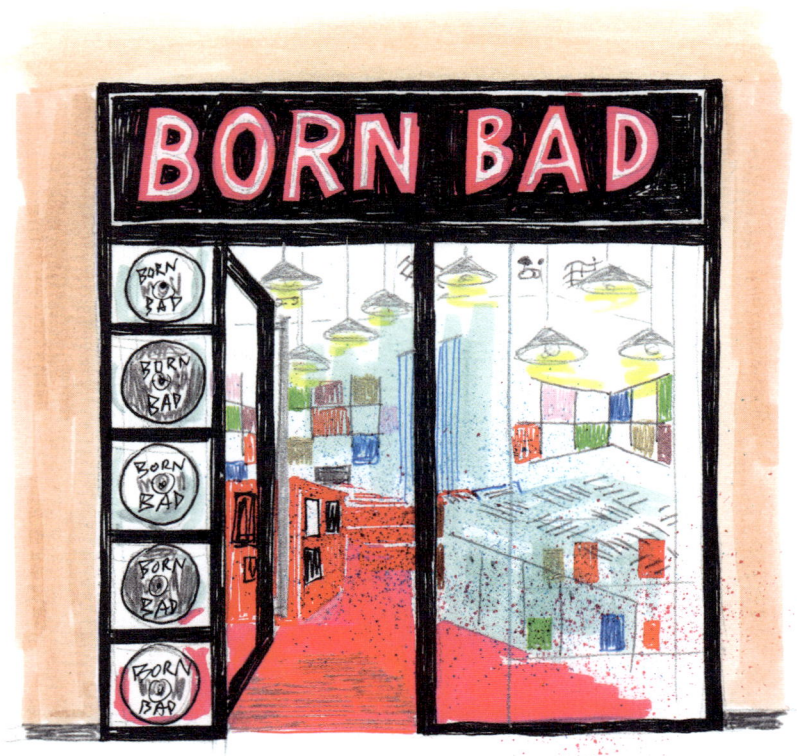

Mangez et Cassez-Vous!

———

Eat and get lost. Scram.

That's pretty much the translation of this burger joint's name, which became social media famous for selling ridiculously inexpensive and tasty homemade burgers (and drawing three-hour-long wait lines). When entrepreneur Aniss Messadek opened the first of four locations in 2018, his aim was to allow those of modest means to enjoy a good burger on the cheap. Though the pressures of inflation have forced him to increase the price, at the time of writing, a burger and fries is still only a few euros. How does he keep costs so low? Everything—buns, sauces, fries, and desserts—is made from scratch. And despite the low pricing, online reviews speak highly about the burgers, which are topped with Roquefort, cheddar, or Munster, and onions. Gamers will particularly appreciate the Boulevard de Picpus location, which is themed after video games.

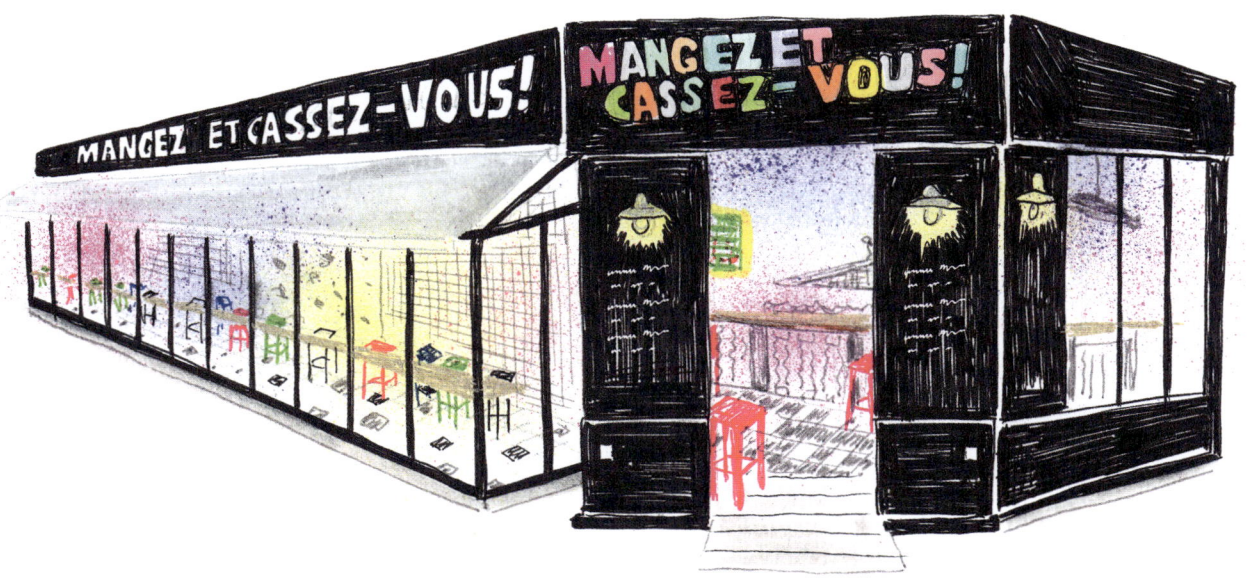

Auberge Nicolas Flamel

———

Fans of the Harry Potter series may recognize the name Nicolas Flamel as the alchemist who created the magical philosopher's stone, which could turn any metal into gold and render its owner immortal. What people may not know is that this storyline was based on an actual French legend and living person.

A rich bourgeois who lived in 14th-century Paris, rumor had it at the time that Flamel's great fortunes could be traced back to a magic stone that he fashioned as an alchemist, which transformed lead into gold—a tale he may have perpetuated himself. For centuries the rumor has trailed him, and he continues to be erroneously described as an alchemist to this day (he was never a chemist, just obscenely wealthy). However, instead of exclusively lining his own pockets, Flamel used some of his money to build a house for the city's poor in 1407, on the condition that the inhabitants recited their prayers twice daily.

That building still stands today at 51 rue de Montmorency, and many say it is the oldest house in Paris.

In 1911, the stone façade was inscribed as a historic monument. Far from being a shelter for the unhoused, today, the ancient edifice is home to a fine-dining French restaurant helmed by chef Émile de France, whose cuisine is described as modern and creative. The restaurant is owned by Alan Geaam (see p. 121).

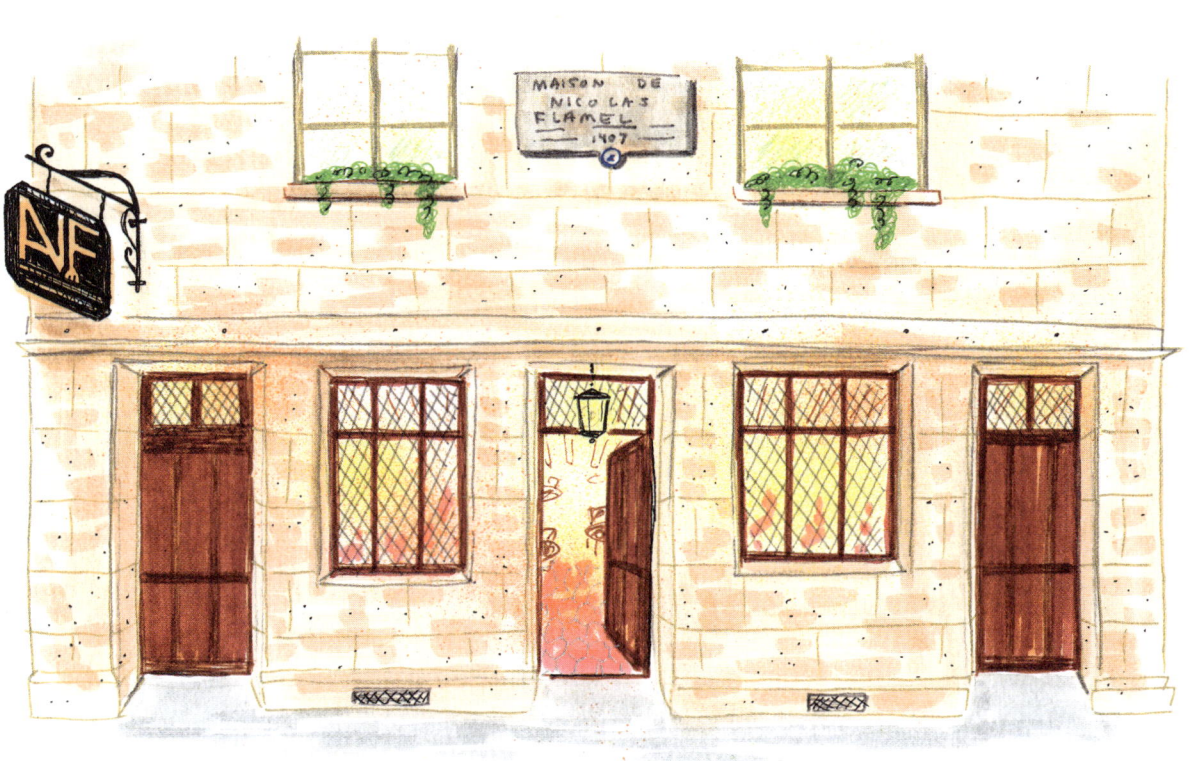

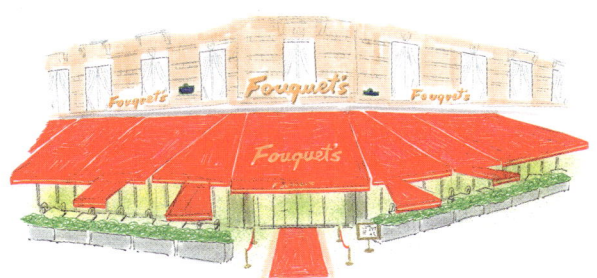

46 Av. George V
8th arr.

La Brasserie Fouquet

Identifiable from afar thanks to its large red awning, this brasserie has been an institution on the Champs-Élysées since 1899. Every year, it also hosts the celebrity-studded afterparty for the César Awards (the French equivalent of the Oscars).

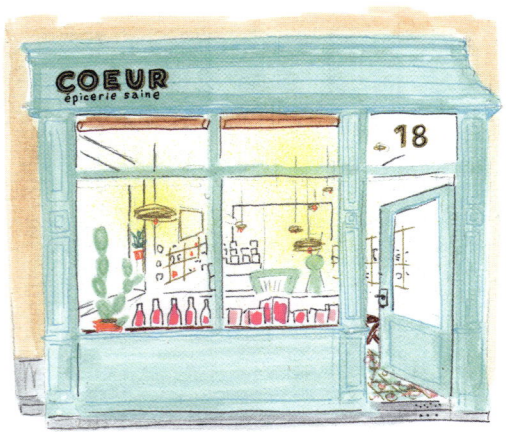

18 rue du Général Guilhem
11th arr.

Coeur

Run by a French-Colombian couple, Coeur, which means "heart," is a bulk health food store that stocks cereal, dried fruit, tea, coffee, legumes, seeds, yogurt, cheese, honey, and jam from local producers.

Place Dauphine, 41 Quai de l'Horloge et 28
1st arr.

Papeteries Gaubert

Since 1830, this stationery store at the picturesque Place Dauphine square has supplied Parisians with everything they need to write. Over time, ink pots and fountain pens have been replaced with gel pens, Moleskine agendas, and premium legal office supplies—their specialty.

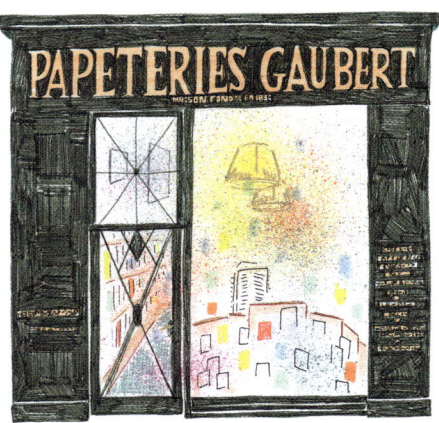

37 Av. de l'Opéra
2nd arr.

Brentano's

All that remains of what was once one of America's largest bookstore chain, Brentano's, is this Paris outpost, which opened in 1895. Today the shop sells English-language titles, home decor, gifts, and stationery.

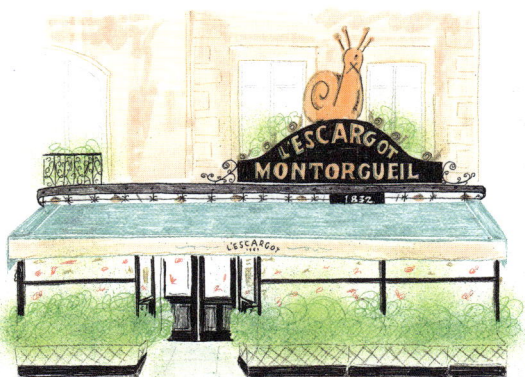

38 rue Montorgueil
1st arr.

L'Escargot Montorgueil

As its name makes plain, this historic restaurant in Les Halles was founded in 1832 and specializes in plump Burgundy snails, which are prepared in classic garlic butter, foie gras, or black truffle sauce.

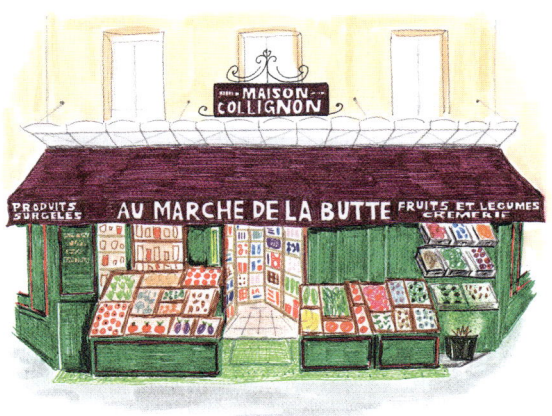

56 rue des Trois Frères
18th arr.

Au Marché de la Butte

Fans of the movie *Amélie* may remember this corner store as the greengrocer run by the dislikable character Collignon, where the heroine loved to plunge her fingers in sacks of dried beans.

41 rue Monsieur le Prince
6th arr.

Polidor

Dating back to 1845, this historic French restaurant near the Sorbonne has hosted dinners for some of the city's illustrious personalities, including poet Paul Valéry, novelist Boris Vian, James Joyce, and Ernest Hemingway.

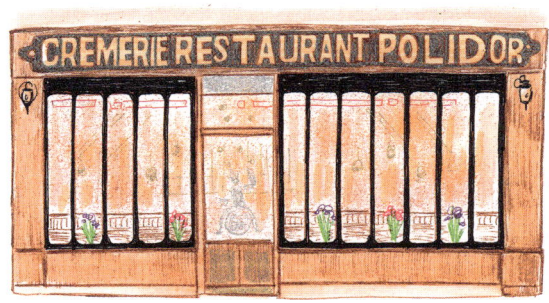

21 rue Copreaux
15th arr.

Le Drapeau de la Fidelité

In 1984, former philosophy professor and political refugee from Saigon Pham-Công Quân opened this modest restaurant. It became a favorite hangout among locals and students drawn to its cheap and delicious Vietnamese fare and Pham-Công's nuggets of wisdom.

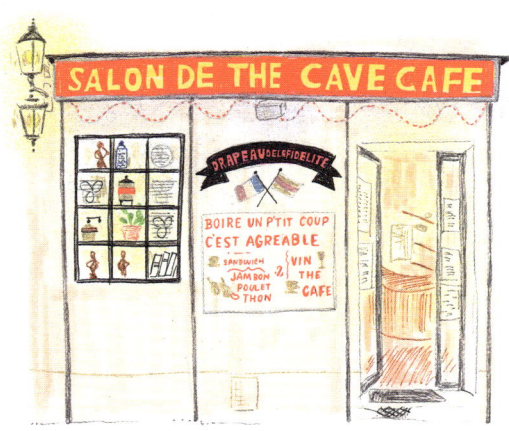

Olive Chicken

———

When word got around among Paris's Korean expat and immigrant community about chef Max Si's generous, authentic, and addictive Korean fried chicken (KFC), his delivery business took off. The concept was basic, austere even: he took orders via a messaging and voice app, KakaoTalk (the South Korean equivalent of WhatsApp), and fried the chicken in his own kitchen. In other words, in the early days, the KFC business was a closely guarded secret known only to the Korean community. But demand soon outgrew his home kitchen, and in 2022, he opened a no-frills brick-and-mortar restaurant that converted local Parisians into loyal KFC devotees. Often called the best, most authentic Korean fried chicken in the city—and rivaling the kind found in Seoul—the menu features classic fried chicken, sweet and spicy *yangnyeom* chicken, and garlic soy fried chicken.

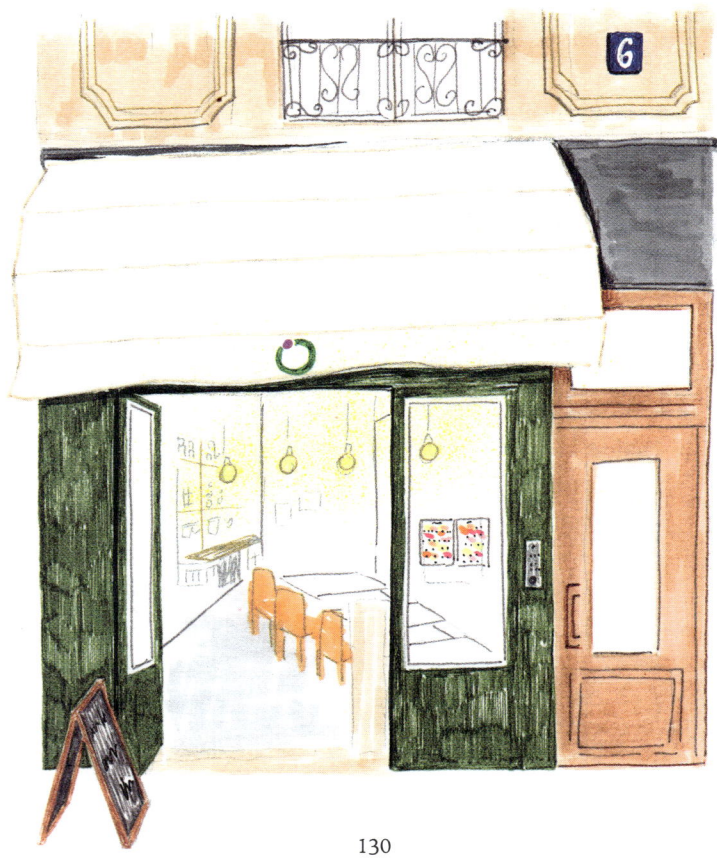

Ground Control

———

The street-level entrance to the food, arts, and community hub Ground Control is deceiving—and disproportionate to what lies within. Because after passing through the single, standard doorway, visitors are led to a sprawling 70,000-square-foot covered hall and outdoor terrace that, since 2018, has served as a hybrid, multidisciplinary space. Inside the former postal sorting center near Gare de Lyon are a dozen food and drink options that include Greek, Chinese, and Italian cuisines, along with craft beer and biodynamic wines. One of the highlights is La Residence, where refugee chefs who have obtained asylum in France cook on rotation; countries represented in the past have included Afghanistan, Cambodia, Sudan, and Eritrea. Depending on the week, the hub may also host yoga classes, photography workshops, themed lectures, DJs, and karaoke nights (all in French).

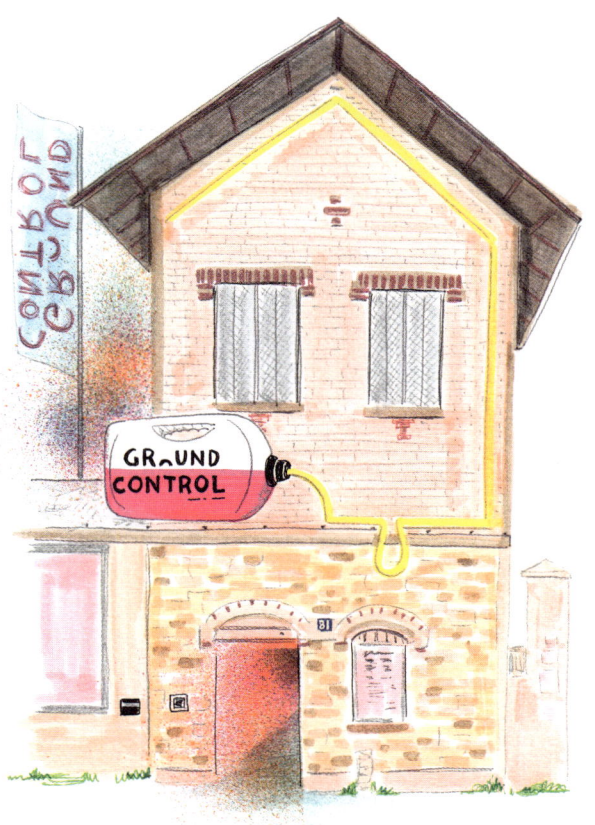

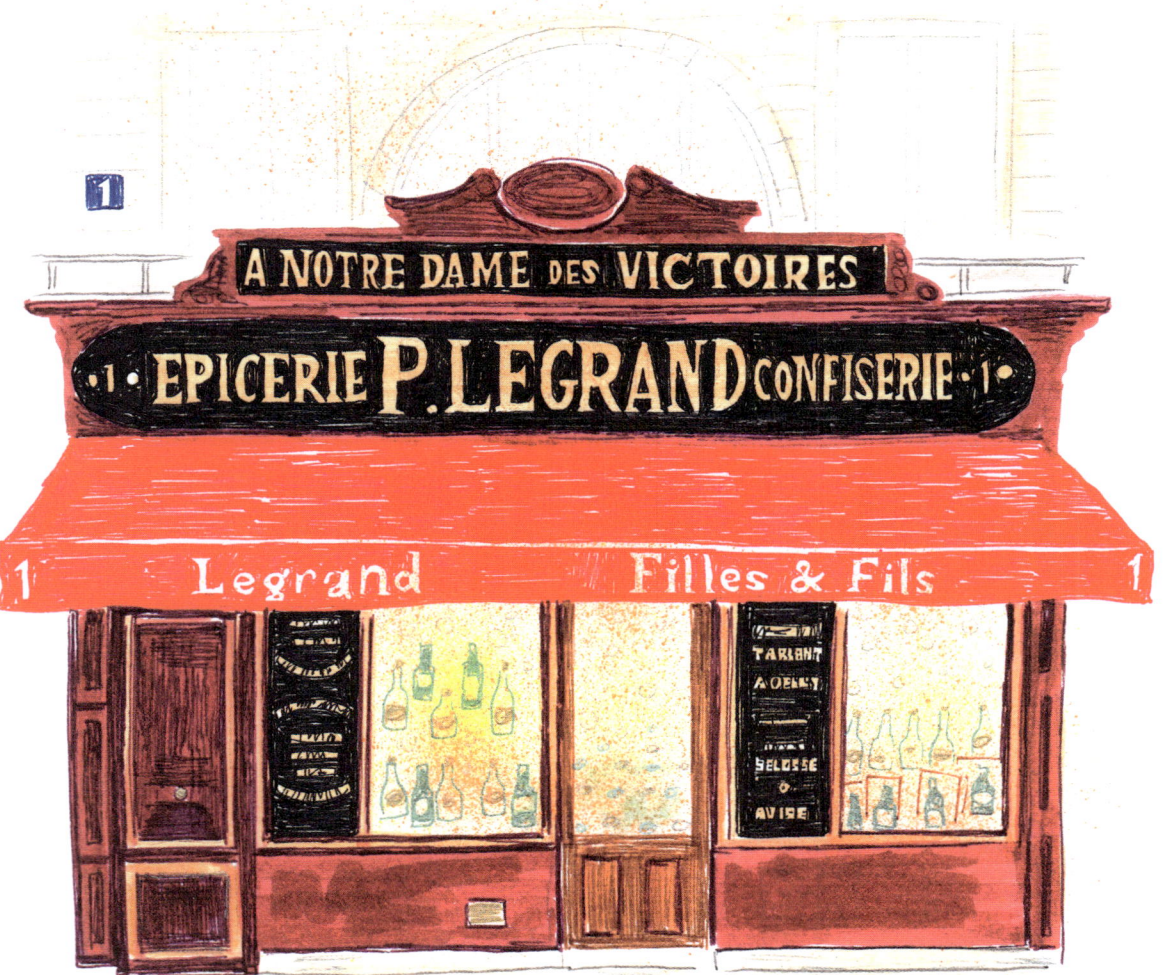

Legrand Filles & Fils Paris

The original façade of this historic wine shop is street-side, and opens into the store—but it can also be accessed through Galerie Vivienne, one of the city's prettiest covered passageways.

Legrand Filles & Fils has long been considered one of the city's most prestigious and trusted wine shops thanks to Lucien Legrand, the business's second-generation owner credited with inventing the modern wine trade.

When his father Pierre bought the shop in the early 20th century, it sold spices, coffee, and teas. After World War II, Lucien took over the reins and started developing a keen interest in wine. At the time, merchants bottled wine they purchased from the Bercy district in southeast Paris, the largest wine market in the world, where barrels were kept in huge storehouses. However, Lucien wanted to do things differently, and traveled throughout the country to meet with winegrowers directly, bringing the best bottles back to the city for his customers. His daughter Francine continued the tradition when she took over in 1986.

As of 2013, Amane Nakashima, president of Japanese agri-food company Nakashimato Co.—which specializes in fine wines, but is best known for their Kewpie mayo—has been the majority stakeholder in the shop. Along with stocking wines from 350 growers across France, Legrand Filles & Fils sells gourmet food and has an adjoining restaurant, where dishes prepared by chef Benjamin Anthoni are paired with one of the shop's wines. The seasonal menu changes weekly.

Maison Goyard

The thing that sets this high-end French luxury bag brand apart is its conspicuous absence of advertising campaigns. In stark contrast to its closest rival Louis Vuitton, for example, Goyard doesn't use celebrity endorsements to peddle its products. Its under-the-radar discretion has even elicited descriptors like "elusive" and "mysterious" from fashion media. But the heritage brand, which was founded in 1853 by François Goyard, has succeeded by word-of-mouth among its target demographic: the most affluent and influential tiers of haute society, who are always seeking exclusivity. Customers have included the world's royals (the Grimaldis of Monaco; the Duke and Duchess of Windsor) alongside the likes of Pablo Picasso, Sarah Bernhardt, and Coco Chanel. The dotted pattern of Goyard's signature logo is a reference to the family's log-driving ancestors, while the Y-shaped chevron is a nod to the central letter in the family name. The rue Saint-Honoré boutique is the brand's original HQ.

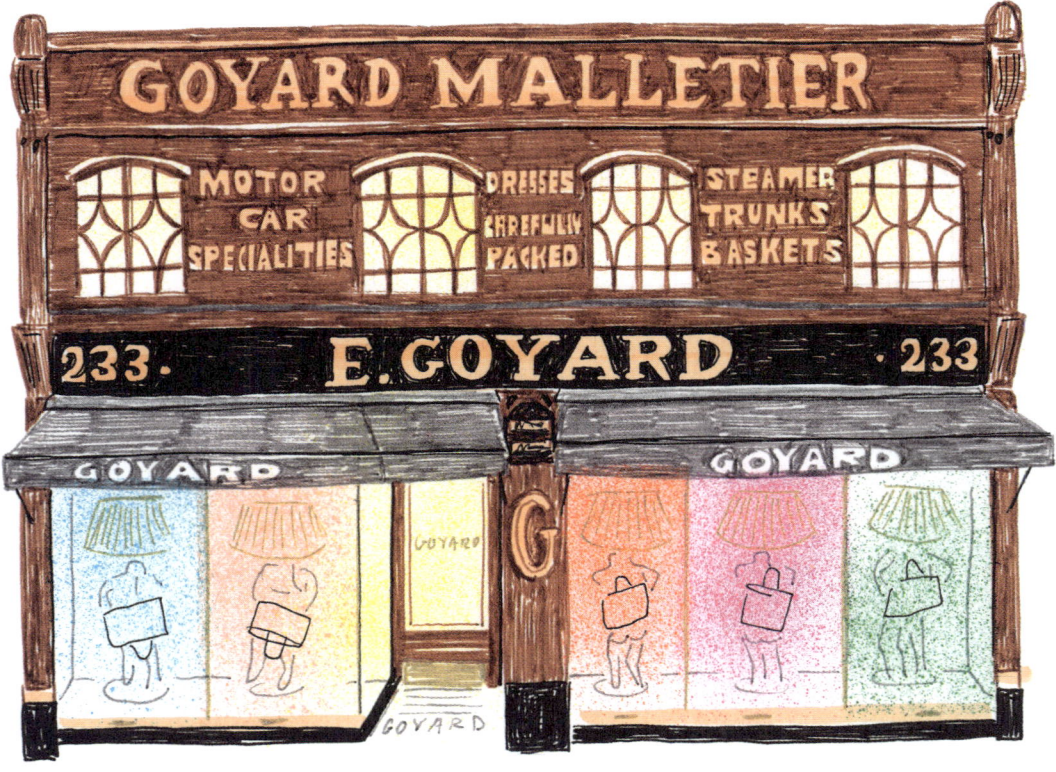

Café Verlet

———

Founded in 1880, Café Verlet is the oldest Parisian coffee company still in operation, and was the first to roast its own beans imported from the West Indies, Africa, and South America. For more than a hundred years, the café's beans have been roasted until they take on the color of "a monk's robe," in accordance with artisanal methods.

Today, owner Eric Duchossoy has carved out a reputation for discovering rare coffees and teas from small-scale producers he meets in Colombia and Guatemala, but also from farmers on lesser-known plantations in countries like Thailand, Burma, and Laos. The Verlet cellar is stocked with 30 single-origin coffees and supplies some of the most luxurious hotels in the city, including Le Meurice, Le Georges V, and Le Brach. The sit-in café serves breakfast, lunch, and desserts.

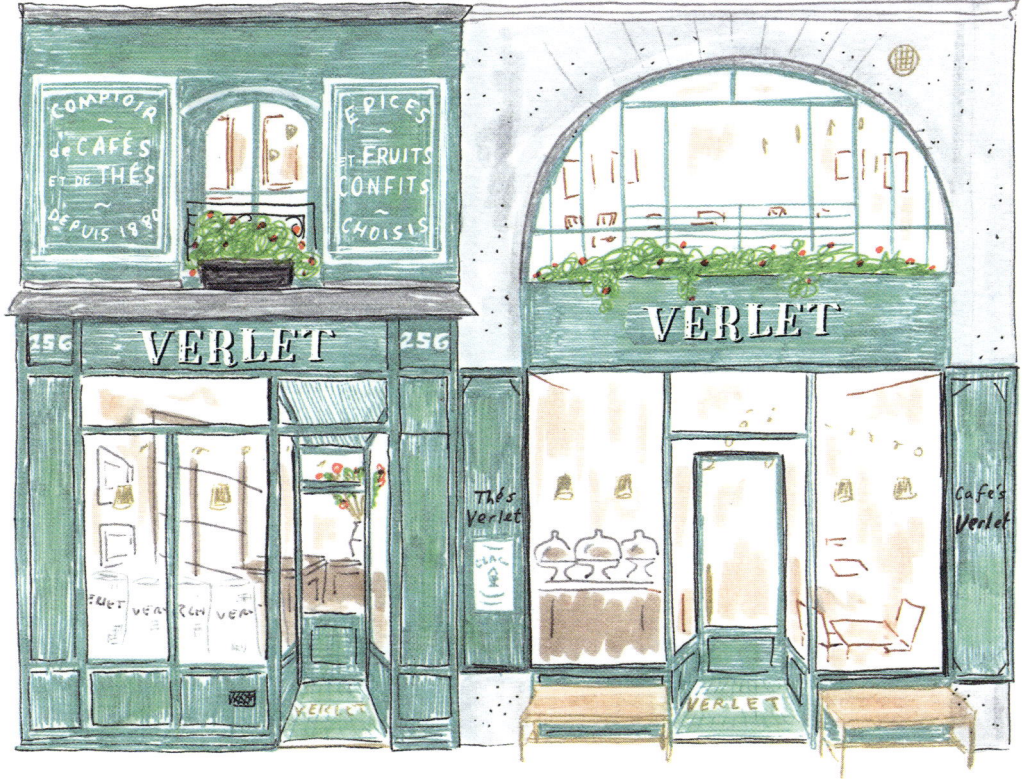

Le Grand Colbert

———

In the 2003 film *Something's Gotta Give*, Le Grand Colbert is a bit of a scene-stealer, diverting attention away from stars Diane Keaton, Jack Nicholson, and Keanu Reeves with its elegant decor during a pivotal moment. In the movie, Keaton's character Erica boldly declares the restaurant's roast chicken to be the best in the world (and in real life, many online reviews also give the dish high marks, calling it "delightful" and "incredible").

Formerly a private mansion and a novelty shop, Le Grand Colbert became a restaurant in 1900 and is named after a minister from the court of Louis XIV. It's listed as a historic monument thanks to its carefully restored Belle Époque decor that includes sculpted pilasters, globe lamps, leather banquettes, and mosaic floors, which echo the tiles of the covered passageway Galerie Vivienne next door.

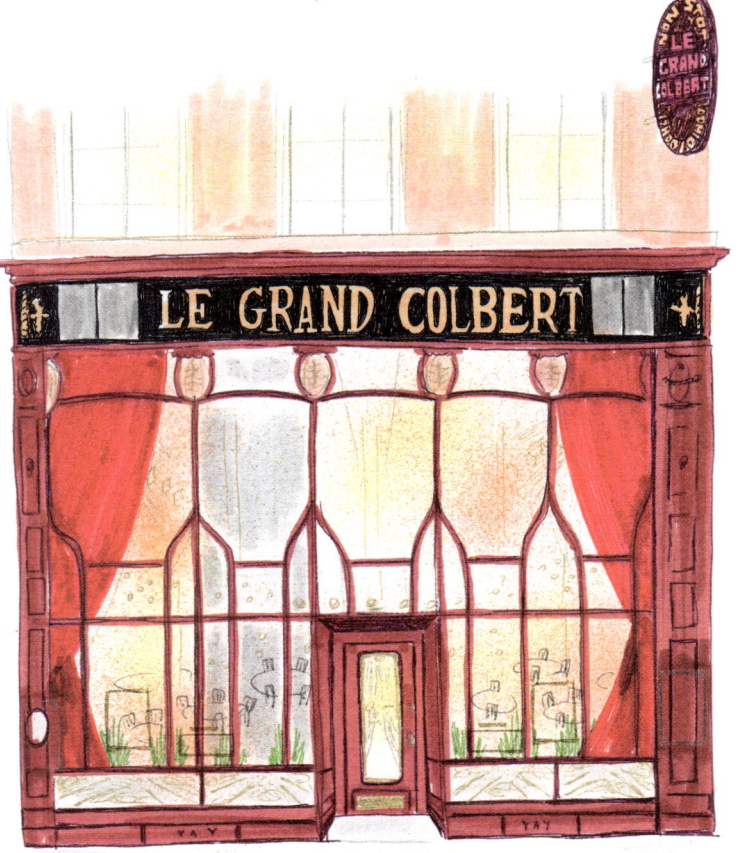

Librairie Galignani

———

Located under the arcades facing the Jardin des Tuileries, Librairie Galignani is the oldest English-language bookshop in Paris. Interestingly, it wasn't a Briton, American, or Canadian who decided that the city needed one, but an Italian man, Giovanni Antonio Galignani, whose Venetian family had been in the printing business since 1520. After living in London and marrying an English woman, Galignani, who also taught foreign languages in Paris, opened a lending library and reading room on rue Vivienne in 1801. There, he published a hugely successful English-language newspaper, *Galignani's Messenger*. The shop then moved to its current location on rue de Rivoli in 1856. Today, the library is run by the same family and is known for its collection of both English and French titles, and for specializing in fine arts. Customers have included Ernest Hemingway, Orson Welles, and Karl Lagerfeld.

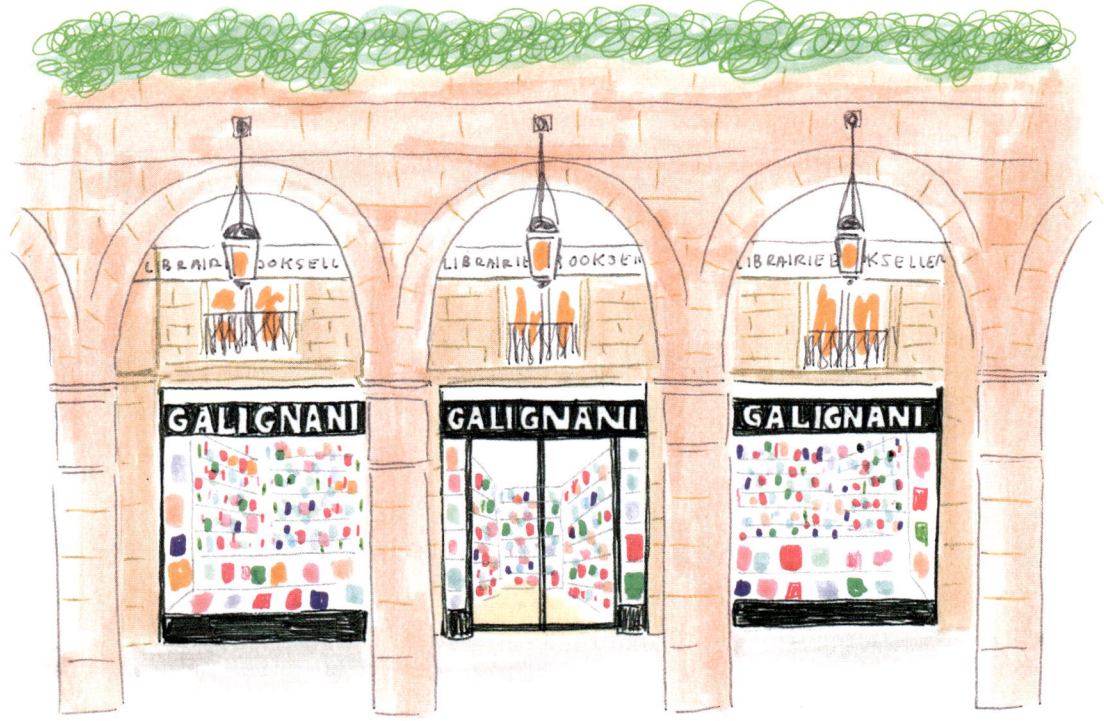

L'Écritoire

———

For Sophie Bastide, owner of this charming stationery store, writing materials run in the family: her grandfather André Tardy was a manufacturer and official supplier of inkwells for the country's national education system in the late 19th century. Between 1975 and 2022, Sophie's shop operated on rue Saint-Martin, where it was identifiable by its red awning. But in 2022 she moved L'Écritoire to its current location, Passage Molière, part of a city-led rehabilitation project which today includes mixed housing, a bookshop, and a poetry performance space—all in an 18th-century passageway. A visit to the bright, modern store may awaken in you a sudden desire to write old-fashioned letters with fountain pens and inkwells on vintage stationery and seal them with one of their many wax seals, or start a journal and practice your penmanship.

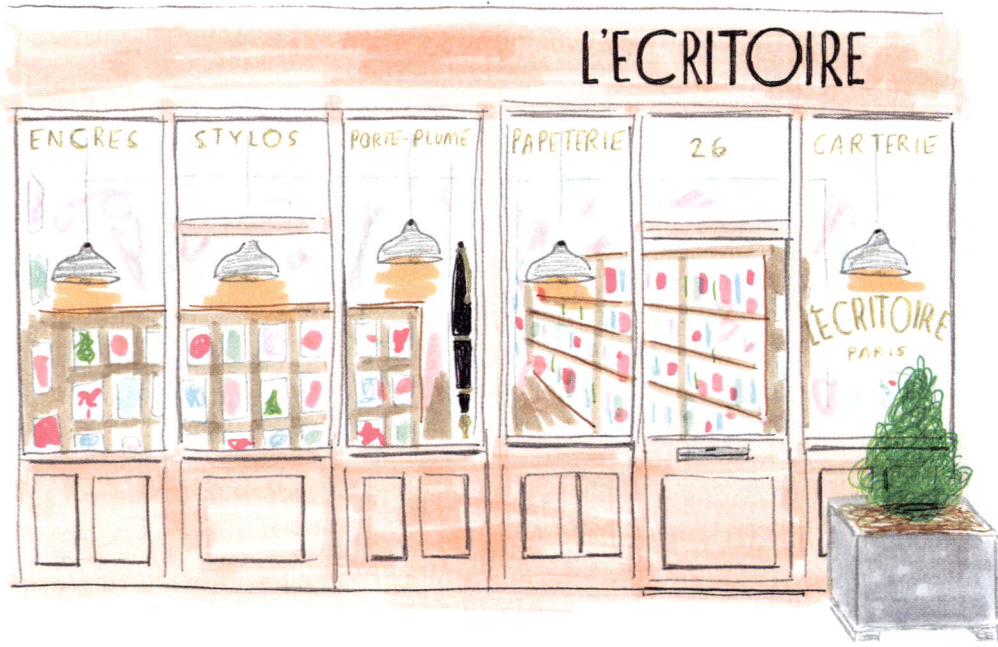

Café Joyeux

———

The cheerful yellow typeface used in the signage for Café Joyeux (which translates to "Joyful Café") couldn't be more apt. Because here, coffees, soups, quiches, and desserts are prepared by employees who have Down syndrome, autism, or other developmental disorders, and served with joy—and zero attitude.

The concept was born in the mid-2010s, when Yann Bucaille-Lanrezac ran a nonprofit that took people with developmental disabilities, the elderly, and refugees on excursions aboard his catamaran in Brittany. When a young autistic man asked him for a job and Yann had to say no, the memory of the young man's disappointment left an indelible mark. This eventually led to the birth of Café Joyeux, which aims to create more inclusive workplaces and integrate people with cognitive differences into mainstream society. Today, there are a dozen cafés across France and a location in New York.

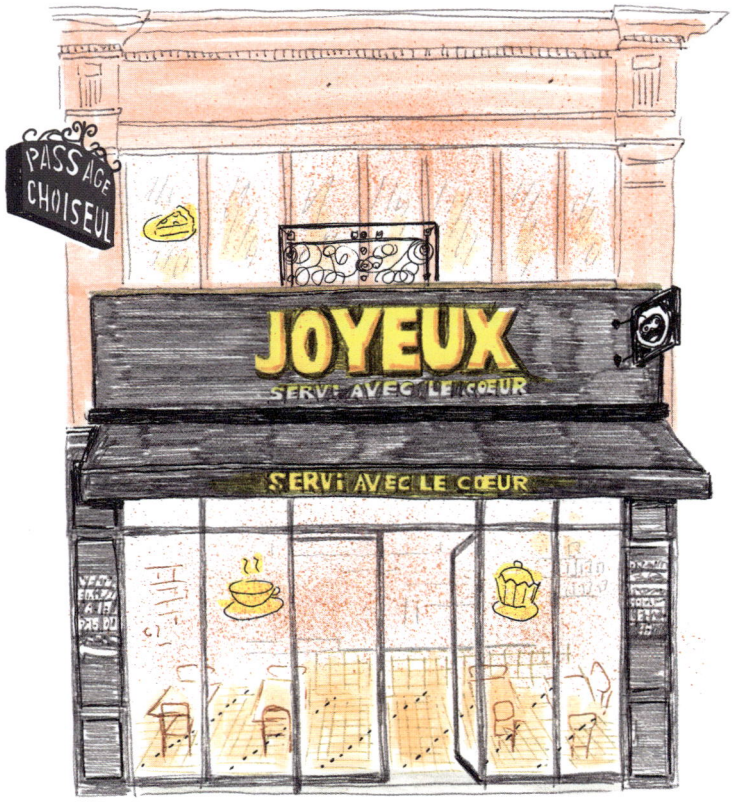

Au Levain des Pyrénées

———

Every year, Paris holds a competition that crowns the best baguette in the city. The winner of the contest—which is judged blind—receives €4,000 and becomes the official supplier to the French president at the Élysée Palace. Winning bakers and their associated bakeries become overnight sensations, with mile-long lines outside their doors daily.

But what makes the 2023 baguette competition so special is the success story of Sri Lankan immigrant Tharshan Selvarajah, who knew nothing about baking when he moved to Paris in 2006.

At the tender age of 21, Tharshan was taken under the wing of a bakery owner. Over the next few years, he learned how to perfect the craft of bread-making and, in 2018, placed third in the same baguette competition. In tandem with his improved skills, though, Tharshan also developed an allergy to flour, which triggers asthmatic reactions. Instead of changing careers as advised by his doctor, he receives treatment to alleviate symptoms.

In 2021, Tharshan managed to buy the bakery at 44 rue des Pyrénées, where his reputation and his victory at the 2023 competition have made him a local hero. "And now, the president of France is eating a Sri Lankan baker's baguette every morning!," he said in a 2023 interview with the *New York Times*.

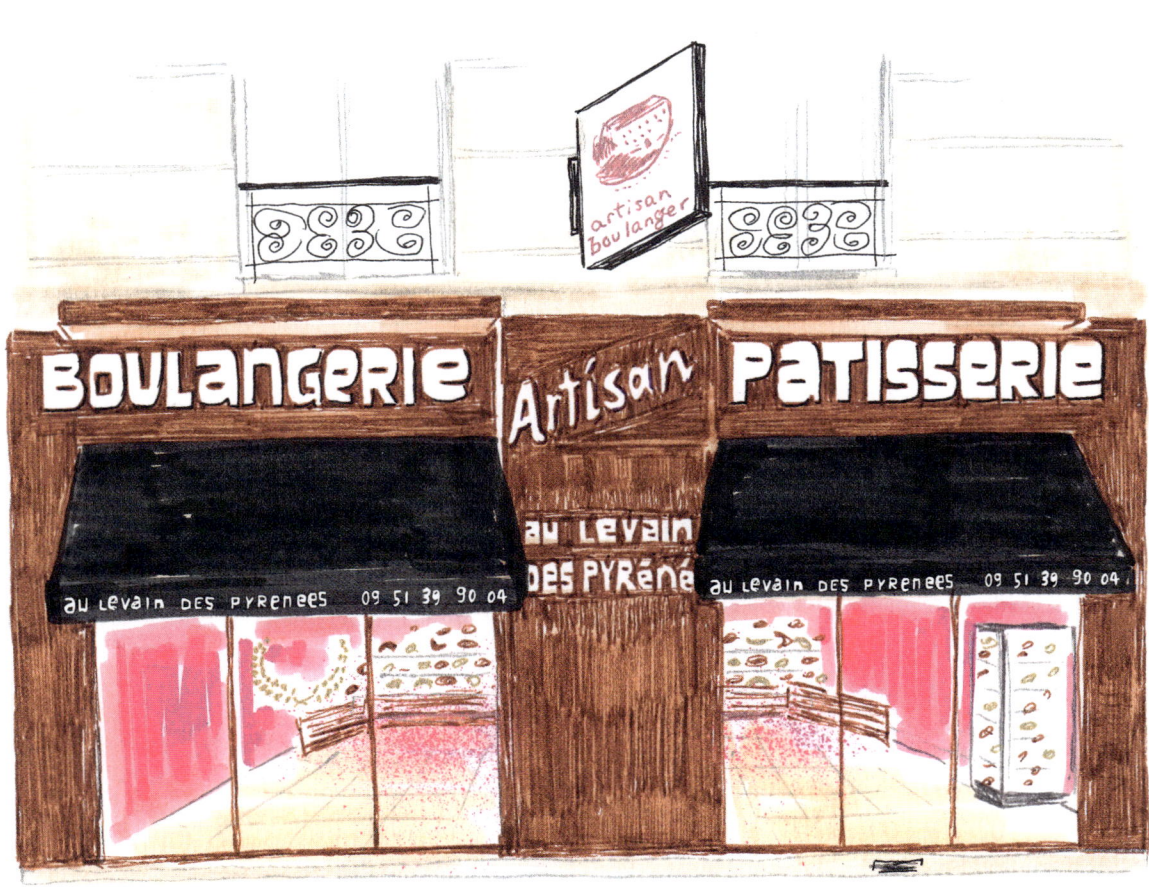

98 rue Legendre
17th arr.

Le Slip Français

—

In 2011, a young entrepreneur founded this underwear brand with the aim of giving the local textile industry a major boost. Specialties like men's boxers, briefs, and pajamas, and women's swimwear, are all made in France. There are other locations around the country, too.

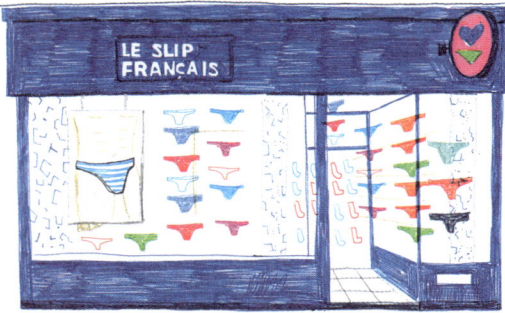

31 rue Cambon
1st arr.

Chanel 31 rue Cambon

—

It's here that Gabrielle Chanel lived and worked, setting up her couture house and fashion empire. The ground floor contains the boutique, while the rest of the building includes fitting rooms, workshops, and Coco's old apartment.

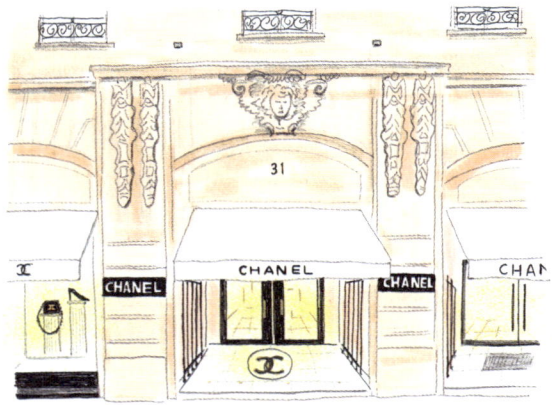

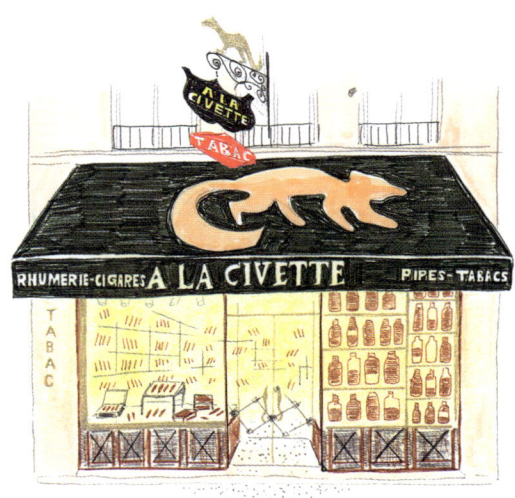

157 rue Saint-Honoré
1st arr.

À la Civette

—

The oldest tobacco shop in Paris, with a history that dates back to 1716, this boutique has served everyone from Benjamin Franklin to Winston Churchill and renowned libertine Giacomo Casanova. Along with tobacco and cigars, it also specializes in rum.

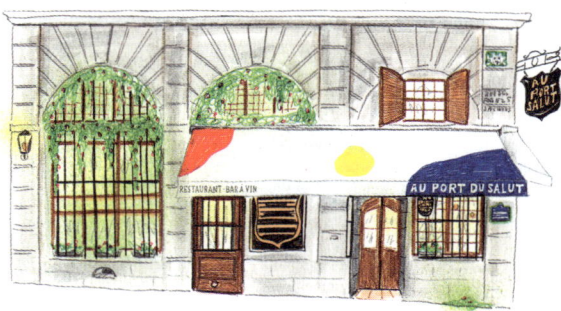

163 rue Saint-Jacques
5th arr.

Au Port du Salut

—

In a nod to its past as one of the most popular cabarets on the Left Bank (singer-songwriter Serge Gainsbourg performed here), this French restaurant brings in a jazz pianist to serenade diners every night.

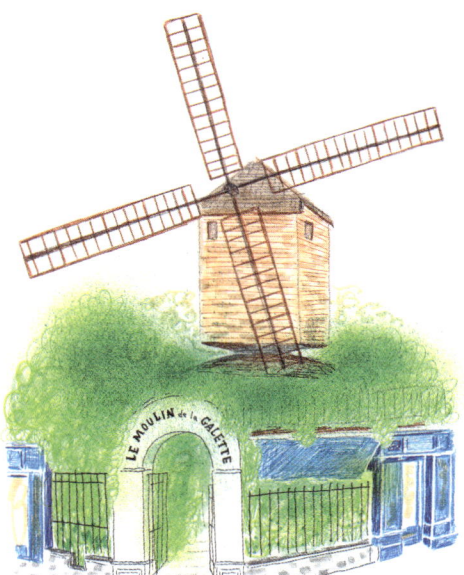

Pâtisserie de Choisy

—

This fourth-generation Chinese bakery sells sweet and savory Asian snacks like taro brioche buns, meat-filled bao, and durian roll cakes by pastry chef Thierry Mac, a graduate of the prestigious Ferrandi cooking school in Paris.

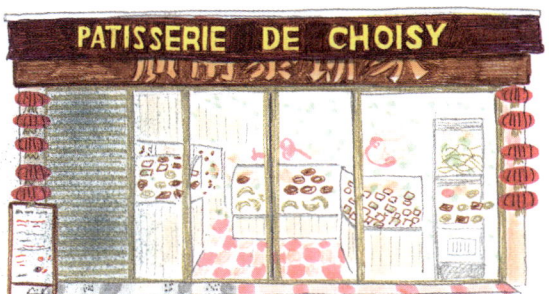

83 rue Lepic
18th arr.

Le Moulin de la Galette

—

Converted from a mill to a *ginguette* (a restaurant with a lively dancefloor) in 1834, Le Moulin de la Galette was once the hottest destination among Parisian revelers, and is famously immortalized in Renoir's painting *Bal du moulin de la Galette*.

35 rue Saint-Louis en l'Île
4th arr.

Clair de Rêve

—

This boutique keeps the 17th-century French tradition of marionettes alive for use in department-store window displays, museums, theme parks, and theatrical stage sets.

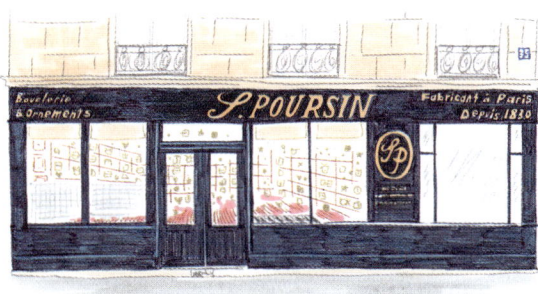

35 rue des Vinaigriers
10th arr.

Maison Poursin

—

When it opened in 1830, this family-run business specialized in buckles and other assorted hardware for horse saddles and harnesses. Today, it also produces buckles for luxury leather bags and belts.

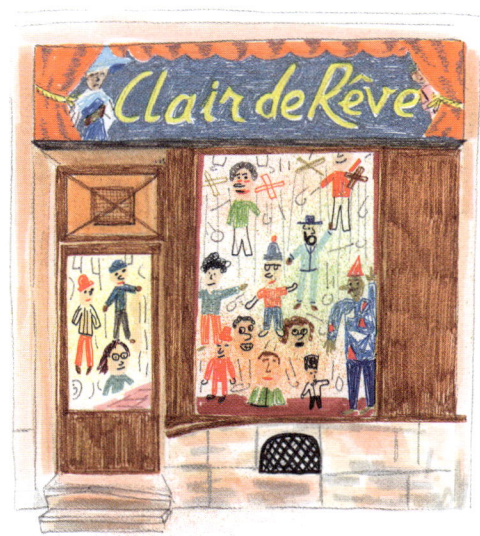

Fou de Pâtisserie

———

This pastry shop actually began as a magazine of the same name (which translates to "Crazy for Pastry") in 2013. The brainchild of indie publishers Muriel Tallandier and Julie Mathieu, the publication was billed as the first of its kind in France, dedicated solely to the country's top pastry chefs and their masterful creations. Three years later, in 2016, the entrepreneurs came up with another novel, never-before-done-in-Paris idea: to open a one-stop boutique where visitors could find desserts, cakes, and pastries from the best chefs in the country, all in one spot—no store hopping required. The pair have been able to get several big names on board from the get-go, including Pierre Hermé, Christophe Adam, Cyril Lignac, and Nina Métayer, who was named World's Best Pastry Chef in 2023. There are two other locations.

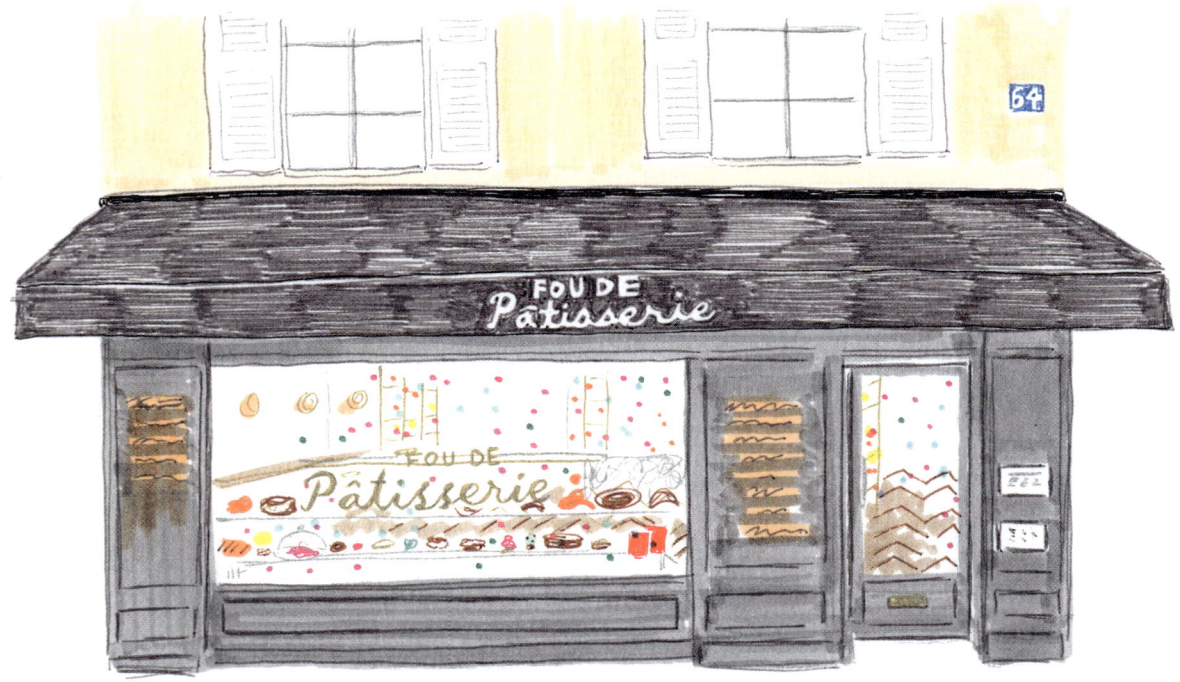

Le Grand Rex

———

With a seating capacity of 2,700 in its great hall alone, Le Grand Rex holds the title of the largest single-screen auditorium in Europe, and is listed as a historic monument for its Art Deco façade. The vision of Franco-Tunisian film producer Jacques Haïk, the theater and concert hall opened in 1932, wowing thousands of spectators with faux stars hanging overhead from the vaulted ceiling, dancing "Rex Girls," and a screening of *The Three Musketeers*. In 1957, it became the first theater in Europe to install a mechanical escalator. Since 1954, one of its most popular traditions has been the annual water and light show *Féerie des Eaux*, involving 2,500 water jets and 26 light projectors. The kid-friendly spectacle takes place onstage before the screening of a Disney film over the Christmas holidays. In 2022, Le Grand Rex's façade underwent a restoration to mark its 90th anniversary.

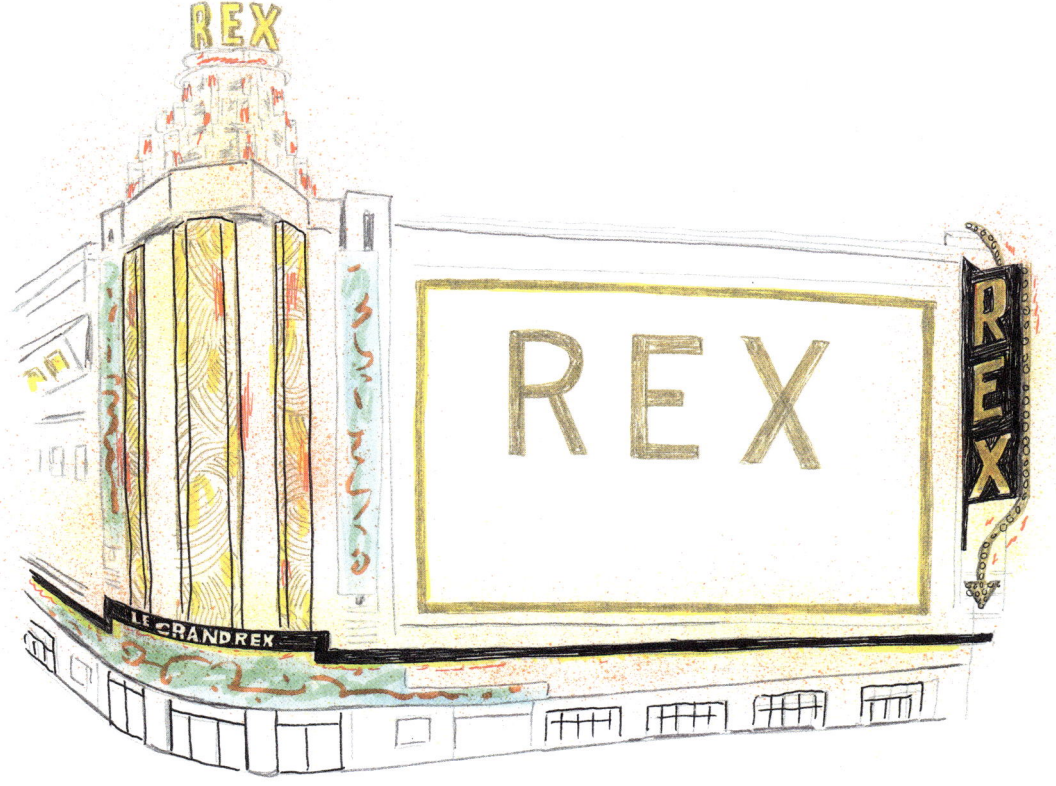

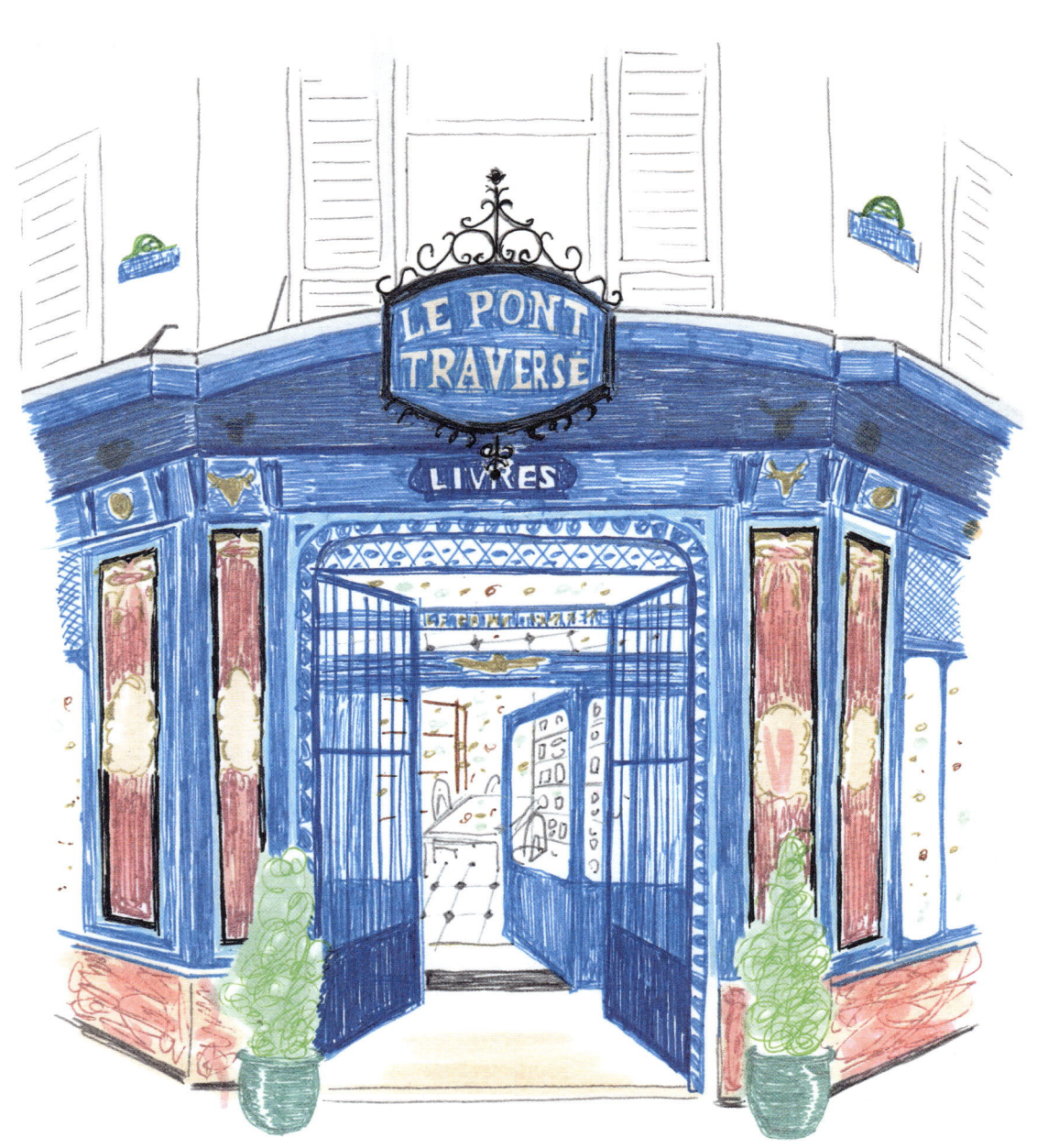

Le Pont Traversé

———

When news got out that the little bookshop Le Pont Traversé (which translates to "The Crossed Bridge") was closing in 2019, it caused a wave of dismay among Paris bibliophiles, particularly lovers of French poetry.

Since moving into what used to be a butcher shop on the corner of rue Madame and rue de Vaugirard in 1973, the quaint store had earned a reputation as a specialist in 20th-century poetry and a purveyor of rare and first-edition books on art and literature. Former French president François Mitterrand was a regular. With its charming cobalt-blue façade, enameled plaques, hand-painted frescoes, and bronze bull heads, the shop was also the pride of the neighborhood. But its owner Marie-Josée Comte-Béalu was retiring, and couldn't find anyone to take it over.

In 2021, along came restaurateur Frédérique Jules, who resurrected the space into a gluten-free café and shop, while (thankfully) preserving the exterior and keeping the same name.

Frédérique is the founder of gluten-free coffee shop Noglu, which has two other locations in the 7th and 11th arrondissements, as well as an outpost in New York. Le Pont Traversé now serves a sweet and savory menu that includes brioche French toast, pizza, quiche, carrot cake, and chocolate cake, all of which are gluten-free. The shop also sells gourmet, gluten-free foodstuffs like pasta, granola, and cake mixes.

Mariages Frères

———

This gourmet brand has earned a reputation as one of the premium tea companies in the world, thanks to a long family history of tea trading. Appointed by King Louis XIV in the 17th century, brothers Nicolas and Pierre Mariage were sent to the corners of the earth—Persia, the East Indies, India, and Madagascar—to seek out the best teas and bring them back to France. Successive generations continued in the trade, and in 1854, brothers Henri and Edouard Mariage opened a tea house in the Marais called Mariages Frères (Mariage Brothers), where they imported the finest teas from as far away as China and Ceylon (now Sri Lanka) for the fanciest hotels and tea rooms in the city. It was only in 1984 that the shop pivoted to become a retail store and tea room. There are locations in other cities around the world.

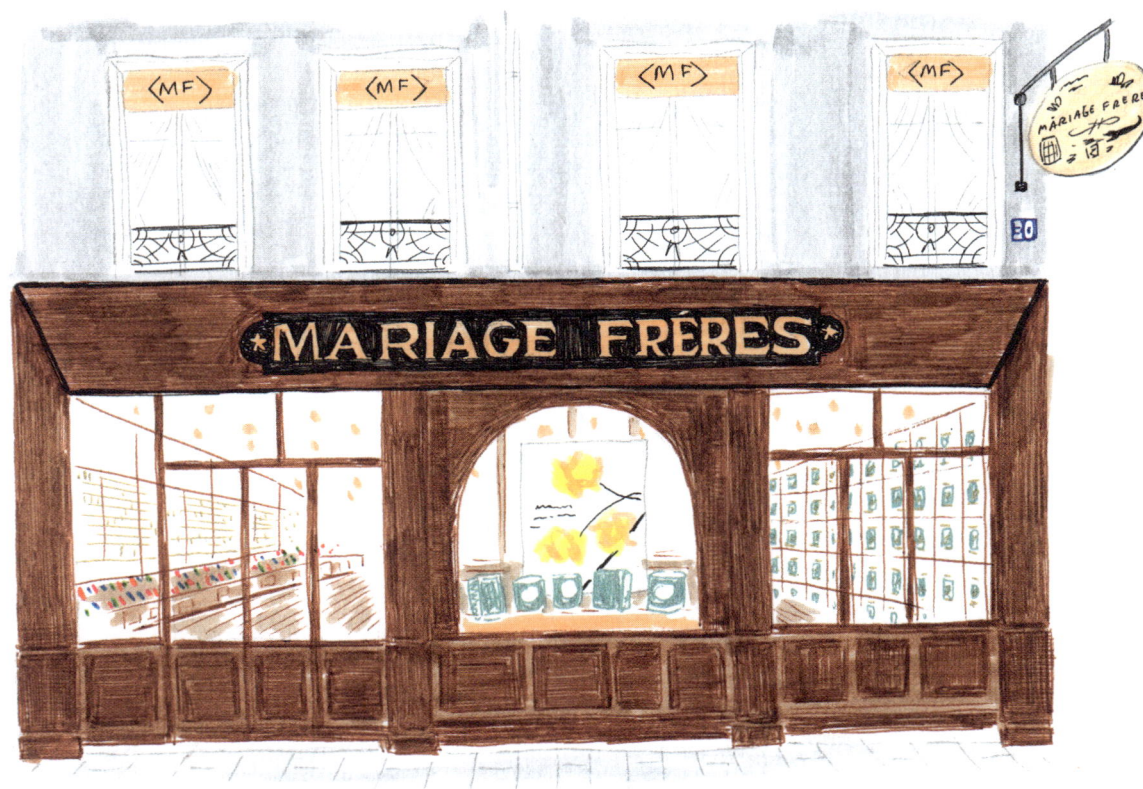

La Belle Hortense

———

The charming blue façade of this boutique in the Marais fronts an equally charming concept: a wine bar and bookshop rolled into one. At La Belle Hortense, wall-to-wall shelves are lined with French and English titles ranging from novels and poetry to cookbooks, and the wine list features organic French wines that are sold by the glass. While it's popular among tourists, the literary bar also attracts French regulars, who greet longtime bartender Brigitte Le Guern by her first name before engaging in a little neighborhood gossip with fellow barflies. Books are curated by Brigitte, who used to work in publishing, while charcuterie and cheese plates are prepared in the kitchen across the street at the equally photogenic café Au Petit Fer à Cheval (both are owned by the same person, Xavier Denamur).

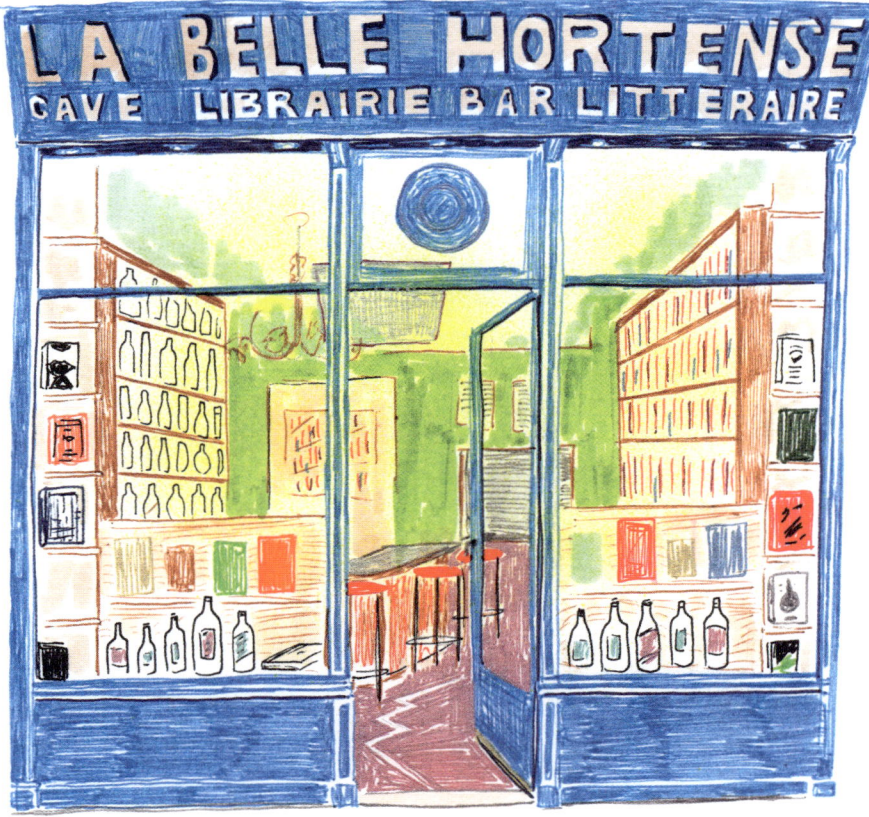

Le Caveau de la Huchette

———

Long before this underground grotto became one of Paris's most legendary jazz clubs, and centuries before its star turn in the 2016 film *La La Land*, it served as a lair for some dark and nefarious activity. Legend has it that the cave was once the meeting place for secret societies such as the Knights Templar, the Rosicrucians, and then the Freemasons. During the French Revolution, prisoners were tried in secret, locked up, and executed in its underground passageways. It wasn't until much later, in 1946, that Le Caveau de la Huchette opened as a jazz club, hosting swing and bebop performances every night of the year. Famous musicians who have played there include Miles Davis, Duke Ellington, Manu Dibango, and Lionel Hampton. The iconic Cavern Club in Liverpool, where The Beatles played in their early years, was modeled after it.

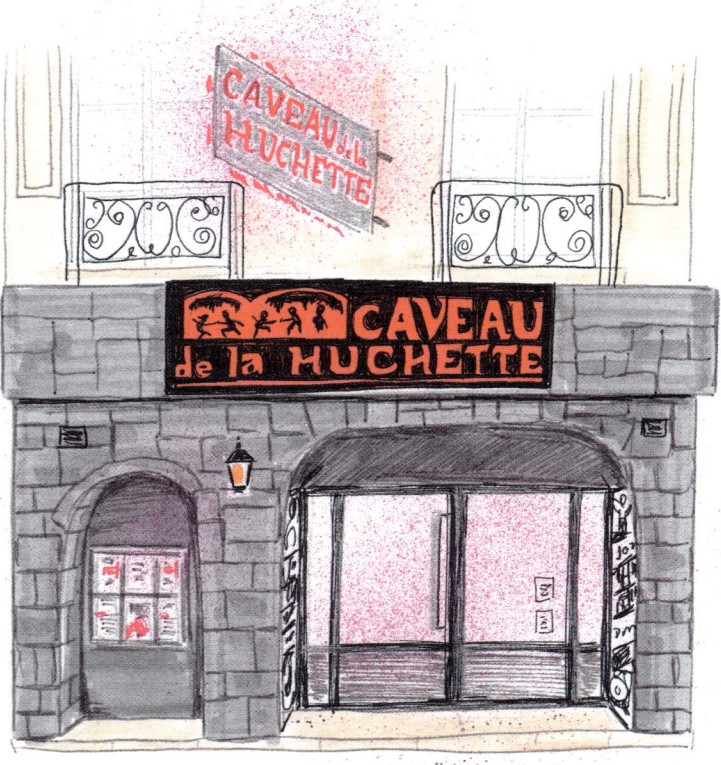

Jixiao's Buns

———

This hole-in-the-wall used to be a closely guarded secret among Paris's Chinese community and neighborhood locals alike, beloved for its plump and savory pan-fried dumplings, until word of mouth gave it away. While the capital has no shortage of *xiao long bao* (soup dumpling) restaurants, Jixiao's Buns specializes in *sheng jian* buns from Shanghai. Unlike steamed *xiao long bao*, these meat or veggie-filled wheat flour buns are pan-fried so that the bottom is golden and crispy.

Before opening his own place, Chef Jun Liu worked in fine dining restaurants like La Brasserie Fouquet (see p. 128) and Le Grand Véfour (see p. 75). Take note that this address on rue Beaubourg only has a few seats outdoors, and is more popular for takeout. A second dine-in address can be found near Notre-Dame on Quai des Grands Augustins.

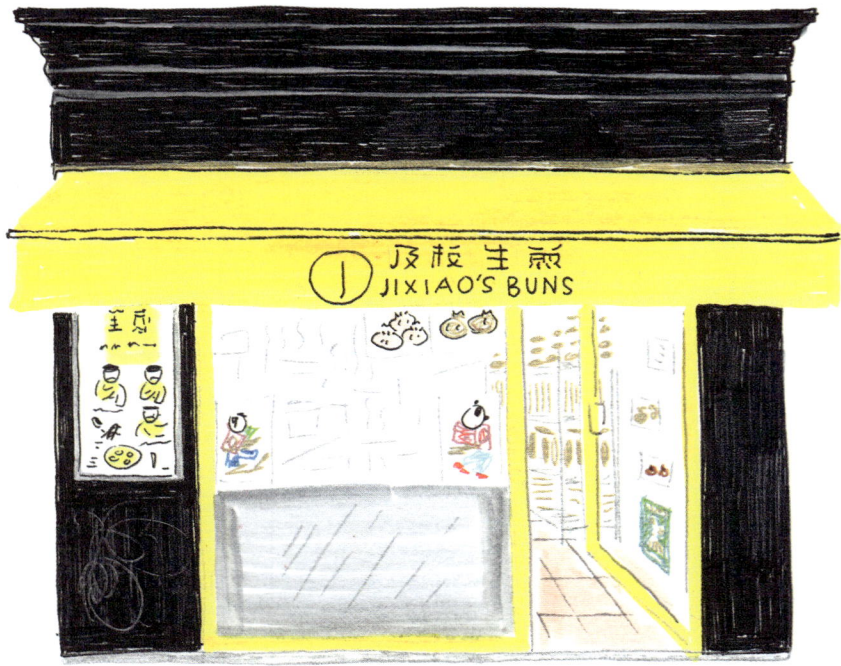

Le Relais de Venise

———

This is the mothership; the place that birthed a beloved *steak-frites* institution across Paris, famous for its steak sauce and generous helping of fries. Though its sister restaurants, all called Le Relais de l'Entrecôte, are perhaps better known, Le Relais de Venise is where it all started.

Founded in 1959 by winemaker Paul Gineste de Saurs, the concept is simple: there's only one menu, which starts with a walnut salad, followed by sirloin steak served with the restaurant's famous sauce and thin-cut fries. The wine is organic and comes from the family's Château de Saurs, near Toulouse. The business's success has been replicated with outposts in New York, London, and Mexico City. In 2021, the chain launched a brilliant street food concept, La Baguette du Relais, in the Marais: *steak-frites* smothered in sauce, stuffed inside a baguette.

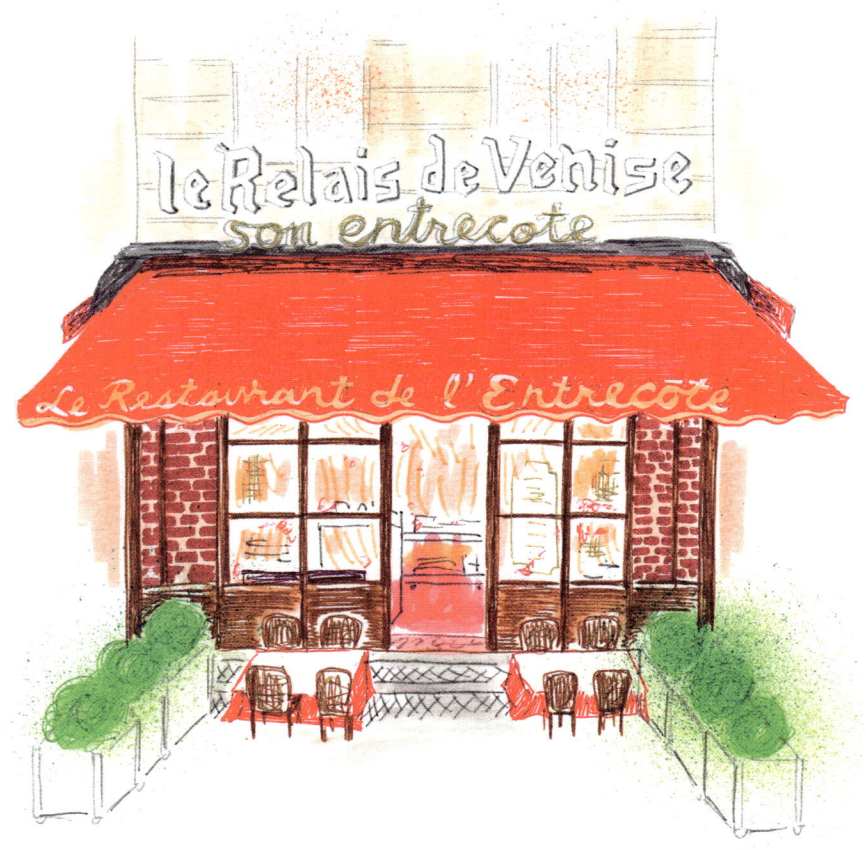

Stohrer

———

Along with being the oldest *pâtisserie* in Paris, Stohrer bakery boasts a few other claims to fame through its founder Nicolas Stohrer, pastry chef to King Louis XV. Before taking on this role for the French court, Nicolas was in the service of the King of Poland, Stanislas Leszczynski, who was living exiled in Alsace. When the king complained that his *kougelhopf*, an Alsatian brioche, was too dry, Stohrer doused it in booze to revive it, and created what we know today as the baba rhum or rum baba. When the king's daughter Marie married Louis XV, Nicolas followed her to Versailles. A few years later, he struck out on his own and opened a bakery on rue Montorgueil, which today is a historic monument due to its elegant period decor. It's owned by the same family who run À la Mère de Famille (see p. 21), Paris's oldest *chocolaterie*. There are five additional locations in the city.

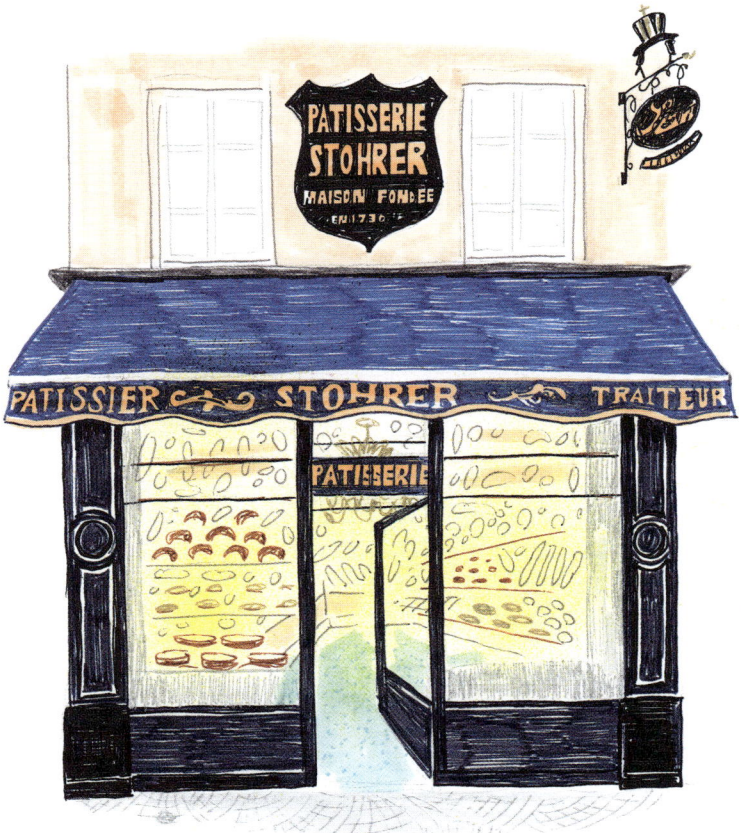

Le Bon Marché

——

It's no exaggeration to say that Le Bon Marché, France's first department store, revolutionized the concept of retail.

Many of today's modern services and shopping experiences can be traced to founders Aristide and Marguerite Boucicaut, who introduced ideas like fixed pricing, home delivery, free exchanges, sales, private concerts (think mall concerts), and reading rooms. When the business opened in 1852, for the first time, the Paris bourgeois could find everything they needed in one place and no longer had to visit specialized merchants. The store sold everything from gloves, dresses, and linens to hats and umbrellas all under one roof, out in the open.

As the years went on, the visionary couple snapped up adjacent buildings and formed what writer Émile Zola described as a "cathedral of modern commerce" in his book *Au Bonheur des Dames* (The Ladies' Paradise). The Boucicauts were also known as generous and philanthropic entrepreneurs: they offered their employees free meals at a staff canteen, retirement funds, weekly paid days off, and English lessons.

The building's steel structure and skylights, which today flood the shoe and women's apparel sections with natural light, can be traced back to Gustave Eiffel, the engineer behind Paris's most iconic monument. In 1986, Le Bon Marché was bought by LVMH, and has since been turned into a luxury department store that stocks high-end beauty, fashion, and design brands.

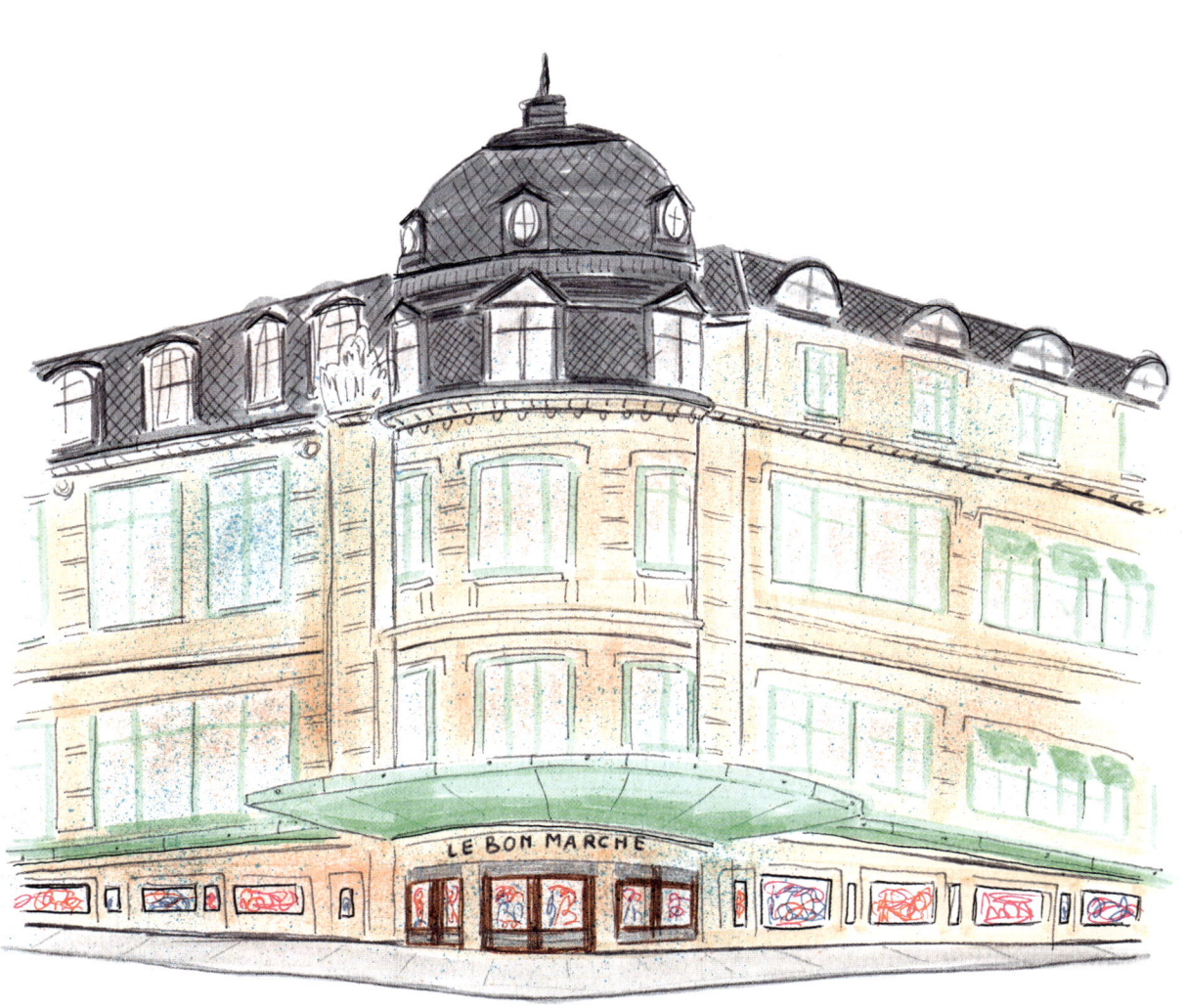

28 rue Yves Toudic
10th arr.

Bonjour Jacob

—

This concept store stocks a large selection of French and English-language indie magazines like *Fare* and *Kinfolk*, alongside lifestyle, art, and design titles including *i-D* and *Monocle*. A coffee counter invites visitors to sit and read awhile. There's another location in the 6th arrondissement.

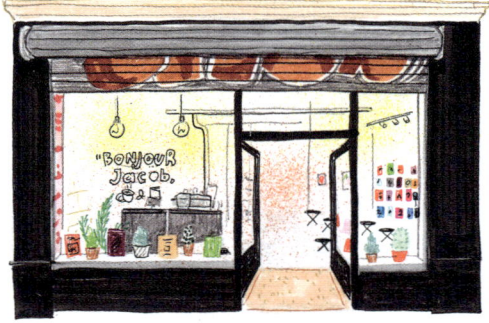

1 Imp. Guéménée
4th arr.

Miyakodori

—

This small, quirky shop may be the luckiest store in Paris. Its specialty is the *manekineko*, or "beckoning cat," a well-known Japanese feline figurine that waves its paw and is a symbol of good fortune.

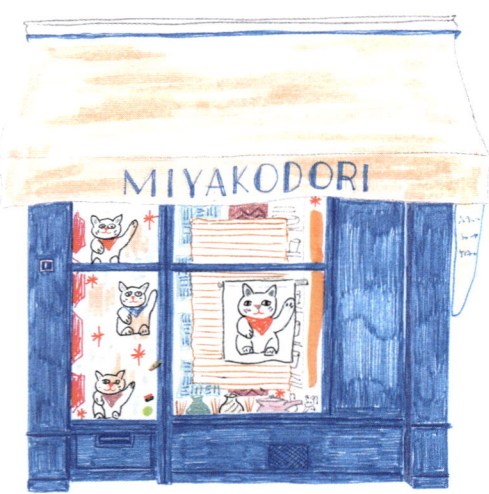

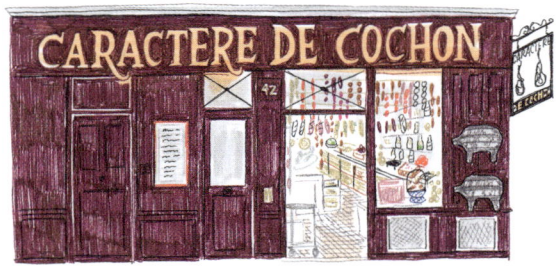

42 rue Charlot
3rd arr.

Caractère de Cochon

—

This delicatessen is famous for its ham baguette sandwiches thanks to its expansive, quality selection of fresh and cured hams infused with truffles or pepper, or smoked with hay. Enjoy at the nearby Square du Temple.

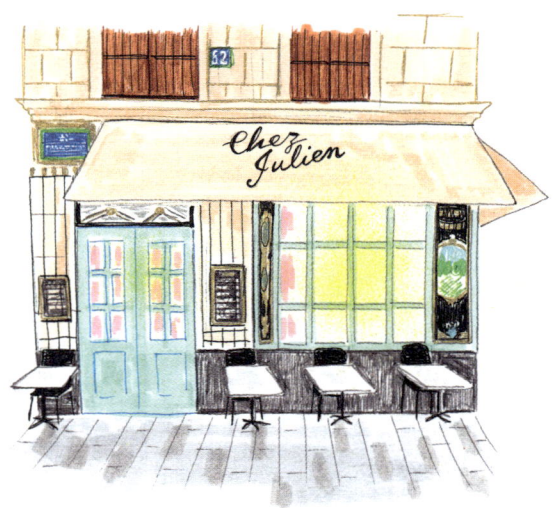

1 rue du Pont Louis-Philippe
4th arr.

Chez Julien

—

Formerly a bakery, this fetching historic monument boasts some of the most coveted terrace seating spots in the neighborhood thanks to its Seine-side location. The Art Nouveau interior is the backdrop for truffle risotto and Chateaubriand steak.

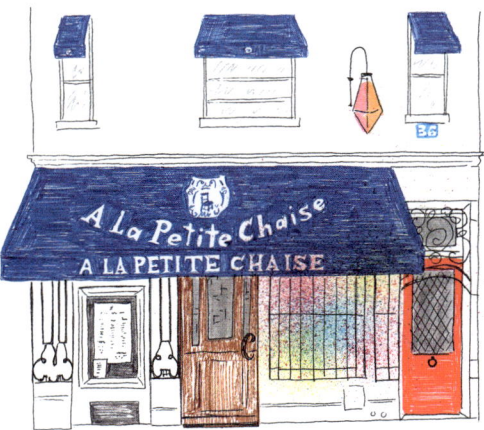

36 rue de Grenelle
7th arr.

La Petite Chaise

Opened in 1680, this restaurant is one of Paris's oldest, and was once a popular meeting spot for writers, politicians, and artists like Alfred de Musset, George Sand, and François-René de Chateaubriand.

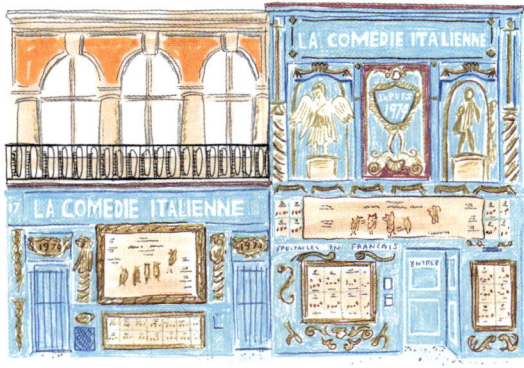

17–19 rue de la Gaité
14th arr.

La Comédie-Italienne

From afar, the blue Baroque façade of this Italian theater, with its depiction of angels, evokes Wedgwood china. The only theater of its kind in France, all plays are exclusively penned by classic and contemporary Italian playwrights.

11 rue Civiale
10th arr.

Ravioli Nord-Est

This modest, no-frills family restaurant is a Belleville institution due to its specialty, *jiaozi* dumplings. Handmade pockets of juicy pork and chive are enveloped in a soft, chewy, pillowy dough wrapper, and are best dipped in a little Chinese vinegar.

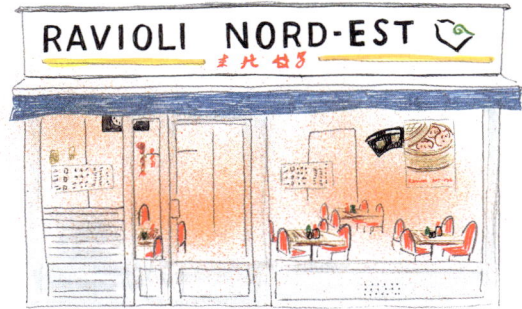

75bis rue des Martyrs
18th arr.

Madame Arthur

At this popular drag club in Pigalle, opened in 1946, performers put on new cabaret shows nearly every week. Entertainers at the decidedly Gallic venue revive a repertoire of classic French songs, and the evening concludes with an all-night club.

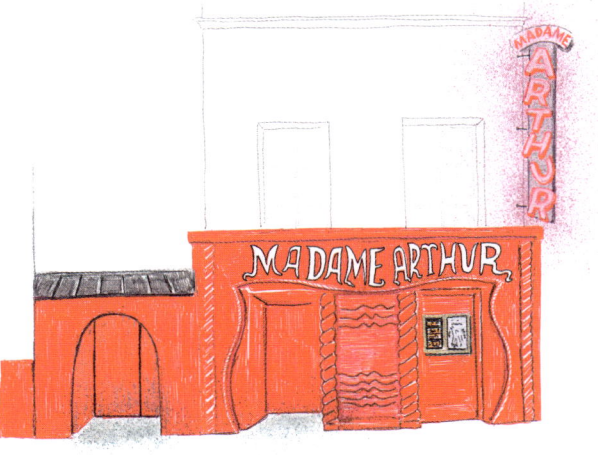

Moulin Rouge

———

When it opened in 1889, the Moulin Rouge was a temple of music and dance, where men got their jollies by watching women kick their legs up in the air and raise their ruffled petticoats. It was where the bourgeoisie and the working class—men and women alike—shared evenings of unbridled, raucous exuberance, rendered famous by the painter Henri de Toulouse-Lautrec.

The Moulin Rouge was the first building to go electric in the capital. It's the birthplace of the French can-can, and is where writer Colette kissed her lesbian lover Mathilde de Morny onstage in 1907, causing a scandal. Today, it's more of a tourist attraction than a den of debauchery, hosting evenings of sequined, topless entertainment as part of its *Féerie* revue. Its most famous performers have included Mistinguett and La Goulue, as well as Josephine Baker, Édith Piaf, Liza Minnelli, and Frank Sinatra.

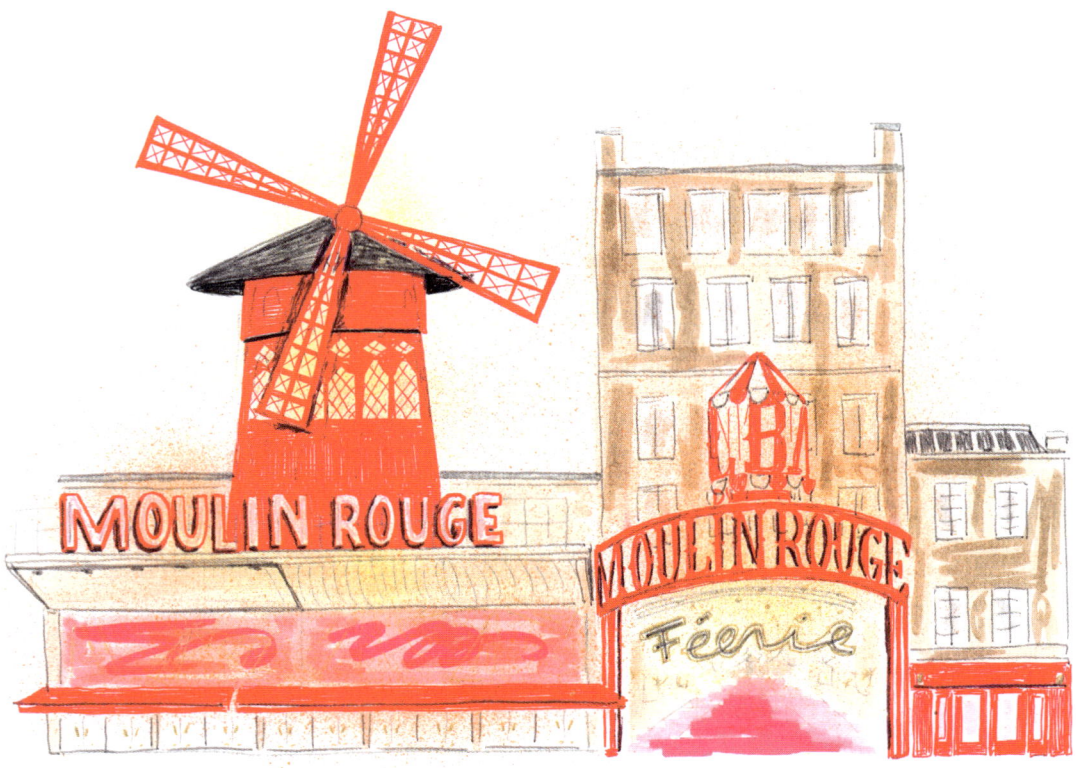

Crazy Horse Paris

———

French newspaper *Le Figaro* calls Crazy Horse the sexiest cabaret in Paris. If the Moulin Rouge (see opposite) is historic and exuberant, Crazy Horse is more sensual and seductive by comparison and, some add, the more artistic of the two. While the Moulin Rouge is located in Montmartre, historically a working-class, bohemian neighborhood, Crazy Horse is positioned not far from the swanky Champs-Élysées. This was a deliberate decision by its founder Alain Bernardin, who opened the cabaret in 1951 as a more sophisticated alternative.

For one of the show's signature numbers performed since 1989, "God Save Our Bareskin," the cabaret brought in a former officer of the British Royal Guard to teach the ladies how to synchronize their marching, head turns, and salutes with military precision. Celebrity performers have included Dita Von Teese, Pamela Anderson, and Lisa, a member of the K-pop girl group Blackpink.

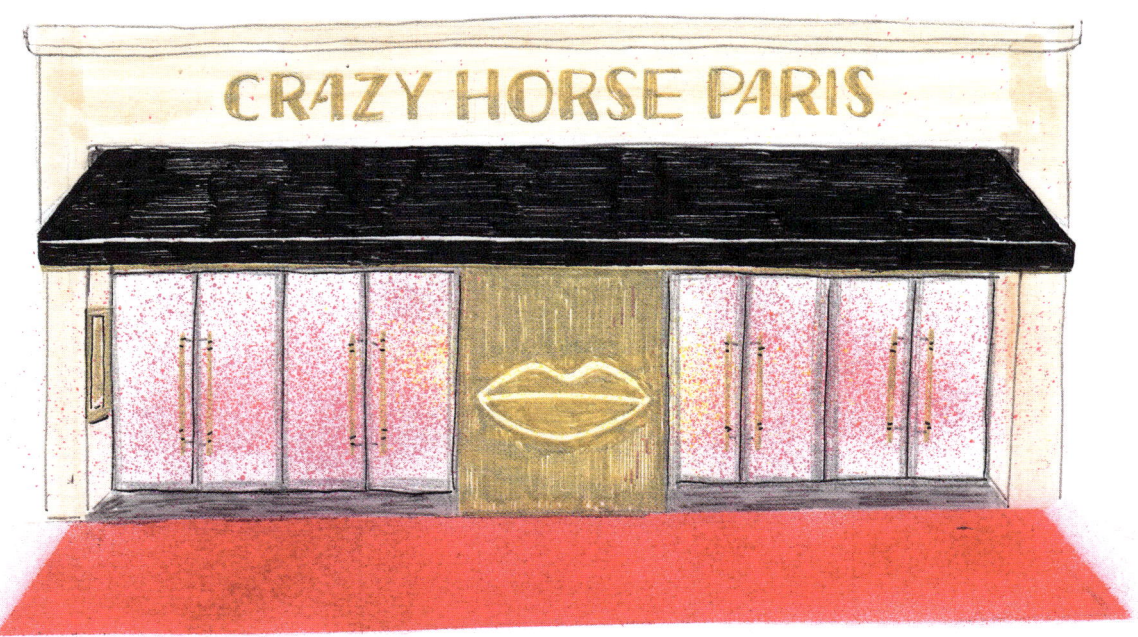

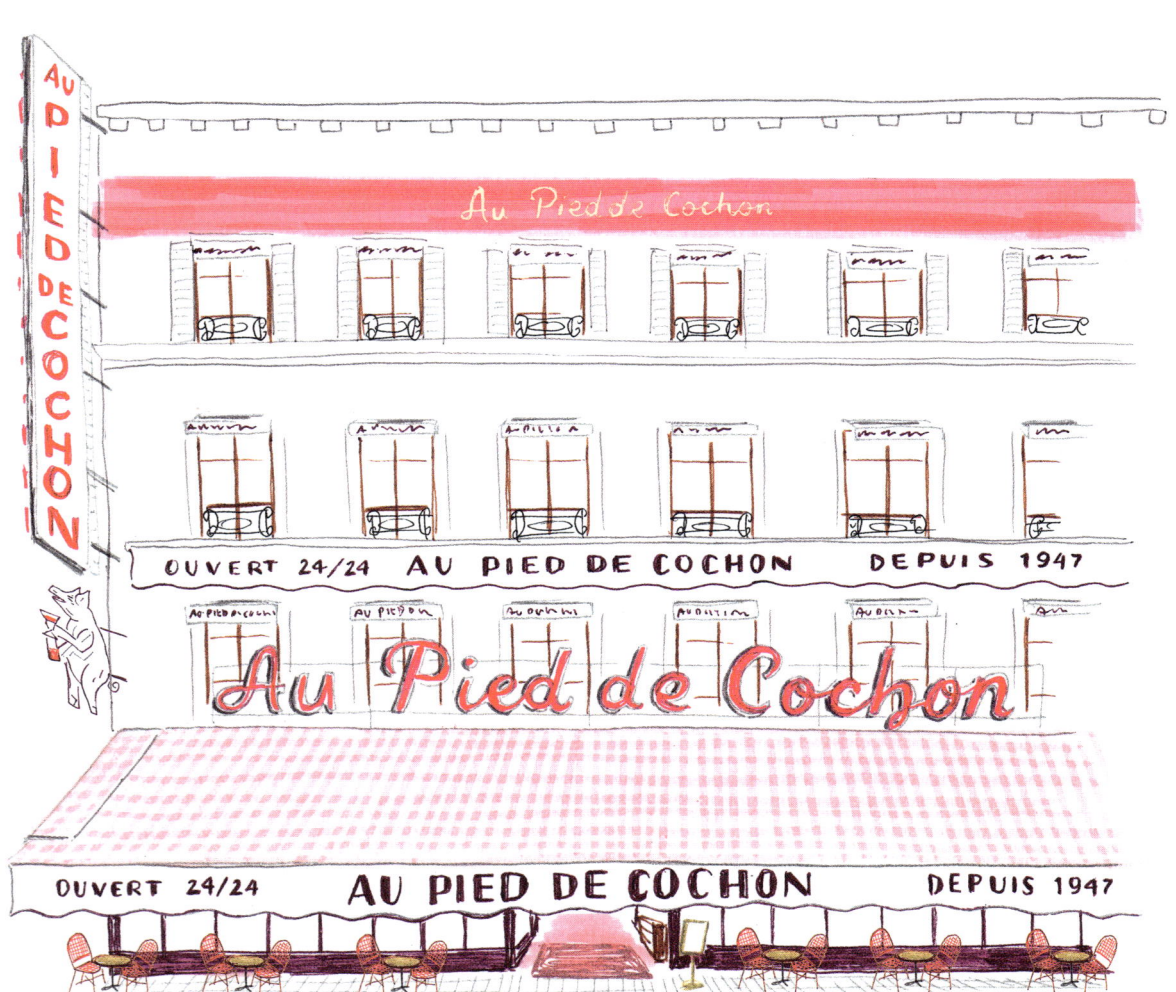

6 rue Coquillière
1st arr.

Au Pied de Cochon

———

A few things set this brasserie apart from the others in the bustling area of Les Halles, which used to be Paris's central wholesale market. First up, as Au Pied de Cochon's French name suggests, the specialty here is pig's trotters, the humble but delicious part of the pig discarded by nearby butchers.

Secondly, when it was founded in 1947, it was the first restaurant to open 24 hours a day, seven days a week. At dawn, it was packed with a motley crew of late-night revelers wrapping up their evenings out, alongside early-morning market workers who were just starting their days. Customers included Josephine Baker, Salvador Dalí, Alfred Hitchcock, and Robert Doisneau. In 1981, François Mitterrand chose to celebrate his presidential victory at the mythic restaurant.

While Au Pied de Cochon now closes between 5 and 8 a.m., it remains one of the few restaurants in Paris to serve food into the wee hours of the morning for night owls and nocturnal merrymakers.

Against a Belle Époque setting featuring red leather banquettes, painted panels, and brass rails, diners tuck into house specialties like grilled pig's trotter with Béarnaise sauce and fries, onion soup, confit pork ribs, and oyster and seafood platters.

Right Bank: 1st, 2nd, 8th, 16th, and 17th Arrondissements

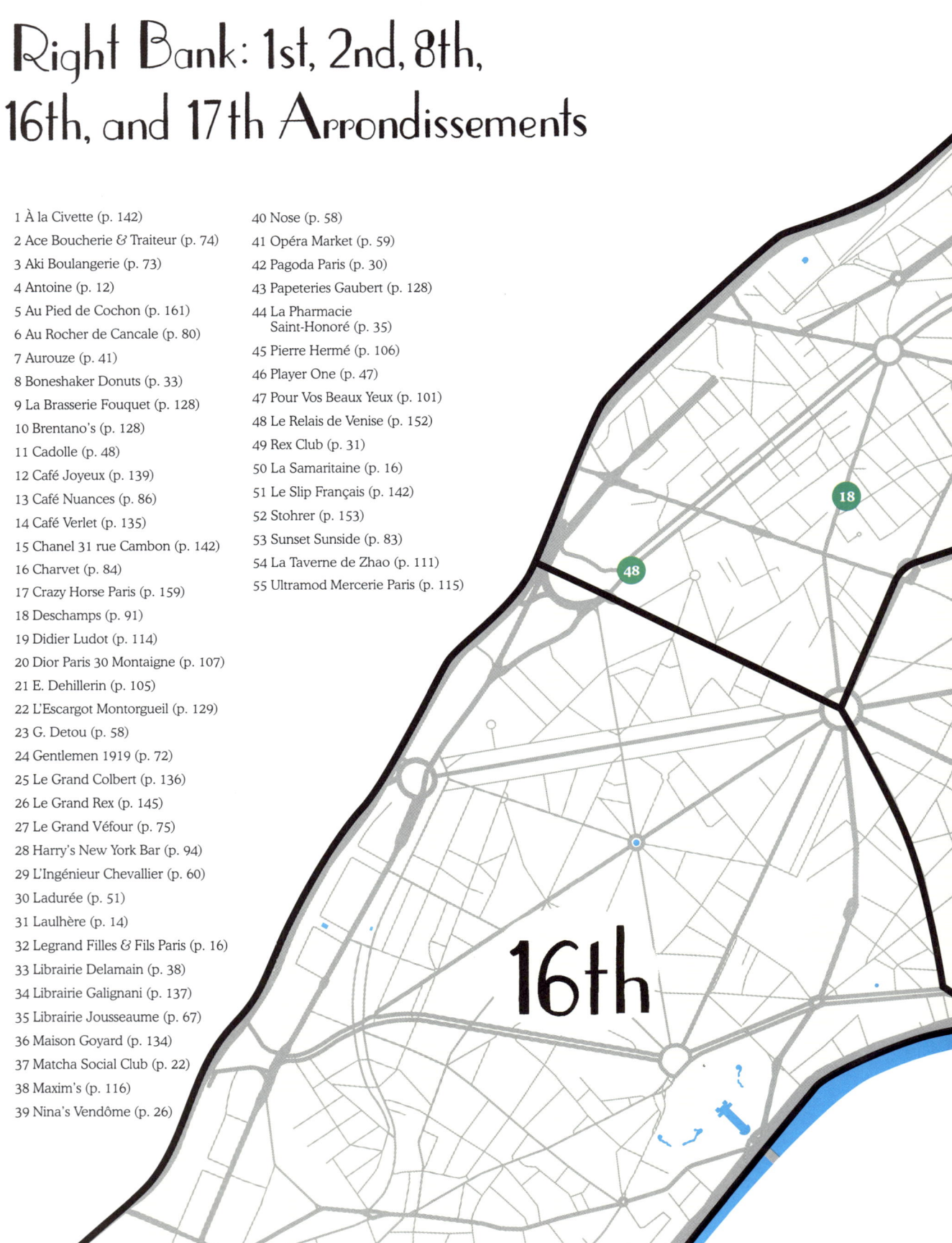

16th

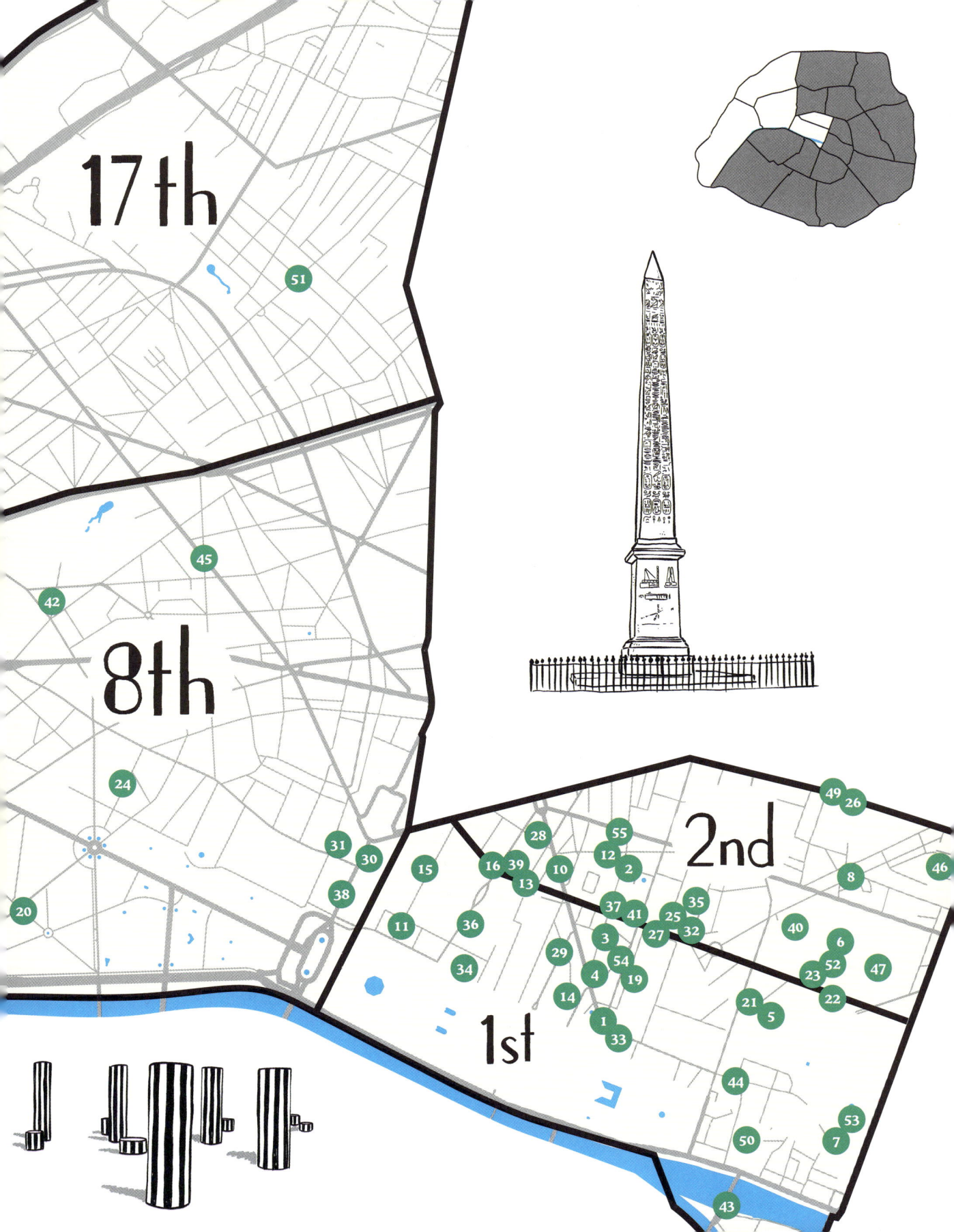

17th

8th

2nd

1st

51

45

42

24

20

31

30

38

15

16

39

13

28

10

55

12

2

37

41

25

35

32

27

49

26

8

46

40

6

23

52

47

22

11

36

34

29

3

54

19

4

14

1

33

21

5

44

50

53

7

43

Right Bank: 9th, 10th, 18th, and 19th Arrondissements

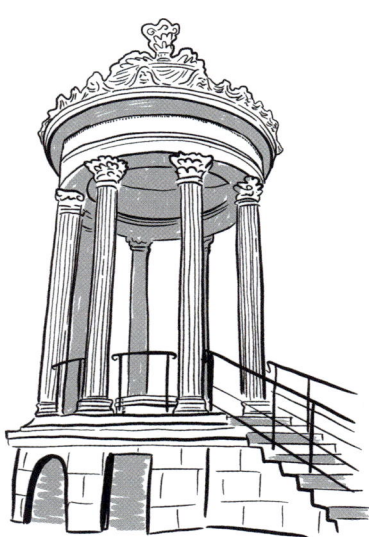

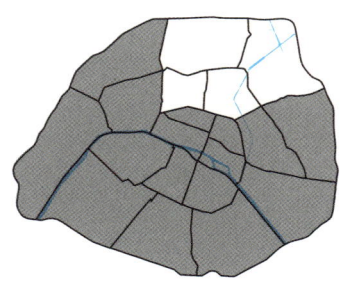

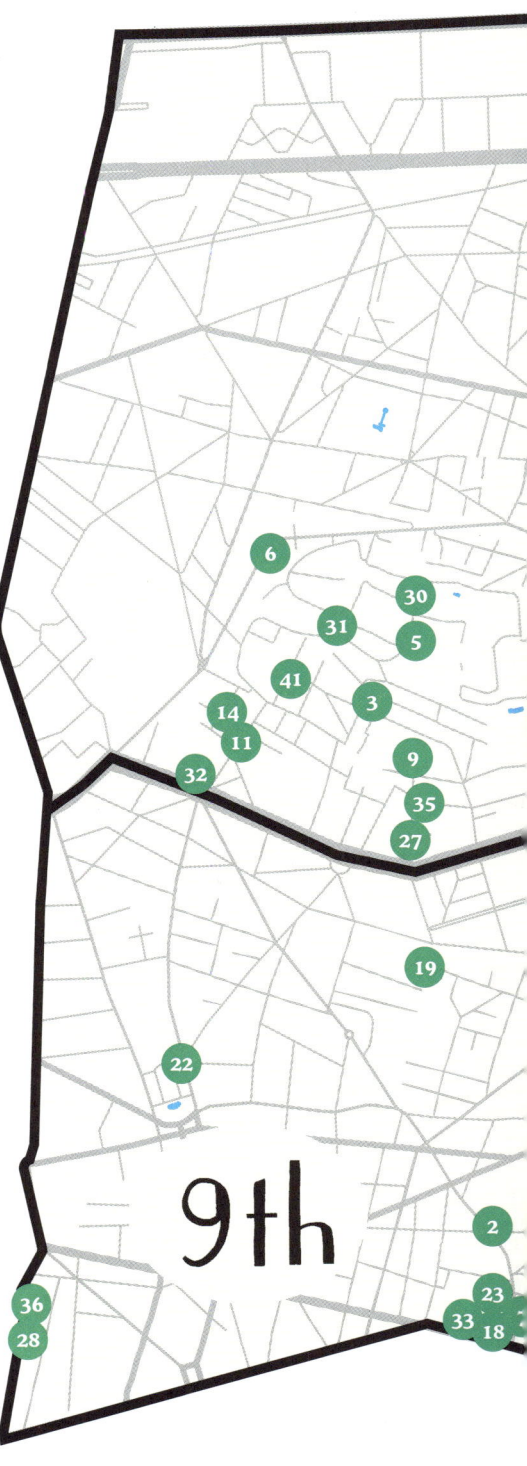

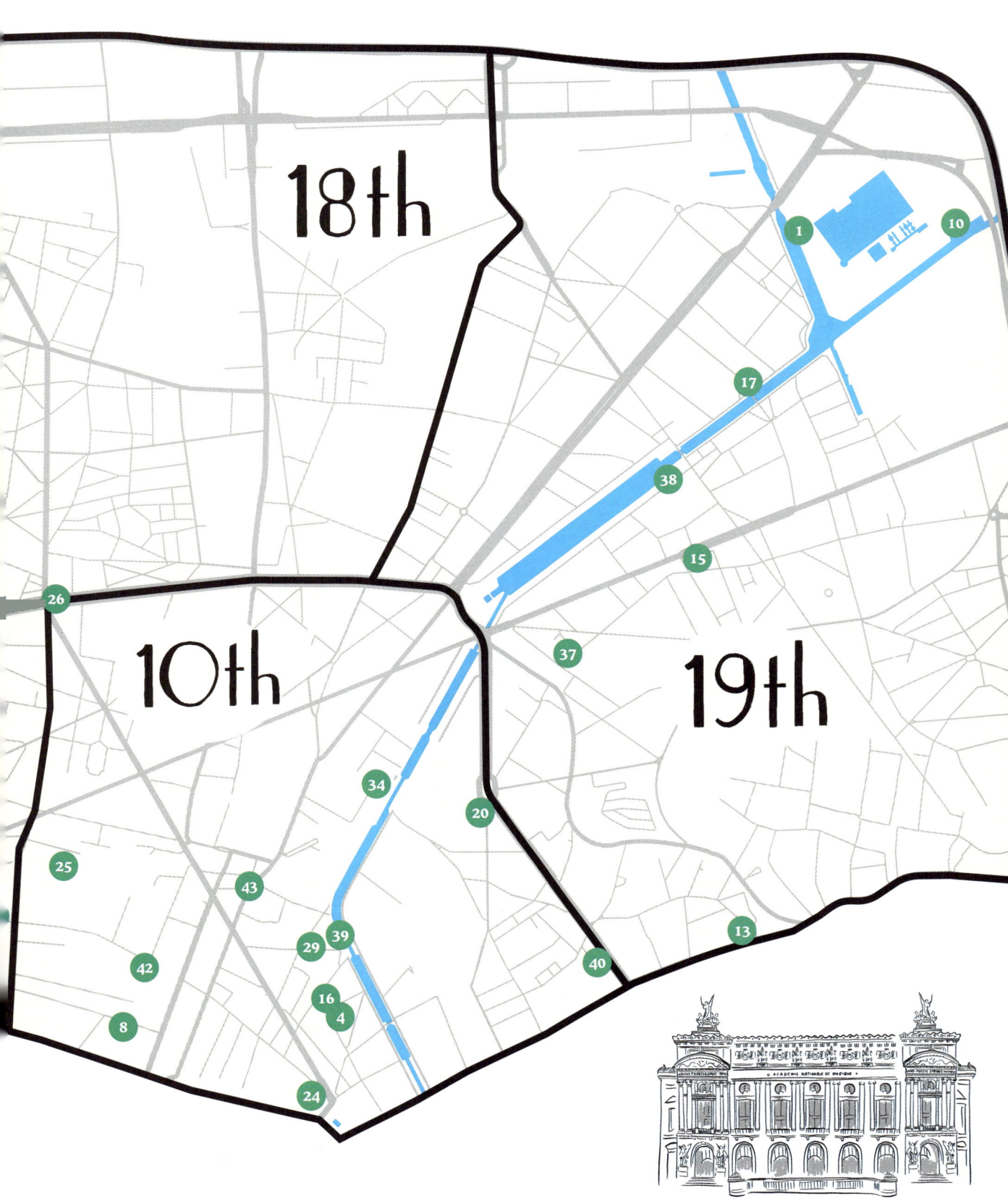

Right Bank: 3rd, 4th, 11th, 12th, and 20th Arrondissements

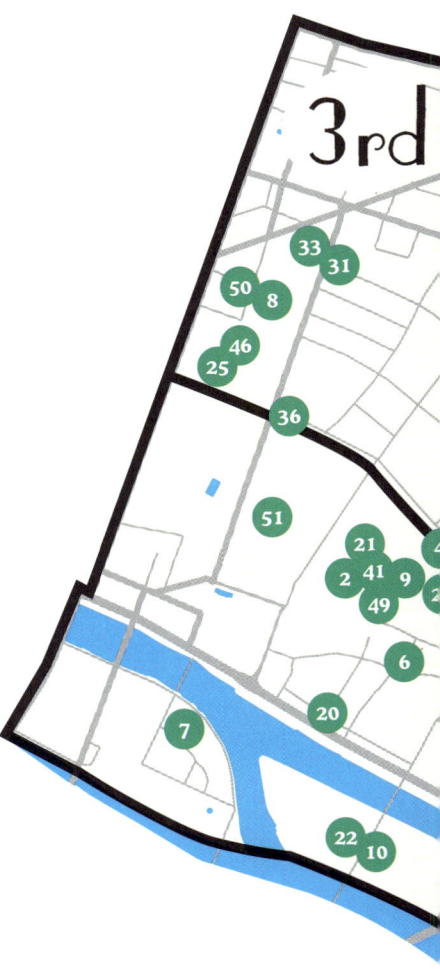

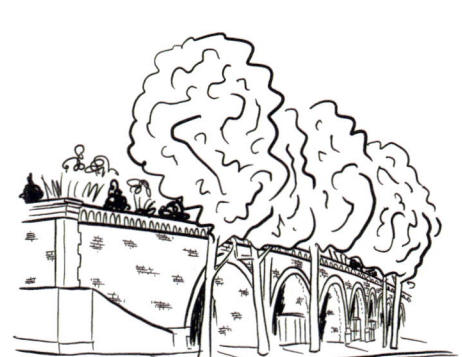

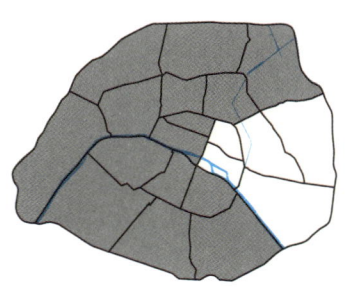

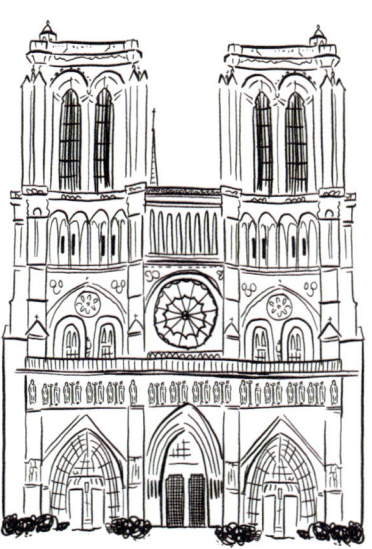

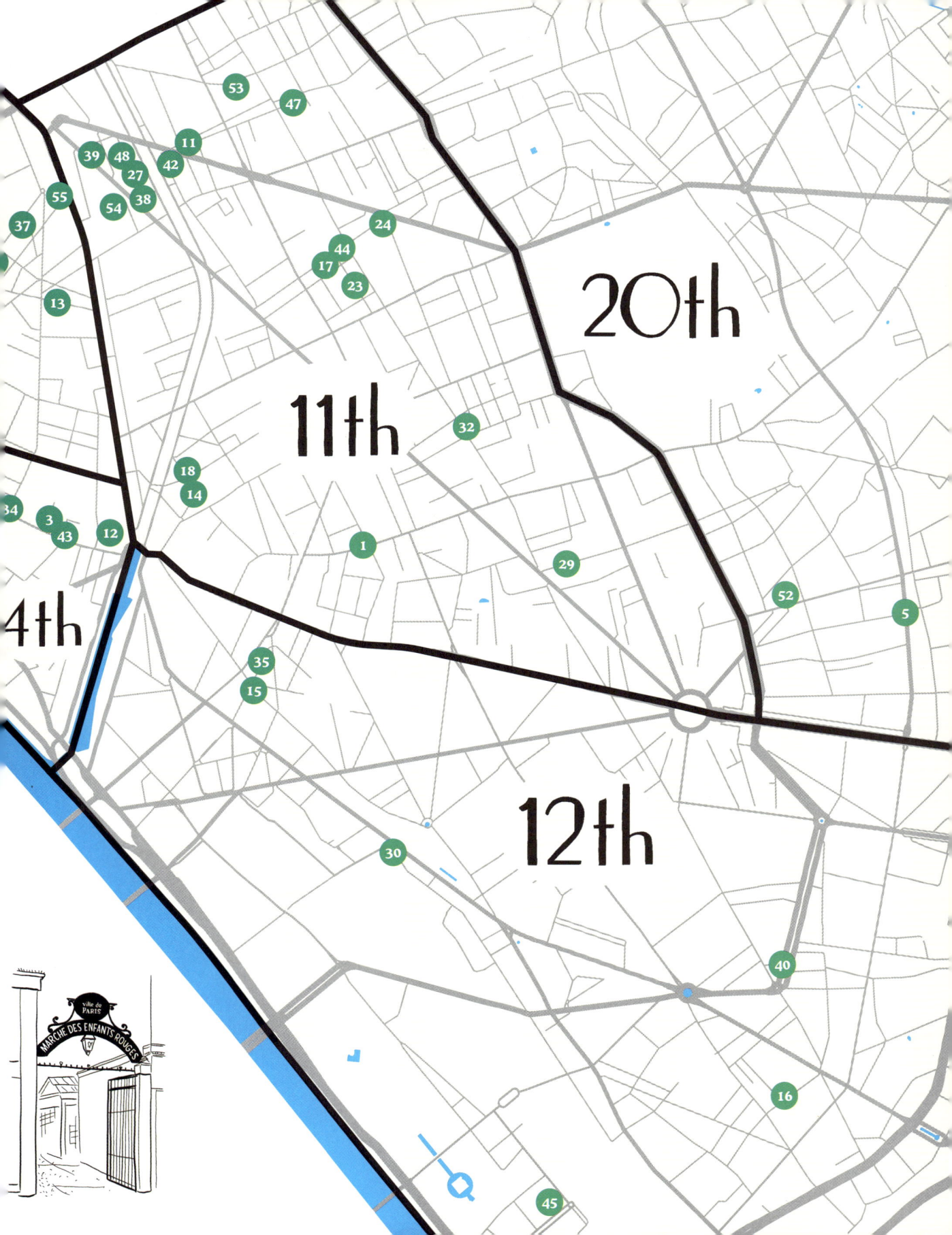

Left Bank: 5th, 13th, and 14th Arrondissements

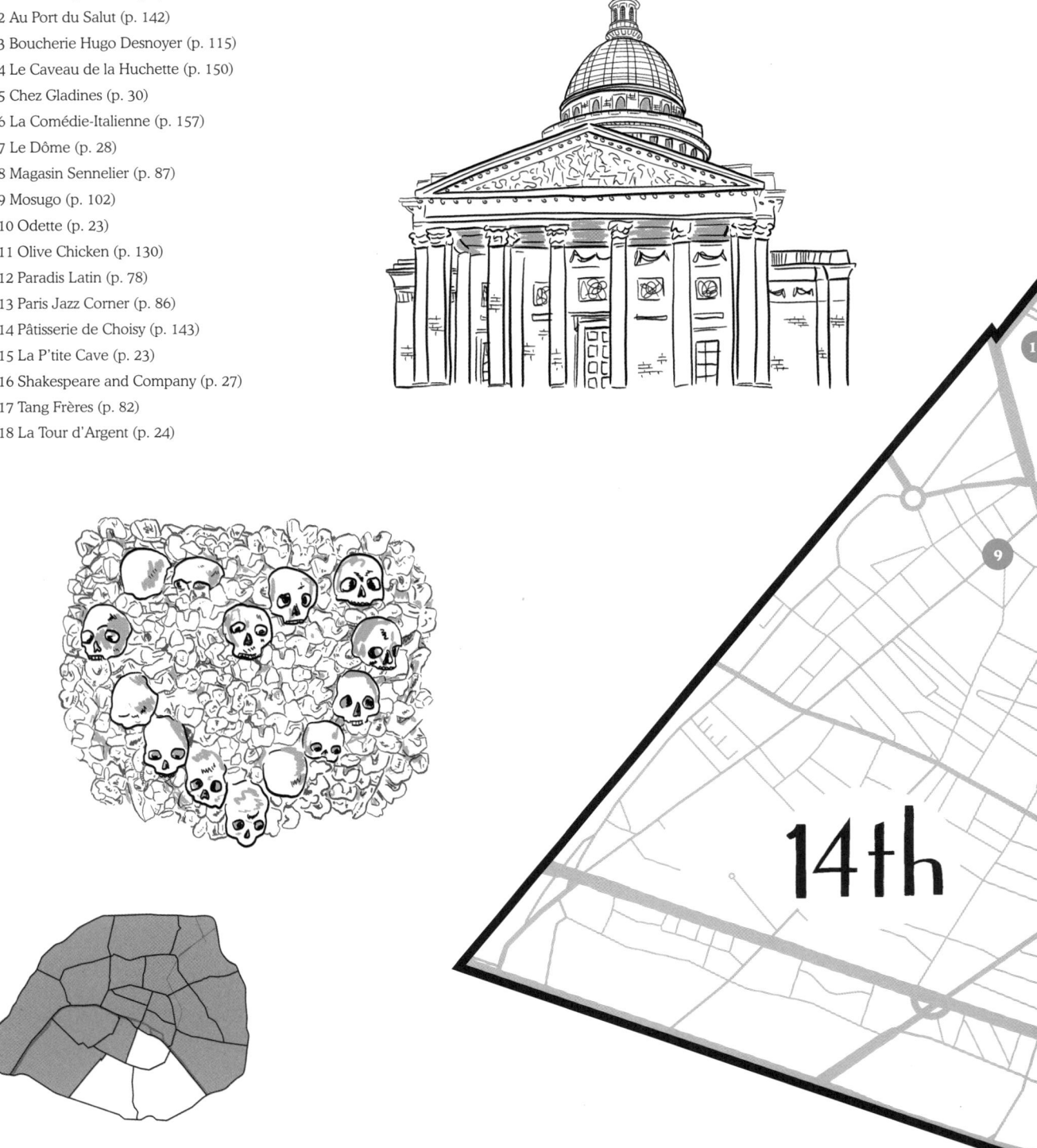

14th

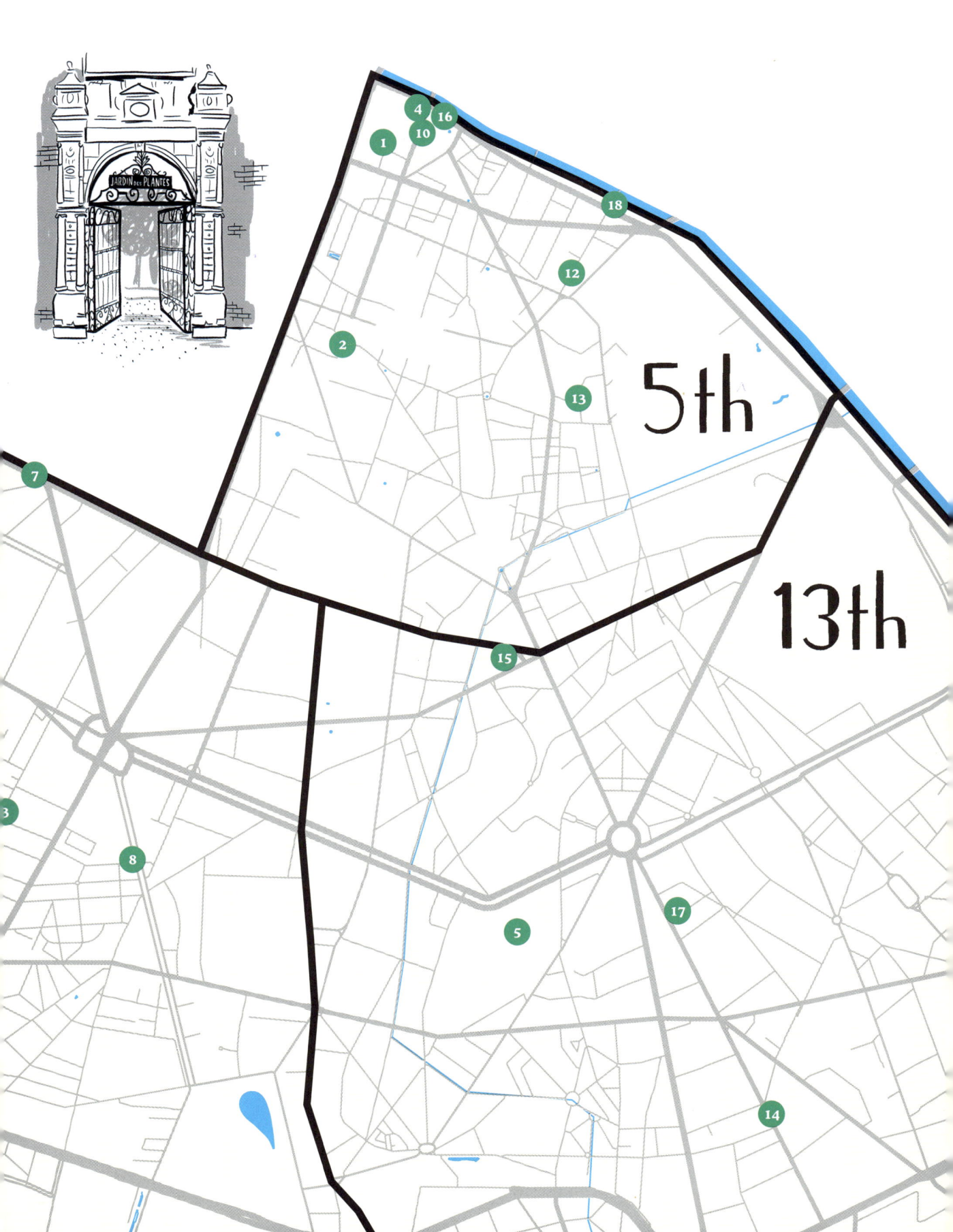

JARDIN DES PLANTES

5th

13th

Left Bank: 6th, 7th, and 15th Arrondissements

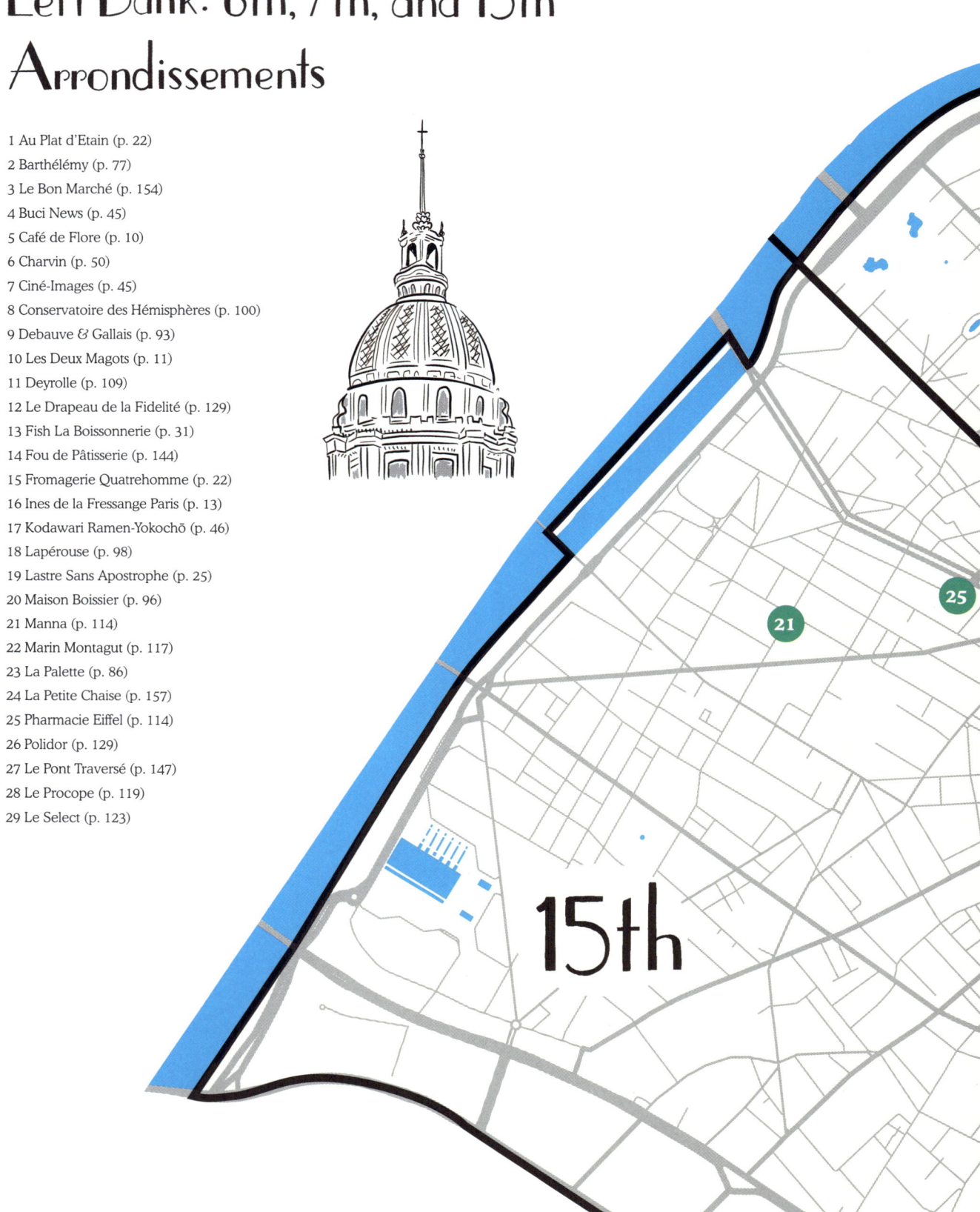

15th

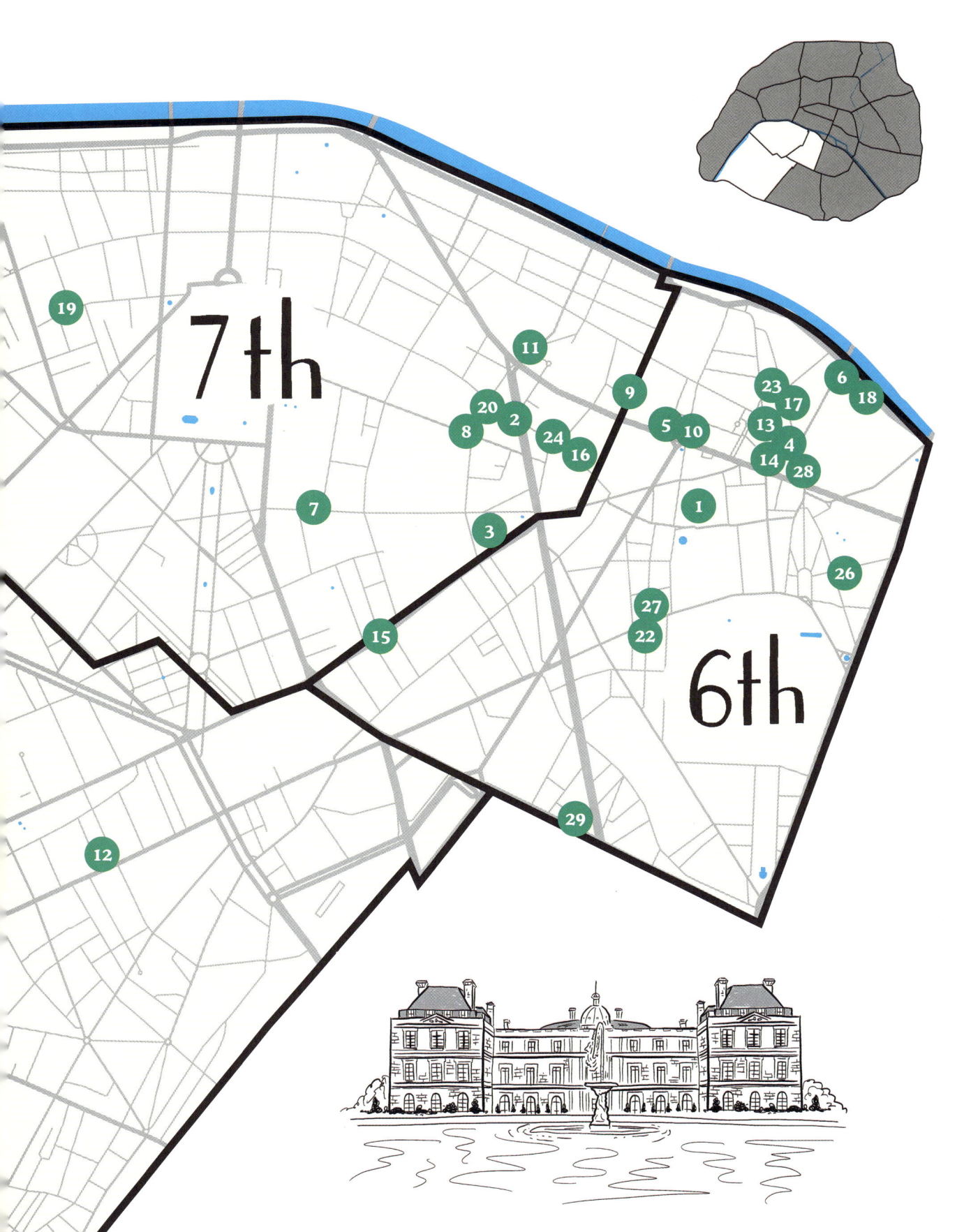

Index

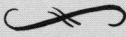

Biographies

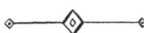

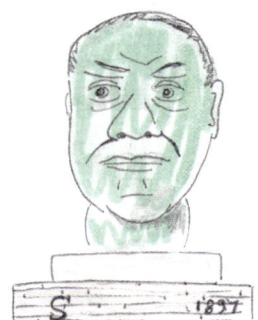

Joel Holland is an illustrator and hand-letterer whose work has appeared in publications including the *New York Times*, the *New Yorker*, *New York* magazine, numerous book covers, and store windows around the globe. His previous books *NYC Storefronts*, *London Shopfronts*, and *Brooklyn Storefronts* (all published by Prestel) pay homage to the small businesses that make those cities so special. He lives in New York City with his wife and two daughters. However, when in Paris, you can find him sitting in a park on a Luxembourg or SENAT chair, thinking about the next cup of coffee or glass of wine. Otherwise, find him on Instagram @joelholland_studio.

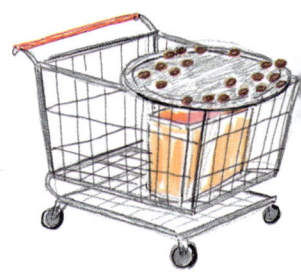

Vivian Song moved from Toronto to Paris in 2010 thinking it would just be for a year, and has since made the French capital her home. In Canada, she started her journalism career as a general assignment reporter at Toronto dailies. As a Paris-based freelance correspondent, her byline has appeared in the *New York Times*, CNN, BBC, *Vice World News*, the *Telegraph UK*, *Lonely Planet*, and *Robb Report*, among many others. In 2023, the Society of American Travel Writers awarded her the bronze award in the category of Travel Journalist of the Year. Even after all these years, she is not blasé about Paris and still finds the city bewitching and inspiring. She speaks French fluently and passable Korean, and shares her love of Paris on Instagram @vivsongviv.

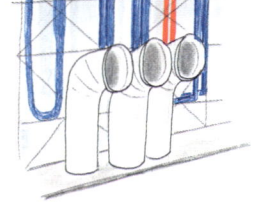

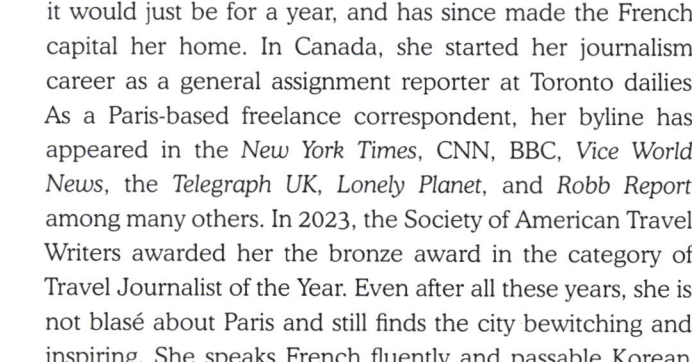

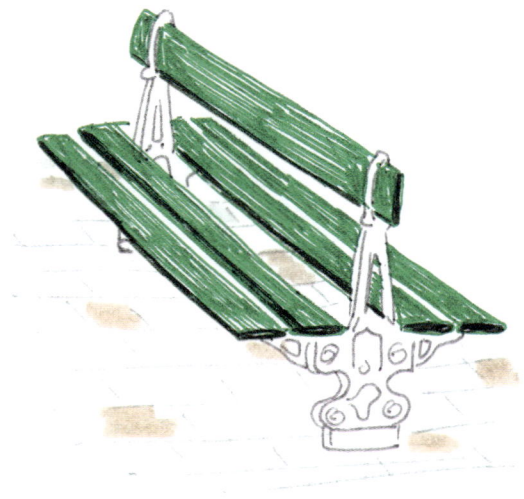

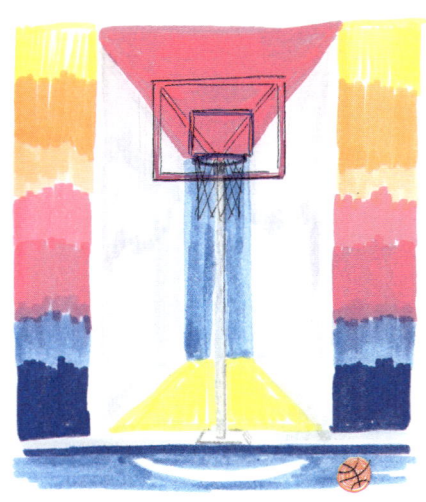

Acknowledgments

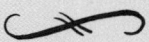

Joel Holland

Thank you to my wonderfully supportive family: my wife Ploy, and our daughters Ella and Nina. You guys are the best, I love our team. Thank you to my parents Blaine and Judy Holland, my brother Stan and his wife Sarah, and their sons Ian and Lars. Also, thank you to my mother-in-law Mallika, and sister-in-law May Milazzo and her family.

Also, thank you to my friends who helped with tips and thoughts from their own adventures: Joseph and Vanessa Setton, Seth Nemeroff, Jira Tontapanish, Big Jitcharoongphorn, Leigh Pasqual, and Sylvia Reutens.

Thank you to Vivian Song for your words, but also your voice and expertise as a Parisian. Reader, there were numerous occasions on which I would suggest a potential shop for our list, only to have Vivian counter with a boots-on-the-ground-verified more diverse business, with an even better story. Thank you. Thanks also to Arnaud Gravade and Sara Taylor for their great shop suggestions. Thank you to Brian Nelson and family, and Nathan Lone and family, for sharing tips from their vacations.

To the amazing team that worked on this project: my extraordinary editor, Ali Gitlow, we did it again! Thank you to proofreading/fact-checking wizard Martha Jay. Thank you to designer Alex Stikeleather for making such a beautiful book, again! And thank you to the team at Prestel: Andrew, Will, Kate, and Naman.

Finally, to the people of Paris, who make these stories possible and maintain such valuable and interesting shops: *Merci beaucoup! Merci bien!*

Vivian Song

A huge thank you to Ali and Joel for inviting me to take part in such a wonderful project. Ali, thank you for shepherding this book through in such a collaborative and positive spirit, and Joel, thank you for bringing these shops to new life with your artist's eye and inspiring in me a whole new appreciation for Paris!

To Hye Ran Song, aka Mamacita Song in Canada, my rock, my biggest cheerleader, and my best friend. I would be nowhere without your support. Thank you for your bottomless love and for being there for me, always. *Sa rang hae yo.*

To my brother Simon and my sister-in-law Ga-eun, thank you for holding down the fort in Canada, I am so grateful. To abba, thank you for being a role model on good work ethics.

Thank you to Bommy, Marilyne, and Audrey, for being my chosen family in Paris. I've shared some of my favorite life moments with you all here.

I am equally grateful to my life-long friends back home in Canada, with whom I still share life updates, time and distance be damned. I'm looking at you, Bon-Hi, Tasha, Tammy, Maria, Anita, Jane, Karen, Janice, Maria, Sabrina, Jackie, Hyun-Jin, Suzan, Esther, and Hyun-Kyung.

And finally, *merci infiniment,* Paris. Thank you for being absurdly beautiful, fascinatingly contradictory, and endlessly inspiring. Paris, *je t'aime.*

© Prestel Verlag, Munich · London · New York, 2025
A member of Penguin Random House Verlagsgruppe GmbH
Neumarkter Strasse 28 · 81673 Munich

© for the illustrations by Joel Holland, 2025
© for the text by Vivian Song, Joel Holland, and Sarah Andelman, 2025
© for the map base: Adobe Stock/Kostiantyn

Library of Congress Control Number: 2024943376

A CIP catalogue record for this book is available from the British Library.

Editorial direction: Ali Gitlow
Copyediting: Martha Jay
Design and layout: Alex Stikeleather
Production management: Luisa Klose
Separations: Reproline Mediateam, Munich
Printing and binding: DZS Grafik, d.o.o. Ljubljana

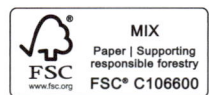

FSC
www.fsc.org
MIX
Paper | Supporting
responsible forestry
FSC® C106600

Penguin Random House Verlagsgruppe FSC® N001967

Printed in Slovenia

ISBN 978-3-7913-9331-5

www.prestel.com

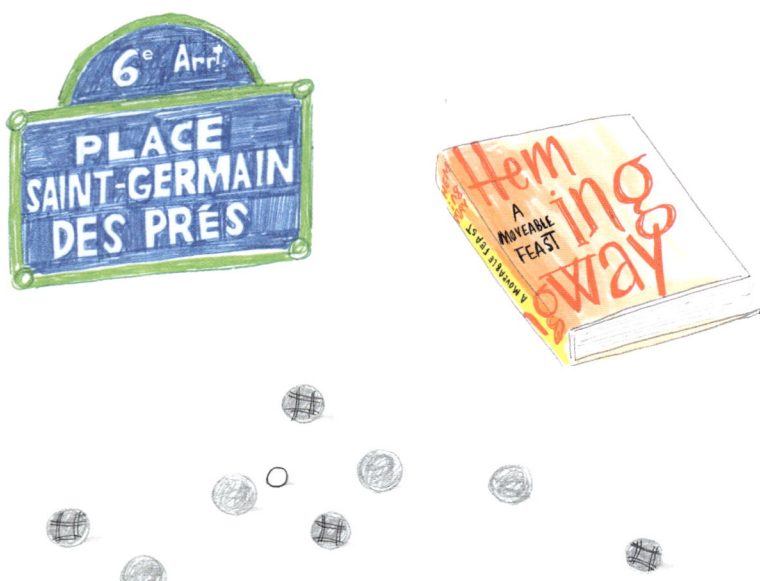

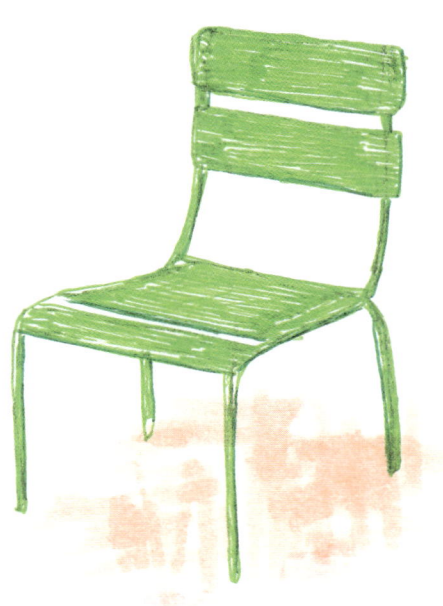